1994

Just Doctoring

Just Doctoring: Medical Ethics in the Liberal State

Troyen Brennan

UNIVERSITY OF CALIFORNIA PRESS

Berkeley / Los Angeles / Oxford

University of California Press
Berkeley and Los Angeles, California

University of California Press
Oxford, England

Library of Congress Cataloging-in-Publication Data
Brennan, Troyen A.
    Just doctoring : medical ethics in the liberal state / by Troyen
Brennan.
        p.   cm.
    Includes bibliographical references and index.
    ISBN 0-520-07333-9 (alk. paper)
    1. Medical ethics.   I. Title.
R724.B73   1991
174'.2—dc20   91-10146
                                                                   CIP

Printed in the United States of America

1 2 3 4 5 6 7 8 9

The paper used in this publication meets the minimum requirements
of American National Standard for Information Sciences—Perma-
nence of Paper for Printed Library Materials, ANSI Z39.48–1984 ⊗

Contents

Preface

This book is motivated by two separate but related inquiries. The first concerns the relationship of medical ethics to the law that governs health care. While it is wrong to talk of a single theory of medical ethics, it seems to me that many ethicists, and especially those physicians who number themselves among ethicists, accept a theory of medical ethics described as "beneficent." The theory of beneficence centers on the altruistic commitment of the doctor to the patient. In a theory of beneficence, "the patient comes first": the physician acts on behalf of the patient and is duty bound to put the patient's interest ahead of her own. Thus the physician acts as the patient's agent.

In return for this commitment, the patient must expect that the physician will at times act paternalistically. Sometimes, she must act on behalf of the patient and help make decisions for him. The patient accepts this paternalistic power of the physician, at least in partial recognition of the fact that sickness tends to decrease his autonomy.

The theory of beneficence contrasts sharply with the trend in nearly every area of health law to increase the prerogatives of the patient and limit the prerogatives of the physician. In areas as diverse as informed consent, medical malpractice law, physician payment issues, and antitrust litigation, we witness decision after decision in which efforts are made by courts to limit physicians' power. The law is suspicious of physicians and evinces little confidence in a beneficence approach to the relation between doctor and patients.

As a physician, I believe that the beneficence model of medical ethics has some, in fact, many, admirable features. As a lawyer, however, I realize that the outstanding aspect of the liberal state is its respect for individual rights, including those of patients. Thus I must ask how the best aspects of the beneficence model of medical ethics can be modified to conform to the morality underlying the liberal state's efforts to reduce physicians' power. In other words, I must ask how the principles underlying medical ethics can be brought into alignment with the moral principles that underlie the law in our liberal state.

The second inquiry that motivates this book concerns the changes in the economic and political structure of medical practice. In the ten years in which I have observed medical practice, there have been very many changes. Those who have observed it for the past thirty or forty years must have seen even greater changes. The world of the individual practitioner, who contracts on a fee-for-service basis with patients, relies on insurers to provide compensation without question, and admits patients to a hospital that defers to the physician decisions on care is now vanishing. The past twenty-five years have seen greater and greater governmental intervention in medical care. And in the last ten or fifteen years market concepts and the influence of competition have been introduced. More and more physicians are employed by health maintenance organizations and other entities that seek to provide managed care—that is, care overseen by administrators of health plans. New incentives to demonstrate appropriateness and cost efficiency in medical care are changing the nature of medical practice. As a consequence, the personal power of individual physicians within the health care system, as well as the overall power of the medical profession, has diminished. The overwhelming majority of middle-aged and older practitioners relate that the practice of medicine is nothing like it was even twenty years ago.

This new structure of medical practice must require new theories of medical ethics. The beneficence theory of medical ethics flourished in an era in which physicians, in their relations with patients, were isolated from economic and political influences. Indeed the traditional structures of medical practice were designed to preserve such insulation. Physicians were free of the restrictions of the market and could literally "do anything" for a patient. Now, physicians must face a variety of political, social, and economic constraints as they practice medicine. Medical ethics must evolve to help physicians address these issues.

In this book, I attempt to develop a new theory of medical ethics, which I call medical ethics as just doctoring. This notion of medical ethics attempts to retain the altruism of the beneficence model of medical ethics. However, this core altruism is placed firmly within the structure and moral principles of the liberal state. It conforms with liberalism and with the laws of the liberal state. Moreover, it addresses the complicated economic and political issues that now arise in the practice of medicine. Medical ethics as just doctoring counts as ethical issues such diverse problems as rationing of care, the role of competition in medical care, limits on care for elderly patients, quality assurance and malpractice litigation, and issues on informed consent. Thus medical ethics as just doctoring represents a somewhat radical departure from traditional notions of medical ethics, which rarely ventured outside the direct doctor-patient relationship.

It is not without some trepidation that I develop this thesis. During the summer I spent writing this book, I had several experiences that helped place the project in perspective. In the early part of the summer, a fellowship program in which I was involved came to a close. The individuals participating in the program came from a variety of different professions and were studying ways to understand and develop professional ethics. All the participants took their work very seriously, and the program provided an atmosphere in which ethical issues arising in the practice of medicine and other professions could be addressed and understood in some theoretical detail. The atmosphere of the program seemed quite distant from the hospital environment in which I practice medicine. I worried that the ideas developed in this intellectual environment might not readily translate to my primary audience—physicians, nurses, and other health care providers.

Just after the close of the ethics program, I served for a month as an attending physician at a university hospital, acting as supervisor and teacher of physicians training in internal medicine, as well as of third-year medical students associated with the team of training physicians. July is an exciting month to be an attending physician. Interns have just graduated from medical school and are taking their first steps as doctors. The internship year is one of total emergence in medicine and the interns work long hours. It is fascinating to watch young people, most of whom have spent the eight years since graduating from high school studying very hard, learn to care for patients. Perhaps most impressive is the set of expectations under which they operate. We all expect, the attending physicians, the directors of the training program, and the second- and third-year residents, that the interns will demonstrate total commitment to their jobs. They will not leave the hospital until all questions about patient care have been addressed or passed along to a responsible individual. Operating under great stress and fatigue, these new doctors evince a commitment to their job unlike that found in any other area of commerce. What is remarkable is that this commitment is standard; it is expected of every doctor in the training program.

Certainly, part of this commitment must spring from a sense of ethical duty to patients. It cannot, it seems, be the mere expectation of gain at some point in the distant future that drives these young men and women. A sense of altruism must be part of the practice of medicine. Yet it is difficult to uncover in conversation with these physicians in training. Indeed, they rarely can articulate the nature of their motivation. The conceptual framework that might link their actions to notions of ethical behavior is missing. Thus it seems important to me to help develop that ethical framework. If one could integrate the moral principles provided by philosophers and ethicists with medical education, perhaps the ethical theory of medicine could be better understood by practitioners. This hope underlines many of the arguments in this book.

In addition to my duties at the university teaching hospital, I "moonlight" in an emergency room at a small community hospital in Massachusetts, where I come into contact with physicians engaged in more traditional medical practice. While preferred-provider organizations and new insurance arrangements increasingly affect their medical practice, many physicians at this hospital still operate under the fee-for-service framework and face little hospital interference. They are also removed from the intellectual atmosphere of the teaching hospital; they work for a living and their living is taking care of patients. The same is true of the incredibly dedicated emergency room nursing staff.

These doctors and nurses constitute another audience I hope to reach. It is, however, an audience quite removed from the ivory tower. It is hard for me to imagine that they would take the time to consider arguments regarding the interrelationship of medical ethics and the liberal state. Moreover, I doubt that they would have any time for discussions of the law and the way it affects medical care. Their view is that the law has to do with lawyers, and they have little interest in dealing with them. Thus, while I can relate to the community physician who has a patient in the emergency room, and in whom I can discern the same commitment to the patient that I see in the fledgling interns, it is difficult to believe that philosophical arguments can change the way he views medical practice.

Nonetheless, I do not start on a pessimistic note. I am hopeful. During the research for this book, I had an opportunity to read Larry R. Churchill's excellent book on rationing health care. The introduction to the book referred to an article that Howard Hiatt, former dean of the Harvard School of Public Health, had published in 1975 in the *New England Journal of Medicine*, concerning whose responsibility it was to protect the medical commons. Churchill believed that Hiatt was appealing to a moral sensibility that largely did not exist and still does not exist in the medical profession. He felt that Hiatt's challenging arguments had been largely ignored, and he feared that his book on justice in the health care system might also fall on deaf ears. Similar notions troubled me during the writing of this book.

Recently, I had an opportunity to speak with Hiatt. I related that Churchill had thought that his article on the commons had fallen on deaf ears. Hiatt reflected for a moment and then said that he had written quite a few articles during his medical career. Some of them had helped define ribose metabolism in human cells. He had also been a coauthor on the paper that first described messenger RNA. He related that none of these biochemical breakthroughs had generated the kind of interest within the profession that this article on the commons had. He seemed hopeful that physicians, even more now than in 1975, would listen and reflect on arguments concerning ethics and justice in health care.

One can only hope for the best. I do not by any means believe that this book has answers to many or even a few of the questions that trouble physicians, nurses, and medical care in general. I mean only to contribute to a debate on the appropriate role of ethics in medicine. Indeed, the important aspect of the work from my point of view is the debate. I believe that physicians must take responsibility. This means responsibility not only for individual patients but also for the set of institutions that define medical care. To do nothing will mean that we will forfeit all responsibility. Thus, while I do not expect my argument to be regarded as a breakthrough in medical ethics, I do intend to stir debate and interest among health care workers, especially physicians, whether they are new interns or cynical and experienced practitioners. In this vein, I offer a notion of medical ethics as just doctoring.

I offer one final word of caution. As a physician, I have a tendency to slide into physician-centric views of medicine. To a certain extent, this is appropriate, as much of what I argue is aimed at physicians. I do not hope to develop a theory of ethics for all health care workers and institutions; rather I am concerned about what is ethical for doctors. As will become clear, however, I believe professional ethics must be public, not a matter strictly defined by the profession itself. Therefore, it follows that all citizens, especially other health care workers, must help define physicians' ethics.

The plan of the book is as follows. In the first four chapters I develop an outline of the liberal state, and the place of medical ethics within it. This will require some summarizing of material that is quite familiar to the bioethicist, but quite foreign to a health care worker. In the following chapters I illustrate the notion of just doctoring by investigating a number of issues in health care that raise legal and ethical questions. I cannot examine every controversy that now arises in medical care—but I hope to have investigated enough difficult ones to reveal the advantages of medical ethics as just doctoring.

Acknowledgments

I am grateful to numerous individuals and institutions for their support and advice. Initial work on some of the themes contained herein was completed when I was a student at Yale Medical and Law Schools. Professor Jay Katz and Dean Guido Calabresi carefully supervised projects that provided a foundation for several chapters. Dr. Robert Levine acted as my thesis adviser and provided insightful critical commentary over a period of several years.

The opportunity to develop and present a variety of impressions in this book is the result of help from numerous individuals at Harvard University. First, my Division Chief, Dr. Anthony Komaroff, was broad-minded and kind enough to be very supportive of the idea of writing a book about medical ethics and health law. Second, Deans James Vorenberg and Robert Clark of Harvard Law School allowed me to teach health law and policy for three years from 1987 to 1990. The probing questions and insightful writing of my students at Harvard Law School have greatly influenced me.

Third, the Program for Ethics in the Professions at Harvard University provided me with fellowship support in 1988–89. I learned a great deal from other participants in the fellowship, most important, Professor Dennis Thompson, the Program Director, who encouraged this project (and carefully read a first draft of chapters 1–5). Without his and the fellowship's help, I could not have undertaken the book.

I am also greatly appreciative of the help of various nameless reviewers who read and commented on a previous draft. Professor Theodore Marmor and Professor Haavi Morreim also reviewed the book and provided me with numerous insightful criticisms and advice. They will recognize their influence in this finished project. My friend Carlisle Rex-Waller provided invaluable editorial assistance. Kim Bruno tirelessly incorporated revisions into the manuscript.

I am in the debt of those numerous physicians who have impressed me over the years with their altruistic commitment to patients, especially Drs. Leo Cooney, John Stoeckle, Marshall Wolf, and Phyllis Jen. They and others provide the idealistic basis for the doctor-patient relationship described herein. I also owe a great deal to the various patients who have taught me so much about human dignity over the last decade. I hope their lessons are reflected throughout the book. Finally, I thank my wife, Wendy, and children, Hannah and George, for all their help and affection.

1

The Liberal State

Newspapers and television often feature controversial subjects arising out of health care. More and more these stories seem to underscore conflicts between institutions and bureaucracies as much as they do the human struggles that were the central focus of such fare ten or fifteen years ago. For instance, a man in Chicago "pulls the plug" on the ventilator that keeps his comatose infant alive. He faces criminal charges. One can barely imagine the emotions and suffering associated with such an act. But the father's decision has come after a hospital lawyer refused to help the family seek a court order to remove the child from the ventilator. The lawyer reasons that since the hospital was not receiving any reimbursement for this child's care, a court might suspect that the hospital's removal of life support was prompted by financial motives.[1]

Consider these other stories: The lover of a movie star who has died of the acquired immunodeficiency syndrome (AIDS) sues the estate and the movie star's physicians because he was never warned that the star was seropositive for the human immunodeficiency virus (HIV). The physicians involved in this case contend that they thought they owed their patient confidentiality. The lover is awarded $5 million. He has not contracted the virus, so observers surmise that the court is sending physicians a message that they must warn individuals who might contract the HIV from one of their patients.

The government agency that determines how physicians should be reimbursed under Medicare, the Physician Payment Review Committee (PPRC), considers capping expenditures. They reason that physicians will then be forced to learn how to ration care, and thus save

1

money for the government. But the American Medical Association (AMA) asserts that this initiative will cause incalculable harm to the elderly.

Each of these examples involves institutions and professions that most physicians are suspicious of, if not contemptuous: the government, the courts, the legal profession, and health care administrators. Yet each of these examples also touches on issues that most doctors would feel are imbued with ethical considerations. This is the dilemma of medical ethics in the 1990s. Most ethical issues that physicians now face are intertwined with legal and political issues.

Most physicians believe they are equipped to deal with ethical problems that arise in the practice of medicine. They would prefer to handle such problems simply by consulting their own sense of morality and doing the reasonable thing. Physicians have tended to isolate themselves from the economic, political, and legal aspects of difficult moral issues that occur when caring for patients. Traditionally, the patient-doctor contract has excluded all extraneous concerns, and thus the focus in medical ethics has been on interpersonal morality.

Today, however, institutions assert themselves in most "ethical problems" facing physicians, inevitably leading to questions on the relation of law to ethics and morality. Notions of justice contend with those of doctor-patient trust. Political philosophers expect conflicts to arise between individuals struggling with ethical concerns and the laws of the state. As Thomas Nagel notes, the impartiality of liberalism, the guiding political philosophy of Canada, Great Britain, and the United States, provides a context for and orders the ethical decision making of the individual citizen.[2] The physician should thus be familiar with the legal and political context of ethical decision making.

What should the physician do when confronted with legal and political issues arising from the practice of medicine? One answer is that she should learn about issues of justice and political fairness. An initial education might involve defining the central terms of such issues. What do the words *law, morality, ethics, justice,* and *liberalism* really mean? Webster's has those answers.[3] *Morality,* on the one hand, is defined as "a doctrine or system of moral conduct." The adjective *moral* is defined as "of or relating to principles of right or wrong" and is synonymous with *ethical. Just,* on the other hand, is an adjective that means "acting or being in conformity with what is morally good or upright." *Justice* is the "maintenance or administration of what is just" and is also the "quality of conforming to the law."

Clearly there is a great deal of overlap in the meaning of these terms, yet they present many different nuances. All deal with correctness of action, and with the qualities of right and wrong. All feature a sense of principled action and of rational relationships. But concepts of morality and ethics do seem less systematic—if you like, less specific—than do concepts of law. Conforming with law is different from conforming with an ethical principle. Justice is institutionalized in a way that morality is not.

What about liberalism? Webster's relates that liberalism is "a political philosophy based in belief in progress, the essential goodness of man, and the autonomy of the individual and standing for the protection of political and civil liberties." That sounds like it has a lot to do with law, justice, and morality; it also sounds like a decent description of the political philosophy that guides the United States, Canada, and Great Britain, to name a few of what I refer to as liberal states. Given the relationship of medical ethics to moral-political concerns in our liberal state, a firm grasp of liberalism must be central to the enterprise of this book. If we can understand what the liberal state is all about, it will be much easier to understand why issues of law and justice are and should be an increasingly important part of medical ethics.

The Core of Liberalism: Negative Freedom

What, then, are the core values of liberalism? Although there is no easy answer, one can probably safely say that liberals believe individuals should be able to make choices, and that the state should be impartial to these choices. Thus liberalism requires an area of non-interference for the individual, or freedom from interference. Isaiah Berlin has called this the sphere of negative freedom and his discussion can help elucidate the essence of the liberal state.[4] Berlin notes that there are two senses of freedom in political discussion. They are as follows:

The first of these political senses of freedom . . . which I shall call the negative sense, is involved in the question, "What is the area within which the subject—a person or group of persons—is or should be left to do or be what he wants to do or be without interference by other persons?" The second, which I shall call the positive sense, is involved with the answer to the question, "What or who is the source of control of interference, that can determine someone to do or be, one thing rather than another?"[5]

Berlin thus constructs two opposing senses of the word *freedom*. One centers on the individual's sphere of action. This sphere is to be quite large and the individual is to be left, to a large extent, unbridled. The other type of freedom, the positive type, is totally different. It involves the use of power or coercion by some in society, or the state itself, to help perfect or improve other individuals. The purpose of this coercion is to allow the citizen to live in accordance with his true self.

Negative freedom operates on the assumption that personal choice affirms one's humanity. Individual action possesses a value incommensurable with other types of action:

There ought to exist a certain minimum area of personal freedom which can on no account be violated, for, if it is overstepped, the individual will find himself in an area too narrow for even that minimum development of his natural faculties which alone makes it possible to pursue, and even to conceive, the various ends which mankind holds good or right or sacred.[6]

These views reflect what I will call "classic liberalism." The classic liberal sense of freedom demands that the individual be left alone with her own projects. The exercise of free choice and pursuit of individual projects are what give life meaning, according to the liberal. Berlin here is echoing John Stuart Mill's conception of society and individual good. As Mill stated, this conception is embodied in "one very simple principle: That principle is that the sole end for which mankind are warranted individually or collectively, in interfering with the liberty of action of any of their number, is self-protection."[7] Of course, this negative freedom, or liberty, is protected by one's political rights.

Mill himself justified the liberal emphasis on negative freedom protected by rights on the bedrock of utilitarianism. His assertion that individual freedom guarantees the maximization of utility rested on his ultimate belief in the greatest good of individual thought. Mill was quite sure that the good of individual thought and action is a far more important consideration than the reasons for limiting individual freedom.

Berlin's rendition of negative freedom certainly concurs with this. Berlin and others do, nonetheless, take a step beyond Mill in their refusal to treat negative freedom and rights as instrumental values, simply justified by the ends served.[8] They argue instead that rights and the liberty or negative freedom that rights preserve are intrinsically good. The individual's liberty cannot be weighed against other goods. Thus liberal philosophers oppose positive freedom, or any form of coercion of the individual in an obdurate fashion. The nature of this opposition further illuminates the content of the liberal state.

According to Berlin, positive freedom issues from a different set of assumptions about what is valuable in society. The adherent of positive freedom sees herself and other human beings as imperfect, yet perfectible. Some human action must therefore be curtailed in order that more perfect arrangements and attitudes can come about in the future. Positive freedom asserts that in order that all may advance, some must be bridled.

Berlin, as a classic liberal, will not accept this. He is a proponent of negative freedom, which he believes is the only true freedom. He argues that societal decisions about the common good are given to misinterpretation and are fraught with the potential for tyranny of the majority, or even dictatorship by a few: "For it is this—the positive concept of liberty: not freedom from, but freedom to, which adherents of the 'negative' notion represent as being, at times, no better than a specious disguise for brutal tyranny."[9] Berlin thus fears positive freedom and seeks to contain it with the concept of personal liberty, or negative freedom.

In medicine today, we are often reminded of the negative freedom of the patient. The patient's freedom from interference comes through most strongly in situations in which patients request that their care be limited. The courts, including the Supreme Court in the recent case of *Cruzan* v. *Missouri Department of Human Services*, have consistently reiterated that when a patient decides that he does not want heroic or lifesaving measures, and the patient is competent, then physicians cannot insist on further therapy. In the courts' analysis, a physician's insistence on therapy would be a violation of the patient's negative freedom, a freedom to refuse further invasive care. Physicians who argue that competent patients cannot understand the importance of their decision to limit their care are seeking, perhaps, to impose their own conception of what is good and to force the patient to accept further care. The courts usually reject this physician assertion of power and reiterate that the patient's negative freedom, or liberty, should be sacrosanct.

Negative freedom can provide the basis for a theory of justice when one links it to an unfettered right to property, the freedom to dispose of what is one's own. Classic liberal philosophy entails that one is free to do whatever one wants with one's possessions. One is free to paint one's own car. One has a right to paint it. One does not lose the freedom to paint one's own car simply because one has no paint. No paint does not mean no rights. Rights are characterized here as formal guarantees, not as material benefits of some sort.

As might be expected, the classic liberal thinks little of positive freedom, which he characterizes as an end-state theory. In this view, although the liberal values a certain, usually egalitarian, pattern of the distribution of goods in society, he also believes that "any distributional patterns with any egalitarian component is overturnable by the voluntary actions of individual people over time."[10] Thus inequality is the natural outcome of rights that guarantee liberties, and the classic liberal accepts this outcome. His belief is that as long as one respects others' rights, then we have no reason to blame him or her for getting wealthier.

Consider Robert Nozick's example of Wilt Chamberlain's ascendancy to fame and fortune. Nozick argues that Chamberlain is not to blame for his own abilities and resultant wealth and that those who would deny him his salary would be constantly trespassing on the personal life of the basketball player. In effect, this means that one can have liberty or equality but not both. Nozick would opt for the former, and he would use the rhetoric of rights to buttress his position. From this argument, it follows that institutions are just only insofar as they promote no interference. In the liberal view, the Internal Revenue Service's interest in Chamberlain's salary, or even the salary caps negotiated by the National Basketball Association with the Player's Association, are unjust.

This position itself represents an evolution of classic liberalism. I will call it "conservatism." A conservative like Nozick or Bertrand de Jouvenal[11] believes that redistribution is ethically wrong because it undermines and weakens notions of personal responsibility. Moreover, conservatives cast doubt on the ability of redistributionist policies to produce the good they intend. In essence, they deny that a central authority can possibly bring about a better pattern of distribution than will free citizens in the market.[12]

The conservative position has been questioned, especially by socialists, but even by other liberals. For instance, some argue that it ignores the impediments that stand in the way of some members of society simply because of the situation into which they were born.[13] Certain members of society will be unable to exercise those liberties granted them because they were born into a deprived setting. While admitting that each citizen may be granted a formal set of liberties outlining a sphere of activity within which he or she can operate, those opposed to conservatism point out that this set remains merely formal so long as people lack the substantive means to realize the potential of their own autonomy and humanity. The idea that formal liberty often fails to become substantive is the outstanding criticism of both classic liberalism and its progeny, conservatism.

There are several other grounds on which to challenge the conservative. Countering his assumption that inequality just happens, that it should be viewed as a natural occurrence, like the weather or volcanic eruptions, some would maintain that it is impossible to generate large amounts of inequality between individuals unless there are significant inequalities of power in a society. This argument is in turn supported by two other propositions. First, people are not all that different in the basic, or if you like, natural, level of talents they have and can offer. Second, inequality is not a result of freedom of choice, but rather of some taking advantage of others. Thus inequality only occurs when some take advantage of inequity of power to use others as means to ends. In this view, liberty and the impartiality of liberalism simply support the appropriation of the means of production by the powerful and the resulting subversion of others.

One need not go to Marxist extremes, however, to fault the conservative for failing to take into account the value of equality, and for overvaluing pure liberty. The conservative statement that rights exist, that they are good, that they should be defended by just institutions, and that the outcome of such a polity is not a concern of justice cannot be logically sustained. It is, quite simply, wrong. Inequality is a result of the set of rights that are allowed in a society, and the inequality is in effect condoned by that set of rights.

The conservative's failure is his lack of consideration for the ways that economic or contractual claims that may legitimately be made by favored individuals in the type of society he values are not available to all its citizens, given a heritage of unequal wealth, education, and health care. This inequality is unjust, and the state must deal with it, not dismiss it as natural. As Albert Jonsen and Andre Hellegers have stated:

When benefits and burdens can be so distributed, the problem of justice arises. Some who will benefit will not bear costs; some who will bear costs will not benefit. When the situation depends not on chance, but on planned and conscious decisions about the structure of the institution, it is necessary to ask, "Why should anyone benefit at the apparent cost to another?" These are the questions at the heart of . . . justice.[14]

Consider, for instance, the newborn child of a mother who has no health insurance and is not eligible for government relief programs. This mother, as a result of her exclusion from such programs, might have received substandard prenatal care for herself and her unborn child. Say that because of this lack of care, the child has suffered some intrauterine growth retardation, resulting in the sort of neurological deficits that good prenatal care is designed to avoid. Thus the existence of inequalities in society has created a situation in which one individual will be unable to take advantage of opportunities theoretically available to every member of the society because he was born with certain neurological problems. An advocate of egalitarianism would argue that this child represents a failure of conservatism, for the enshrinement of negative freedom has failed to guarantee him the enjoyment of life, at least from the point of view of classic liberalism.

While conservativism is a natural evolution of classic liberalism, there are other offshoots. The most prominent is what I will call "modern liberalism," so as to distinguish it from classic liberalism and conservatism. Modern liberals recognize the arguments made by those who point out the importance of egalitarian programs. They realize equality must be balanced with liberty in the modern liberal state. It can be said that conservatives see themselves as defenders of liberty, while modern liberals are more concerned with equality.

The modern liberal realizes that granting greater liberty by placing an emphasis on rights allows for more inequality within a society and also realizes that liberty can bring rewards only if the material means to pursue that liberty are available. Modern liberals, while still valuing liberty, envision a society that can establish greater equality. In pursuit of this end, they would not balk at interference with certain individual liberties if a larger proportion of the society would benefit as a result.

Liberty, Equality, and Market Impartiality

Classic liberalism gives rise to a number of different moral-political philosophies, in particular, conservativism and modern liberalism. The core of liberalism, whether classic or modern, concerns liberty and impartiality. The concept of liberty guarantees the individual a sphere that is his or her own. Liberty provides an area in which one can operate unencumbered by the strictures of the society within which one lives. The state remains impartial to the individual's choices in this sphere: it guarantees liberty.

Given this core, how does modern liberalism address inequality? Liberal notions of equality celebrate the belief that all people are the same in their humanness, that no matter what physical and mental differences exist between us, society accepts each and every member as beings of incomparable worth. Thus, the concepts of both liberty and equality can represent the optimistic belief in perfectibility that characterizes liberalism of all flavors. Yet, as noted above, classic liberals and especially their conservative offspring might see some conflict between the values of liberty and equality. To understand this potential conflict, let us define liberalism more closely.

In the liberal state, an individual's liberty is primary, and the individual enjoys and utilizes his "freedom from" interference to develop his notion of a good life. This liberty is guaranteed by rights. Each citizen, in a model liberal polity, has an equal set of rights that includes an equal right to opportunities. The individual's liberty should not be, or should only minimally be, hampered by the policies of the state. The classic liberal conception assumes that a free market will provide the means for maximizing an individual's free choice. The government tends to stand aside and let the market order societal relations, allowing its citizens to take advantage of their liberty.

The classic liberal state is therefore fundamentally impartial. It allows the citizen to formulate her own notions of goodness, and to pursue them with little interference. As John Rawls notes, the liberal citizen need possess only two moral powers, a sense of justice and a notion of the good.[15] There are no special notions of virtue that underpin liberalism. Rather, liberalism encourages pluralism. Each citizen is allowed to develop and pursue her own sense of morality in the ideal liberal state. The government stands by impartially, making sure that the free market economy remains in place.

Of course, as modern liberals recognize, this state is only an ideal. The impartiality of liberalism does not empty the society of its sense of community. The liberal state is a polity, and its citizens realize they must live together, and so there are constraints on liberty. Instead of a formal impartiality and rampant pluralism of moral ideals, the modern liberal state features what Rawls calls an "overlapping consensus."[16] So long as there is some degree of consensus, the liberal state is a place where many views are tolerated. Certain views of moral behavior, such as those that call for racial purification, are excluded. Every Nazi or white supremacist cannot be allowed to take action based on his own sense of morality. While the liberal state does not preclude any view of society, it does exclude putting some into effect. Absolute liberty is thus diminished for the sake of the community. The modern liberal state is accomplished only through a series of compromises with the traditional liberal ideal, compromises between equality and liberty.

The classic liberal ideal overlooks the fact that natural differences between persons are unavoidable. To bring about equality, it is thus sometimes necessary to have the state interfere in the pursuit of individual projects. Notions of equality thus tend to restrict liberties; in particular they restrict free choice in the market.

The liberal state, then, must carefully weigh the competing values of liberty and equality. Rights often act as the operators within this negotiation. The nature of the rights to which a citizen is entitled tends to outline the compromise between equality and liberty that has been reached within a society. On the one hand, a society that creates a right to health care that requires a great deal of government subsidy to realize it, will probably sanction a more than modest interference with liberty. On the other hand, a society that sanctions a fundamental right to personal property and that prohibits takings by the government will probably largely prohibit interference with liberty.

Indeed, different liberal states, each of which is based on the notion of what I have termed modern liberalism, will make different sets of compromises and sanction varying rights. Thus, while an ideal state can be imagined that more or less perfectly reflects classic liberalism, conservativism, or modern liberalism, real liberal states are not so pure. The United States, Great Britain, and Canada are all liberal states, yet they reflect different renditions of liberalism. (I will argue that the

United States is a modern, or should be a modern, liberal state, though certain aspects of it reflect conservative views.)

The classic definition of liberalism tended toward a state in which liberty was emphasized. The impartiality of classic liberalism extended beyond a mere tolerance for different moral points of view, to a true impartiality of the state with regard to individual activities, especially economic activities. In this sense of liberalism, a right to health care does not seem comprehensible as a right. Classic liberalism's rights were simply rights claims staking out negative freedom. Historically, John Locke's contractual ethics seem to condone this attitude toward rights, portraying them simply as properties of individuals that protect their liberty, a notion that is quite powerfully emphasized in conservatism.[17] Rights were not really thought of as the operating concepts of a compromise between the principles of liberty and equality, but rather as a means for asserting one's liberty. The rise of personal liberty was central to the forms of liberalism-pluralism that developed during the eighteenth and nineteenth centuries and that were so well characterized by John Stuart Mill.

The modern liberal state cannot, however, allow rights to guarantee liberty without regard for equality, nor market impartiality to remain entirely unfettered. Moreover, pluralism cannot run rampant. Both the free market and the choice of moral enterprises must be limited for the liberal state to be a political community. For the former, some regulations of economic activity and taxation will be necessary to promote equality. For the latter, constraints regarding the important differences between beliefs and truths in political dialogue are necessary to maintain the transcendent objectivity central to liberalism. In other words, to paraphrase Nagel, one who asserts that his moral beliefs are grounded in truth must be able to present that truth such that others accept it as true. This invalidates the claims, for instance, of the racial supremacist.

Perhaps the most fruitful way to conceive of the modern liberal state is to say that it takes as its constitutive ideal that citizens should be treated as equals.[18] Of course, treating citizens as equals can be two very different things. In one sense the government treats citizens as equals by treating them with equal respect and concern. Alternatively, the government treats all as equals in a very different sense by ensuring that goods are distributed in an equal manner. The former is a regulative principle, while the latter is a substantive principle.

The end state of distribution is critical to the substantive principle of equality. It requires that the government define the nature of distributive equality. This is no easy task. Consider, for instance, the distribution of health care. Some of my patients are quite well disposed to medical care. They want tests and have questions and welcome treatment. That is their choice. Others tend to avoid visits, do not want to undergo tests, and do not wish to take medications for minor or even major ailments. How would the state go about distributing health care equally? If it is distributed on the basis of need, we must recognize that choice will play a role in some people's needs. Clearly, equal distributions are not easily accomplished, and they often have very little to do with choice.

The liberal can accept only the regulative principle of equality as constitutive of the liberal state. Individual choice is critical to liberalism, and end-state theories of equality must be based on governmental determinations of equal distributions. The liberal cannot tolerate this lack of impartiality. This does not mean that the liberal must become a utilitarian fanatic who relies on the unfettered market economy for formal equality, maximizing only the average welfare of all individuals. It is of no solace, and provides little meaning for modern liberals, that some members of our society have millions while others go without proper medical care because they have no insurance.

So in what sense can equality, defined as equal concern and respect for each person, act as a constitutive principle for liberalism? First and foremost, as we have seen, liberal equality must be neutral or impartial. Only official, governmental neutrality can allow the choice and liberty central to liberalism. Specifically, liberal equality cannot be based on any particular notion of the good life. One citizen must be free to choose to avoid medical care. Another must have the liberty to seek the medical care she can afford.

Given equal concern and respect for every citizen, and official neutrality regarding the good life, what kind of state does the modern liberal countenance? How does he distribute the goods and services available in society? It is doubtful that he will rely wholly on a market to distribute goods. Nor does it seem likely he will allow the government to make all distributional decisions. With his commitment to individual choice and also to equality, he will want resources distributed roughly equally, modified by the caveat that individuals must be able to exercise their preferences and transfer goods for those they value more.

Rough equality and maintenance of individual preference (negative freedom) are difficult values to satisfy mutually. Suppose, for the sake of argument, that all people have roughly equal talents and that each starts life with the same resources as everyone else. Given these rather unrealistic conditions, the modern liberal acknowledges that the market is the best way to conserve free choice and also maintain rough equality.

Consider again two patients. One values medical care and wants to purchase as much as possible. She invests in special diets, takes part in fitness programs, and requests medications that may be of only partial or marginal benefit. She wants above all to stay alive and directs her physician that should she become incompetent, she wants every possible measure to be taken to keep her alive. She develops leukemia at an advanced age. She has saved her money, giving up the enjoyment of sports cars and exotic travel, and she wants to spend her savings on a bone marrow transplant. In the ideal world in which we all start out with the same resources and same talents, her free choice or negative freedom is respected, and she purchases what she wishes. Yet our second patient has decided that eating well, smoking good cigarettes, and in general living a fast life is the best use of resources distributed to him. He does not seek therapy for his high blood pressure or his high cholesterol, and he develops heart disease. He has not saved for a heart transplant, and so he cannot purchase it. He dies of his heart disease, but he started out life with the same resources and same talents as the first patient. He exercised his negative freedom in an appropriate fashion, and he bought what he wished.

These examples reveal the ideal manner in which the market acts as a means for guaranteeing a roughly equal distribution of goods and services to individuals. In our example, the woman chose to trade aspects of a "good life" for more medical care. The man's choices were just the opposite. They had freedom to choose, and their use of resources was roughly equivalent. The difference was in their values, not in the distribution of goods. We do not have to feel sorry for the man who cannot have a heart transplant, nor do we feel uncomfortable about the elderly woman's bone marrow transplant. The choice of the market revealed equal concern and respect for both individuals, and the choices they made.

But we live in a real world, and political theories for ideal worlds are only of limited help. In any real liberal state, there are inequalities of talent and resources at birth. For example, on any given morning, I have several patients scheduled. One I see is a twenty-year-old man. When I asked him about his occupation several years ago, he told me he "hustled." It turns out that hustling includes a variety of illegal activities, the most profitable of which are male prostitution and the cocaine trade. While hustling, he contracted the human immunodeficiency virus (HIV). He is one of seven children from a home without a father. His mother was and is very insistent that I be firm with the patient, as she had already lost two sons in drug-related deaths. He has not always taken good care of himself, but now he appears to recognize that some medical follow-up is important. He is applying for general relief but is hampered by the fact that his reading skills are minimal.

Another of my patients is twenty-two. He is a junior at a local college and has sought medical treatment because there is a familial pattern of high cholesterol. He has had several sessions with the dietician in our office and now returns periodically for follow-up cholesterol tests. He studies mathematics, and in fact he derived a negative binomial statistical test for me so that I could win a bet with an epidemiologist friend. He, like my other patient, is both charming and decidedly entrepreneurial.

Without engaging in too great a "Prince and Pauper" fantasy, I do not find great differences in these two gentlemen. Although I would probably not ask the former to babysit for my kids at this point, I can imagine that he might perform in much the same manner as the other fellow if he had the same opportunities. While some might dismiss this as Pollyannaish, as a modern liberal, or even a classic liberal, I have to have some faith in the perfectibility of man and the value of each individual. Given that disease strikes people from all walks of life, I, like other physicians, have become well aware of the inequality in starting points for many people. And these inequalities of birth tend to disrupt the sense of equal concern and respect that the market can provide.

Thus the modern liberal state must address the inequalities in skills and birthright of individual citizens. A modern liberal citizen would like to develop an economic system that allows some inequalities, in particular the inequalities that reflect market choices, but not allow others, such as those that result from biological or social differences. In our liberal state, the market allows both types of inequality; indeed it is difficult to imagine any system in which the former inequities exist

without the latter. Since the liberal, even the modern liberal committed to equality, cannot give up the principle of individual choice, he
will probably stick with the market, or at least with simulations of the
market, in his construction of a social order.

But if the market is to be retained, it must be modified through
reforms that help develop a more equal distribution of goods while
leaving in place the value of economic choice. In medicine, this could
be done through taxation and development of a series of welfare programs so that people like my HIV seropositive patient have a fighting
chance to live the best lives possible. However, if one spends a lot of
time with the urban poor, and others generally disenfranchised by the
market, even the most liberal person may begin to argue that the
market itself should be done away with in large segments of society
and replaced by a socialist system. Negative freedom in this scenario
would be protected by simulations of the market in the pricing structure developed by the government. In any event, recognition of the
inequalities that occur in a market regime, and realization that the
market perhaps overvalues negative freedom, forces the modern liberal
to reflect on the values of a modified market, and even on the value of
socialist alternatives to the market.

Of course, the liberal need not fear that the particular mix of market
and nonmarket aspects of the economy is to be decided autocratically.
He will rely on representative democracy to decide the best way of
dealing with the inequality that arises from the market, or the lack of
equal respect and concern that develops when the socialist approach
curbs free choice in the market. Every individual, and groups of like-
minded individuals, will be able to lobby for changes in the mix of
market and socialism that they believe are appropriate. In this manner,
the liberal state reinforces its commitment to equality by giving each
individual an equal vote.

I am not so naive as to think that my vote counts as much as the
small campaign contribution I might make to my favorite elected official. Nor do I think that my contribution matters as much as the
much larger contribution that the AMA's political action committee
makes to a candidate. The liberal legislature can, however, create a
more equitable political sphere by passing legislation that prohibits
campaign contributions above a certain level. The legislature would
thus address inequality by trading free choice (of the members of the
PAC) for greater equality (between voices of citizens).

There is no doubt that democracy can still result in the majority's abuse of minorities. Not infrequently, the majority decides that it cares little about the equality of a certain insular minority. For instance, say the legislature in Massachusetts decides that the best way to deal with the budget crunch is to cut off disability and general relief for drug users. This would mean that my patient will not be able to qualify for Medicaid. His uninsured status means he will not be able to get drugs that will slow the affect of HIV in his system. His death will be hastened, and he will be treated with less respect than an insured patient. One unfortunate justification for this unequal treatment is that the average drug user is not a campaign contributor; indeed it is unlikely that he votes.

To avoid the inequities of majoritarianism, the modern liberal must advocate a set of civil liberties that will help maintain equal concern and respect—the principles at the heart of liberalism. He must also advocate a set of welfare rights to guarantee that poor people will have a right to aid, medical care, and legal representation. Insofar as our state fails to provide these rights, it fails to guarantee the equality central to modern liberalism. It is thus not illiberal for us to advocate wider civil liberties to guarantee the equality that gave rise to the market and representative democracy as the major institutions of our society. As Ronald Dworkin notes:

The familiar idea, for example, that rights of redistribution are justified by an ideal of equality that overrides the efficiency ideals of the market in certain cases, has no place in liberal theory. For the liberal, rights are justified, not by some principle in competition with an independent justification of the political and economic institutions they qualify, but in order to make more perfect the only justification on which these other institutions may themselves rely.[19]

That justification is an equal concern and respect for individuals.

Justice, Law, and Morality

Civil liberties have to define modern liberalism's notions of justice. Justice is the first virtue of social institutions. Justice governs institutions; it is conceptually distinct from the virtues that govern personal action. "The principle of justice for institutions must not be confused with the principles which apply to individuals and their actions in particular situations."[20] Thus personal morality is separated, as in classic liberalism, from the attributes of a just state.

Liberal justice is based on the fairness of a contract between equals; it is a contractualist theory. The notion of wrongness in contractualism has been defined by Timothy Scanlon as follows: "An act is wrong if its performance under the circumstances would be disallowed by any system of rules for the general regulation of behavior which no one could reasonably reject as a basis for informed, unforced, general agreement."[21] The justice of institutions derives from the fact that equal individuals, impartial about their attributes, accept a set of rules as fair. This is justice as fairness.

The modern liberal, such as Rawls, can integrate the ideals of equality, fairness, and impartiality into an overarching theory of justice using the construct of the "original position." In the original position, the fundamentally equal citizens of a society gather together and select the principles that will guide their later decisions concerning the shape of the institutions they will populate. These principles will give life to the laws and institutions that will govern the way people must treat one another. The citizenry remains ignorant of their own attributes in the future society. In this manner, the impartiality and equality of respect of liberalism are fundamentally rooted. Rawls calls the lack of knowledge of the future society, and one's position within it, the "veil of ignorance." The veil hides present circumstances from the original position. Thus the citizenry must select principles that will guarantee fairness, and, as their final position in that society cannot be known ahead of time, they all will want a fair share in the society they build.

The primary principle governing the society that is to be created by the modern liberal citizens of the original position is this: "Each person is to have an equal right to the most extensive total system of equal basic liberties compatible with a similar system of liberty for all."[22] This principle has two parts. The first is equal liberty and fair process. The second part concerns substantive inequality. Since one does not know which position one will be in as a member of the society-to-be, it makes sense that everyone would want the same liberties and a just legal system. Moreover, no one wants to be discriminated against from the outset, or to be born with deficient resources. To militate against such eventualities, Rawls puts a limit on inequality. "Social and economic inequalities are to be arranged so that they are both (a) to the greatest benefit of the least advantaged, and (b) attached to offices and positions open to all under conditions of fair equality of opportunity."[23] The right to equal liberties and the limit on inequality are, then, the two subprinciples that liberal citizens in the original position would select.[24]

But, the modern liberal must move beyond these formal considerations and discuss the general motivations of citizens in a given society. The first major concern will likely be the attainment of primary goods. The founders of the original position would develop a list of such goods. These primary goods would then be distributed through a modified marketplace. The market would be modified to prevent any action that increases inequalities without benefit to all. The justice of the institutions that develop to distribute primary goods is guaranteed by the principles embedded in such institutions from the start.

Institutions are just insofar as they reflect the impartiality of the original position. This impartiality is translated into principles that promote liberty and constrain inequality. Clearly, constraints on inequality will diminish liberty and the extent to which limits on inequality bind liberty should be a subject of active political discussion. The lines of battle will shift as this is debated within the liberal state. The modified market thus is valuable to the liberal state insofar as it helps bring about the compromise between negative freedom and equality. In turn, market mechanisms should be constrained when they produce inequality in society without a compensating increase in liberty.

Again we can return to the example of medical care to illustrate the place of the market within the liberal state. In our liberal state, we rely on private insurance to finance medical care. Private insurance is supplemented by nonmarket governmental interventions such as Medicare and Medicaid. Nonetheless, some individuals are still without insurance for medical care. As a result of decreased access to medical care, they may suffer higher rates of mortality. At present, there is a debate within our society about the best way to address the question of the uninsured. Some would argue that we should increase taxes and use the revenues to purchase insurance for them. Others suggest that health care providers should care for uninsured patients without expectation of compensation. The decrease of the liberty of a few—either through higher taxes or through economic penalties for health care providers—is justified by a decrease in the overall inequality in our society. The operation of representative democracy in the liberal state must provide answers about the best approach to such problems. These are the concerns of liberal justice.

While the principles of justice shape institutions, they do not define personal morality. Liberal institutions allow individuals to develop moral stances freely, so long as they do not interfere with justice. To define in more detail the nature of liberal justice, one must address the law. As Dworkin has noted, the law is justice translated into the real world.[25]

There is inevitably a moral dimension to law.[26] While this statement on first sight seems a truism, it is not a given in jurisprudence. Indeed one of the most important theories of the relation of morality to law denies any necessary such relationship. Positivism holds that the propositions of law are largely dependent on notions of authority and that valid laws need not express nor be derivable from morality. The law is backed by the power of the state. Liberals, however, insist that law bears a complicated relationship to morality, and that the nature of that relationship is critical to an understanding of the place of ethics and morality in the liberal state.

A modern liberal might argue that there are two types of morality: majoritarian and public morality. The former is the conception of shared morality held by the majority of a group or society. The latter concerns the "general moral principles used in the criticism of actual social institutions including [majoritarian] morality."[27] The modern liberal argues that although people may disagree about the content of morality, there must be some agreement on the fundamental principles that underlie the state. Thus the modern liberal conceives of both a morality of the majority, and a public moral infrastructure made up of critical principles that may restrict that morality.

Public morality constitutes the principles that in turn constitute justice. As we have seen, in a liberal state these principles are quite narrow and maintain an impartiality regarding the individual's outlook. Individual moral views must, however, conform to the public morality insofar as a consensus of views is necessary for society to exist (the overlapping consensus discussed by Rawls).

The modern liberal advances these arguments concerning morality and the law without the positivist's detachment of law and morality. However, he rejects a model of law and morality, such as proposed by Patrick Devlin,[28] that implies that the judiciary must be willing to take account of all the prejudices, rationalizations, and inconsistencies that make up the majority's belief about a legal or moral issue. This, the modern liberal asserts, is not what the law is about. Legal questions should not be a report of prejudices or feelings. They should be settled through reasonable argument. The law must have moral integrity.[29]

Rather than consult the majority, the modern liberal, whether the legislator or jurist, is charged to think and to analyze. She "must sift these arguments and positions, trying to determine which are prejudices or rationalizations, which presupposes general principles or theories vast parts of the population could not be supposed to accept, and so on."[30] This reasoning process is based on the public morality of the state, not on the collection of individual moral views that constitutes a majority. Discussions of the correctness and rightness of a law must draw upon analysis that leads to the study of principles, not the study of prejudice and irrationality. The principles that constitute the public morality of a liberal state are those pertaining to impartiality, individual choice, equality of respect and concern, and civil rights that protect minorities and work against inequality.

There are, of course, limits to liberal impartiality and tolerance. While most liberals would agree that "the identity and continuity of a society reside not in the common possession of a single morality, but in the mutual toleration of different moralities,"[31] they would also recognize the potential for anarchy in such a society. The public morality of the liberal state both celebrates and constrains the individual's autonomy, and thus the choice of individual moral viewpoints. The law is the product of rational consideration of the public morality. The plurality of moral views that the public morality allows, indeed encourages, can be called the social morality.

Thus the relation of morality to law is quite complicated. The principles of justice constitute what can be called a public morality. They define the relationships between institutions and citizens within the modern liberal state in an effort to bring about the "right" or the "good." The law is the result of rational consideration of the principles of justice, the instantiation of these principles. The law does not, however, exhaust the totality of potential goods, or of correct relations between persons. People enjoy and pursue moral activity above and beyond the requirements of the law. Liberalism encourages such activity, within the purview of liberty. While the law has moral content, there is much moral activity beyond the concerns of law and justice. The aggregate of individual moralities is the social morality. The moral outlook that constitutes a majority of individual viewpoints on any one issue is the majoritarian morality. A just liberal society requires that there be a relationship between law and public morality, but no relationship between law and majoritarian morality.

This is not, however, to say that every law of a particular state necessarily reflects liberal values. Just as there is variation between real nations that we might call modern liberal states (the United States, Canada, and Great Britain), so too is there variation in the "liberalness" of various laws in those states. A liberal state and its individual laws can be scrutinized from the point of view of the principles of liberalism. This chapter then provides a summary of the notions of liberalism we will use to study medical ethics in a liberal state, especially, but not solely, our modern liberal state in the United States.

At the beginning of this chapter, I noted that many of the moral problems in medicine raise political and legal questions. Physicians and patients find themselves bumping into a number of governmental institutions and often face concerns of justice. As a result, I argued, it was important for one concerned with medical ethics to understand the liberal state.

The modern liberal wants to maintain a broad range of negative freedoms for individuals. He wants the state to remain as impartial as possible toward the choices that go into the pursuit of a good life. But, the modern liberal is also committed to treating each member of society with equal concern and respect. He realizes that talents and opportunities are spread unevenly within society and that as a result great substantive inequalities can occur in the liberal state. While the liberal is willing to use a market economy to distribute goods, and indeed believes that the market itself can bring about the best compromise between equality and negative freedom, he is willing to modify market approaches substantially if they lead to significant inequalities. The liberal relies on representative democracy, supplemented by a set of entitlements and civil liberties, to develop the best possible mix of equality and individual freedom.

The modern liberal understands that the principles underlying the liberal state constitute a public morality. The essential values of this public morality are liberty and equality of each individual. The liberal state allows the growth of personal morality; it accepts and indeed encourages individuals to develop their own choices regarding a moral life. Nonetheless, this aggregate of personal moralities, called the social morality, must not conflict with the public morality that issues from the principles underlying the liberal state. The law and the justice of institutions thus constrain social morality. Individual rights not only protect the sphere of negative freedom for the individual but are a way to counter the threat of inequality that shadows such liberty.

This outline of liberalism can bring the paradigms discussed at the

outset of this chapter into focus. The individual who killed his comatose son was acting on his own morality and ideals, which had brought
him to the decision that his son's life was not worth living. He was
prosecuted by the state because there is a concern that his personal
morality conflicted with the public morality of the state. The hospital's
decision not to terminate care was based on concerns that its motives
might be misinterpreted, that it would be perceived as being unduly
influenced by the market. In short, hospital officials were afraid the
public would view the hospital as willing to countenance murder if the
patient were unable to pay his bill.

The court decision on the lover of the man who died of AIDS
reflects the court's willingness to protect individual or negative freedom. He had been placed at risk for infection, a risk to which he had
not consented. The individual autonomy central to liberalism's negative freedom implies full knowledge of risks, or at least is adverse to
misleading information about risks. Thus the court's award of damages
reflects the liberal state's interest in autonomy.

Finally, one can understand the government's decision on prospective budgeting of physicians' payments under Medicare. The government funds Medicare as a means of creating more equality within our
society. The market cannot provide decent insurance for elderly people. Therefore, the government intervenes and constrains the market in
order to bring about more comprehensive insurance and better care for
members of society who would otherwise be treated unequally. The
representative democracy must decide who will bear the burden—the
loss of liberty—for this effort to provide greater equality. In the past,
general tax revenues have been used to fund Medicare. Now it appears
the government will have the burden fall more selectively on health
care providers, who will be expected to provide necessary care, some
of which will not be compensated.

The outcome of each of these cases makes sense when one consults
the public morality of the liberal state. We have noted, however, that
the public morality of the liberal state is different from the individual
moralities selected by its citizens. Physicians have long assumed that
important moral issues in medicine are the concern of the patient and
the physician. But I will argue throughout this book, that American
medical care takes place in the liberal state. The political economy of
health care cannot be distanced from liberalism. Moreover, the indi-

vidual relationships between doctors and patients must be constrained by the public morality of liberalism. With this understanding of liberalism, let us turn to a discussion of medical ethics.

2

The Medical Enterprise and Medical Ethics

At the beginning of chapter 1, I discussed a number of newspaper stories dealing with tragic events. In each, doctors and patients were involved. The government, the legal system, and health care institutions also played a role. The stories raise questions of social values and correct or right action; in other words, they involve moral issues.

A physician reviewing these stories about a family withdrawing care from their child, about the integrity of the doctor-patient relationship, or about problems with the availability of care, would see them in terms of morality. That is, she would assume that the right action would be for the attending physician to consult her professional ethical code and make her own decision. A professional ethical code is not a part of the law; it is a more personal concern of the professional group. The physician's considerations are thus matters of social morality.

Others might have a different view. For many, the first news story would raise questions about the proper extent of criminal law and the role of technology in prolonging life. They might see the physicians who failed to inform a lover of a man with AIDS about the patient's disease as wrongdoers, and they might regard the distribution of primary goods, in this case, the rationing of care for the elderly, as a set of social decisions. Cast in this manner, these problems seem to be concerns of public morality. They require consideration of what is just for society as much as or more than they require consideration of one profession's social morality. They are problems central to the liberal state.

Physicians have tended to treat such problems as a matter of professional ethics. Increasingly, society must treat them as political and legal problems. As the care of patients and the medical enterprise become more complicated and require more and more supporting institutions, medicine moves into the realm of public morality. Justice plays a larger and larger role, and the mandates of the liberal state loom larger in what used to be essentially private decisions. Indeed, it may very well be that some aspects of medical ethics are illiberal, and that the public morality should constrain and modify medical ethics. The liberal state may require doctors to take quite different actions from those of traditional medical ethics. Indeed, I would argue that the public morality of the liberal state conflicts in no uncertain terms with many tenets of medical ethics as they are traditionally understood. Why this is so is the question I address in this chapter and the next.

The Functional Analysis of Medical Ethics

The special nature of the traditional doctor-patient relationship, particularly the inequality of knowledge and the vulnerability of the patient, is central to an understanding of the evolution and function of medical ethics. Without an ethical context emphasizing physician duty and fidelity, concepts somewhat separate from the principles of the liberal state, many physicians would assert that doctor-patient communication cannot occur.

D. Barnlund has outlined the obstacles to communication between doctors and patients.[1] He notes communication is inhibited in situations that touch upon the patient's sense of self, such as discussions of physical inadequacy. Communication is also difficult when there are great differences in knowledge, as is usually the case in encounters between doctors and patients. The same is true when status differences exist between people, as is likely in a medical setting. The different things that doctors and patients want to say, and the different ways in which they say those things, create emotional distance between them.

These differences are exacerbated by verbal manipulation and by ambiguity of language. Without some sort of special relation or special attention to communication, these problems could tend to overwhelm the possibility of patients understanding physicians.

In their now-classic article on the doctor-patient relationship, T. Szasz and J. Hollender provide a description of the kind of interaction that can overcome these problems. The first, and what the authors characterize as the oldest, model is that of activity-passivity. The doctor is active and dominates the relationship, giving orders to the patient. The patient is to follow the doctor's order—he is essentially a nonparticipant in the relationship. The second model discussed by Szasz and Hollender is guidance-cooperation. Both participants are "active" in this relationship. There is, however, an unequal balance of power in that the doctor can overrule the patient. The third model represents the opposite of the active-passive model. It is called the mutual participation model. The authors note that

mutuality rests on complex processes of identification—which facilitates conceiving of others in terms of oneself—together with maintaining and tolerating the discrete individuality of the observer and observed. It is crucial to this type of interaction that the participants (1) have approximately equal power, (2) be mutually independent, and (3) engage in activity that will in some ways be satisfying to both.[2]

The other two models need not demonstrate any of these characteristics.

Each of these models can describe doctor-patient relationships. The first model, the active-passive relationship, represents the traditional therapeutic paradigm. In this type of relationship, the doctor takes control of the patient's free choice, and directs the patient back to health. In a sense there is a psychological merging of the doctor and patient, with the physician retaining the prerogatives of choice in the fused identity. This fusion, as Robert Burt has noted, provides the psychic basis for the therapeutic effect.[3] But it also puts a great deal of power into the hands of the physician, and it requires that there be an enormous trust in the doctor's decision.

Szasz and Hollender imply that doctor-patient relationships are moving away from this pole, toward that of mutual participation. They assume that patients want more control over the course of their treatment. However, until quite recently, the commitment of physicians to a doctor-patient relationship that approximates the mutual participation model has been questionable.[4] The inequality of power and knowledge always tugs the doctor-patient relationship toward the active-passive model, investing the physician with great authority.

The relationship between doctors and patients that is suggested by this review of ethical codes and doctor-patient communication is not typical of relations between the citizens of a liberal state. Traditionally, doctors have seen it as their duty to make decisions on behalf of patients. The reason such dutiful action was necessary was the power of the physician over the patient, a power held by virtue of greater knowledge and the patient's vulnerability. Medical ethics has helped ensure that this power was used benevolently.

This kind of power relationship based on inequity of knowledge is typical of professions. As H. S. Becker has noted, "Professions are occupations which possess a monopoly of some esoteric and difficult body of knowledge. Further, this knowledge is considered to be necessary for the continued functioning of society."[5] Along with the monopoly of information goes control of the professional relationship. Thus "physicians consider it their prerogative to define the nature of disease and of health, and to determine how medical services ought to be distributed and paid for."[6] The professional realizes that she possesses a great deal of power over the client. The client is unable to judge the professional's abilities because of the inequity of knowledge. As a result, the client's only recourse, is a blind trust in the professional: "The client is to trust the professional; he must tell him all secrets which bear upon the affairs in hand. He must trust his judgment and skill."[7] Thus the patient/client is expected to give in to the rationality of science, suspend at least partially his liberty to pursue his own values, and accept the physician's authority.[8]

Authority is conceptually linked to reason.[9] A person will accept authority when he accepts the rationality that underlies and infuses it. An example of an authority is a dictionary. One accepts it as such because of the rationality that it exemplifies. The same is partially true of a doctor and a patient. The patient accepts the physician because of the rationality that underlies medical science. The dictionary analogy does not provide much insight, however, into those decisions a physician makes that involve nonrational issues concerning the patient's personal values. Thus authority based simply on rationality will neither provide justification for the physician-professional prerogatives nor for the active-passive model of doctors and patients.[10]

Talcott Parsons has developed a more comprehensive theory of doctors' and patients' relations and of medical professional authority.[11] Parsons's approach demands that the various actors in any relationship play specific roles that serve certain functions. The patient plays a sick role. The doctor plays the healer. In a simplistic analysis, physicians must help the sick, while the sick, must try to get better. But the sick person is not expected to be able to get better on his own: he has a "condition," not an "attitude." In return for his special status or "condition," which relieves him of other social responsibilities, the patient must seek technically competent help, namely, that of a physician, and he must cooperate with her in the process of trying to get well. It is here, of course, where the role of the sick person as patient is enmeshed with the role of the physician as healer.[12]

The physician's role is perhaps more complex.[13] First of all, it reflects achievement values that are intended to guarantee technical competence. Another set of values is designed to preclude physician behaviors that might take advantage of the patient's vulnerable position. Functional specificity demands that the physician deal only with those aspects of a patient's life that are necessary for a cure. A physician must be affectively neutral, meaning that he must treat the patient only within a technical rubric. Involvement with the patient on other levels is prohibited. These aspects of his role protect the physician from "transference" and allow him to enter the patient's private life without compromising the openness necessary for the relationship. As Jeffrey Berlant has put it: "Fundamentally, the physician gains access to the patient's private life by maximizing trust, emphasizing competence, asking health related questions, and segregating the context of professional practice from other contexts."[14]

The patient must also be protected from the possibility of a physician's economic greed. Since the physician makes many of the decisions about the kind of care that the patient needs, the possibility exists that the physician will prescribe unnecessary treatments for her own profit. This temptation is mediated by what Parsons calls the "collectivity orientation" of physicians. The profession sees itself as a collectivity; its orientation is to the group as a whole, rather than to individual members.

The ideology of the profession lays great emphasis on the obligation of the physician to put the welfare of the patient above his personal interests, and regards commercialism as the most serious and insidious evil with which it has to contend. . . . The profit motive is to be drastically excluded from the medical world.[15]

This orientation, Parson believes, should prohibit the physician from advertising, bargaining over fees, and refusing patients because of economics. Thus the doctor's authority is not "legitimized without reciprocal collectivity orientation in the relationship."[16] These sentiments echo the codes of traditional medical ethics.

In summary, Parsons posits that the technical competence of the physician is the way to understand the doctor-patient relationship. It is this technical competence that leads the patient to seek the physician. In turn, the physician's role is defined by the attitudes and subroles that protect the patient from the "built-in institutionalized superiority of professional roles."[17] Such orientations lead to "an association in which the status of the participants is declared to be formally equal."[18]

Parsons's theory of the doctor-patient relationship is remarkably broad, containing both normative prescriptions and sociological descriptions. Any theory of this breadth is open to some criticism, but one is especially telling. In Parsons's discussion of the doctor-patient relationship, he puts too much emphasis on its expert-layperson aspects. As was noted above, the physician's technical expertise, for Parsons, is the linchpin of the other subroles that define the doctor-patient relationship. Other sociologists have argued that different dynamics provide the primary context of this relationship. Eliot Friedson, for instance, notes that

the basic interpersonal paradigm of a problematic doctor-patient relationship may be seen as a conflict between perspectives and a struggle for control over services. . . . In the case of medicine in the recent past of the United States, the marketplace has been organized for a fee-for-service basis, practitioners being entrepreneurs, nominally competing with each for the fees of prospective patients. The merchant-customer relationship has been emphasized.[19]

Friedson allows that there are also expert-layperson and bureaucratic official-client relationships within the doctor-patient interaction. He nonetheless asserts that the merchant-customer relationship is foremost.

Parsons had assumed that the collectivity orientation would prevent physicians from playing the merchant role. In *The Social System*, he refused to address the medical profession's advocacy of the fee-for-service economic structure of private practice. In a later essay, "Social

Change and Medical Organization in the United States," he portrayed
the fee-for-service system as an embarrassment, and as something that
would disappear as professionalism grew. Moreover, he noted that the

insistence by the official spokesman of "organized medicine" that the individual fee-for-service mode of organization is the morally ideal one lays the
profession wide open to the charge that they have abandoned their ancient and
honorable devotion to the welfare of the patient.[20]

In his refusal to accept the pronouncements of "organized medicine"
Parsons was obviously being prescriptive rather than descriptive. Thus
his analysis of the doctor-patient relationship at least partially fails
because it is a model of what he thinks reality should be, rather than
what it is.

From the vantage point of Parsons's ideal role of the physician,
however, it is easy to understand the importance of medical ethics.
Medical ethics summarizes and embodies the ideals that Parsons says
must guide the physician: the patient is to "come first," before any
consideration of economic gain. The physician must enable the patient
to trust her and must fulfill her obligations to the patient faithfully.
The patient's trust is thus not based solely on the doctor's knowledge,
but is justified by the doctor's benevolence. Jonsen has argued that the
doctor's power is based "on the assumption that physicians [are] not
only skilled in medical arts, but [are] also benevolent, that is, [have]
the intention and the motivation to use medical arts to the benefit of
the patient. Skill and benevolence [have been] the titles to the right to
control the physician-patient relationship."[21]

Perhaps more important, the functional role of medical ethics designed by Parsons requires "honorable devotion to the patient" that is
not to be affected by financial pressures. Thus Parsons himself could
not reconcile medical ethics with fee-for-service practice. Yet many
physicians who support Parsons's understanding of the correct doctor-
patient relationship also support fee-for-service arrangements. Indeed
they might argue that such arrangements were ideal from an ethical
point of view because they provide insulation from market constraints,
and, as I will argue, from the public morality of liberalism. This in turn
would enable a duty-based ethic to thrive. To understand how this is
so, let us turn to a discussion of traditional medical ethics.

Doctors, Patients, and Codes of Ethics

Medical ethics, like justice, liberalism, and freedom, is not easily defined. Engelhardt refers to it as the "taken for granted webs of moral values that constitute the character of everyday life-worlds of medical practice."[22] He also refers to medical ethics as canons of proper conduct for physicians. But what is proper conduct for physicians? What are the moral values of medical practice? How do they relate to the public morality of liberalism? The medical profession has a long history of ethical codes, most of which are regarded with great respect. A complete discussion of these codes is impossible here, but an overview can provide some insights into the medical profession's view of its moral relations with patients.[23]

The Hippocratic oath, adopted by a small group of Pythagorean physicians in the fourth century B.C., is usually the starting point of an analysis of physician codes.[24] As Robert Veatch has thoroughly discussed, there are several major themes within the oath. The first, which Veatch calls the Hippocratic tradition, commits the physician "to producing good for [the] patient and to protecting that patient from harm."[25] The second major theme is paternalism. The Hippocratic ethic gives remarkable authority to the physician to use her judgment to decide what will be beneficial: "I will follow that system . . . which according to my ability and judgment, I consider for the benefit of the sick."[26] Third, the Hippocratic oath "is remarkably silent on the question of whether the physician has duties to the sick of society, or only to individual patients with whom the physician is engaged."[27] The Hippocratic ethic, taken as a whole, is thus well summarized by Tom L. Beauchamp and James F. Childress who note that it views physicians as independent, self-sufficient philanthropists who give a gift of noble behavior to their patients.[28]

The Hippocratic tradition can be traced through nearly two thousand years of patient care to the widely accepted beginnings of modern medical ethics, the code of which was written by Thomas Percival. Percival's discussion of professional conduct in general practice contained advice in six areas: "trust building, consultation among physicians, taking over another physician's patient, economic policy, promoting the honor and interests of the profession, retrospection, and miscellany."[29] Where Percival's code went beyond the Hippocratic theme, it was usually in terms of etiquette rather than ethics. Many of his admonitions were meant to contain intraprofessional strife and to develop self-regulation.[30] His rules also tended to minimize competition between doctors, further diminishing the need for outside regulation. Thus, with Percival, the medical ethical code became a device for professional cohesiveness.

The first code of ethics developed by the AMA in 1847 drew heavily upon Percival's lead.[31] Subsequent American codes paid increasing attention to the role of fees in medical practice and to the concept of fee splitting. In the 1903 code, physicians were for the first time ethically bound to collect fees; again, however, there were firm rules against competition.[32] Moreover, the ethical code frowned on group practices, as they were thought to dilute the individual doctor-patient relationship.[33] In 1912, the new code was even more specific:

It is unprofessional for a physician to dispose of his services under conditions that make it impossible to render adequate services to his patient or which interfere with reasonable competition among the physicians of a community.[34]

Thus the emphasis on patient trust, doctor control, and economic noninterference was institutionalized.

By 1949, the profession could no longer ignore the inroads of "third parties" into the practice of medicine. Nonetheless, the 1949 code stated that the

physician should not dispose of his professional attainments or services to any hospital, by body, organization, group or individual . . . under terms or conditions which permit exploitation of the services of the physician for the financial profit of the agency concerned.[35]

If there were to be profit in a health care setting, it should devolve to the physician, not to a third party. More to the point, a fee-for-service practice effectively excluded outside influences from the doctor-patient relationship, enabling physicians to devote full attention to patients.

More recent codes of ethics have avoided strict prescriptions as we shall discuss in a later chapter. But even today the prescriptions noted above would sound appropriate to many doctors. Hippocrates' traditions, Percival's etiquette, and the principles of the AMA code all contain insights into what many practitioners undoubtedly feel is special about medical ethics. In particular, these codes emphasize physician duty to patients. This fidelity to the work of healing, to the medical needs of the patient, seems to entail a certain disrespect for the

negative freedom of the individual and hence for one of the fundamental values of our liberal state. In addition, the medical professional
codes, with their emphasis on noncompetition and an opposition to
third parties who seek to profit from the doctor-patient relationship,
reflect suspicion of market relations in medical care, with the exception
of the patient fee for the doctor and the need for independence from
extraclinical pressures. Indeed these observations suggest that medical
professional ethics have required that the relation between doctors and
patients be independent of the principles underlying liberalism. The
emphasis has been on duty to the patient, not respect for liberty.

Any code of ethics must be grounded in a more philosophical theory of morality. Of course, it is not really possible to talk about a
theory of medical ethics, or even theories of medical ethics. As Veatch
has noted, "To be realistic about it, 'theories of medical ethics' is too
pretentious. What we really have before us is a series of unsystematic,
unreflective, ethical stances of traditions."[36] The variety of codes, essays by physicians, theologians, and philosophers, and ethical and
moral assumptions that are termed medical ethics is enormous. Nonetheless, there are some values or ideals that are fairly consistently found
in these essays that undertake the task assigned to them by Parsons's
functional interpretation.

These values or ideals center on the physician's responsibility to the
patient—a physician is said to act morally when he or she places the
patient's welfare above all other considerations. Beauchamp and
Childress have stated this principle in the following manner: "The
physician is not a policymaker. His or her primary responsibility is to
the patient, and society has good reasons for insisting on the primacy
of this responsibility of personal care."[37] The well-being of the patient
must be the doctor's primary concern, and his attention to any other
ethical issue is usually discouraged.[38] In this regard, sociology enters
the province of moral philosophy. "The physician is thrust into a paternalistic role on numerous occasions by the questionable condition
of patients, by their enormous regard for his or her knowledge of their
conditions, and partly by their unwillingness or inability to make hard
decisions."[39] As Parsons assumed, medical ethics orders the physician's
relations with patients in a manner that increases her own prerogatives.
While the "patient comes first" in terms of the physician's ethical code,
it is the physician who is the decision maker. Thus, in essence, the code
emphasizes physician regard for patient welfare, not patient autonomy
per se.

This is not, however, to say that medical ethics is only justified by its practical application. Indeed, many advocates of traditional medical ethics would say that medical morality is not grounded in utilitarian considerations, but in the goodness of the morally correct relation between two people.

The most eloquent of such theories of medical ethics is the covenant-fidelity model proposed by Paul Ramsey. Ramsey writes that "in the language of philosophy, a deontological dimension or test holds chief place in medical ethics, beside teleological considerations."[40] His characterization of medical ethics as deontological means that the moral worth of the doctor-patient relationship is contained within the relationship itself, not in the possible ends of the relationship. In other words, the goodness of the relationship cannot be explained by the outcome of the relationship; the goodness must reside in the immediate interaction of doctor and patient.

Ramsey develops his theory by emphasizing the loyalty between doctor and patient. Rather than the blind trust purportedly demanded of clients by professionals, Ramsey states that there is reciprocal trust between doctors and patients. Their relationship is a cooperative agreement: "Faithfulness among men—the faithfulness that is formative for all covenants or moral bonds of life with life—gains specification for the primary relations peculiar to medical practice."[41] This kind of mutual trust allows the healing relationship to occur. "Men's capacity to become joint adventurers in a common cause makes possible a consent to enter the relation of patient to physician, or of subject to investigator. This means that partnership is a better term than contract in conceptualizing the relation between patient and physician or between subject and investigator."[42] What we described above as a unification of personalities forced by the physician's much greater knowledge becomes, in this context, a free choice by two people. The physician's authority is generated by the patient's free choice and by the mutual trust and faithfulness of the relationship.

In some ways, the mutuality of the doctor-patient partnership is akin to that generated within Kantian ethics.[43] Bernard Williams concurs with this conclusion. Each patient, Williams writes, is "owed the effort of understanding, and that on achieving it, each man is to be abstracted from certain conspicuous structures of inequality in which we find him."[44] Thus both Williams and Ramsey agree that the doctor-patient interaction must reflect a relation between people as

ends in themselves, and that it must demonstrate the duty-bound action and radical equality entailed by that sort of relation.

What does it mean to say that medical ethics are Kantian? A full-
blown discussion of this subject is beyond the scope of this book. Of
great importance, however, is Immanuel Kant's statement, in chapter
1 of his *Groundwork of the Metaphysics of Morals*, that "it is impossible
to conceive anything at all in the world, or even out of it, which can
be taken as good without qualification, except a good will."[45] He
rejects any thought of moral action that is based on the good the
action may produce. A good will is not good simply because of what
it causes, but because of its intrinsic value. Moreover, a will that acts
for the sake of duty is a good will. Hence, Kantian moral activity
springs, not from inclination, but from duty.

In turn, duty that is defined by a categorical imperative can be
stated in a number of ways, but the most coherent is this: "Act in such
a way that you always treat humanity, whether in your own person or
in the person of any other, never simply as a means, but always at the
same time as an end."[46] Dutiful action is action done out of respect for
a law that emphasizes one's respect for others. Thus moral activity
turns, not on what the activity produces, but on how one treats one's
fellows.

It is predictable then that some find Kantian ethics to be especially
applicable to the moral relationship between doctors and patients.[47]
The doctor's task is to help the patient back to good health. This
activity involves her deeply in the life of the patient. The doctor also
possesses, as we have seen, a special knowledge that makes her, in
some ways, superior to the patient. The patient must rely on this
knowledge and trust that the physician will not abuse the power it
gives her. A Kantian theory of medical ethics posits that both patient
and physician will treat one another as ends in themselves. This will be
understood by the physician as dutiful behavior. She will act in accordance with the dictates of the duty she has to the patient. In Hans
Jonas's words:

In the course of treatment, the physician is obligated to the patient and no one
else. He is not the agent of society, nor of the interests of medical science, nor
of the patient's family, nor of his co-sufferers or future sufferers from the same
disease. The patient alone counts when he is under the physician's care. By the
simple law of bilateral contract . . . the physician is bound to not let any other
interest interfere with that of the patient in being cured. But manifestly more

sublime norms than contractual ones are involved. We may speak of a sacred trust; strictly by its terms, the doctor is, as it were, alone with his patient and God.[48]

Again, it is argued that the doctor's sense of duty and the trust between patient and physician supersede the concerns of other interests.

What then are the details of this duty-based medical ethics? S. Twiss describes the special demands of the doctor-patient relationship as pertaining "mainly to the fulfillment of duties designed to further the welfare of others, albeit a defined class of others."[49] He notes further that "these duties are often nonpreemptive in character (that is, not claimed as rights) because they enjoin the kinds of actions that are not performed out of loyalty, devotion and respect. . . . These duties represent moral requirements that fall under a general concept of concern, concern for another's welfare."[50]

Medical ethicists often refer to this interpretation of the doctor-patient relationship as the theory of beneficence. Unfortunately, the definition of beneficence is sometimes murky. For instance, Edmund Pellegrino and David Thomasma define it as a shorthand for the best interests of the patient, including in those interests both respect for the patient's autonomy and calculations about his quality of life.[51] This makes beneficence sound as though it is partly Kantian, partly utilitarian. Later, however, they note that for beneficence to work, the physician must pursue a course of self-effacement; agapeistic ethics are the norm.[52] Indeed, Pellegrino and Thomasma reject the contractual model of the doctor-patient relationship for one of fidelity. Virtue, for a physician, is placing the good of the patient before her own good.[53]

It is clear that these notions of medical ethics conflict with some of the principles that guide action in a liberal state. While the formal equality between doctor and patient is emphasized, the patient's individual liberty is not essential to the partnership. A sphere of free action is not guaranteed the patient; rather, the partnership's mutual trust involves the physician in the most profound aspects of the patient's life. The physician's self-effacement and commitment to the patient is the solution to the inequities in power and knowledge noted by sociologists. The patient trusts the physician and the physician is duty bound to treat the patient with complete respect. The emphasis on duty thus sets the relationship off from the values of the liberal state. Patient autonomy is not entrusted to the patient, but rather to the doctor. In many ways, "the patient comes first" means the doctor decides.

In summary, the beneficence model of medical ethics squares nicely with a functional explanation of medical ethics. The inequality of doctor and patient in knowledge is overcome by patient trust and the physician's sense of duty. Of course, for both sociological and philosophical reasons, the relationship must be insulated from the pressures of profit. The beneficence model assumes at least a conceptual discontinuity between the treatment of patients and the principles of the public morality of liberalism as well as an insulation of doctors and patients from market influences. The fee-for-service payment helps isolate the therapeutic endeavor from the market economy, because only the physician is subject to financial incentives, and he withstands these owing to his commitment to dutiful action.

In the next section, we will present an overview of the institutions that nurtured the therapeutic encounter, insulating it from liberalism and the market. We will then see how these institutions have changed and diminished and how others are growing up in their place, and we will outline a medical morality that can accommodate the new medical realities that are firmly grounded in the liberal state.

The Medical Enterprise of the Past

In the United States, the medical profession has always insisted on a fee-for-service system of reimbursement and opposed any third-party interference with doctors and patients. This is apparent from the earliest history of our country. The subject of the government's involvement in health care issues was raised soon after independence, when the president and his entire cabinet were forced to flee Washington in 1793 because of a yellow fever epidemic plaguing the East Coast. Many believed that the epidemic would have been more effectively controlled if the federal government had been empowered to act. But legislative proposals designed to implement federal control of some public health programs were met with challenges from states' rights advocates. The Supreme Court's decision on the matter affirmed the principle that states were to control health care matters.

Within the states, medical societies modeled on the British Royal College of Physicians were soon established. Before independence, the Royal College had enjoyed a legal monopoly on licensing in the colonies. Beginning with the incorporation of the Massachusetts State Medical Society in 1781, the licensing function was taken over by statewide organizations of physicians.[54] As Berlant has noted, the power of the medical societies was restricted throughout the first three decades of the nineteenth century, largely because of a general hostility toward corporations.[55] The medical societies were also opposed by medical school administrators, who were rivals for control of the profession. Nonetheless, by 1830 most states had societies that controlled their licensing and state laws that restricted the unlicensed, thus giving the profession some control over who could practice medicine, as well as over the type of medicine that could be practiced.

Growing public discontent with the performance of physicians and widespread fears of monopoly led to the repeal in the 1830s of many licensure laws. This development, combined with the proliferation of medical schools, threatened the medical societies' control of the practice of medicine. In 1847, the American Medical Association (AMA) was founded and immediately adopted a strategy designed to cope with the problems threatening the profession's control.[56] Its leadership argued that education and licensing should be separated, with licensing controlled by a state-appointed board of physicians that would be dominated by the state medical society.[57] Physicians would have to have a diploma from a certified medical school before they could apply for a license. The licensing board strategy defused monopoly charges to a large extent and, as a result, as Berlant argues, "The medical societies could go a long way toward dominating the medical schools, using the diploma as a simple means of entry into the profession, and laying the infrastructure for the restriction of the size of the medical profession."[58] These reforms were not immediately instituted, but by 1900 all states had medical practice restriction laws patterned after the AMA model.[59]

During the last half of the century, the AMA emphasized that health care for individuals was the domain of the private physician. This was especially clear in the opposition of the medical profession to public health services for individuals. State and metropolitan health boards were first established in the mid- to late-nineteenth century.[60] Physicians supported this development, helping to set up the American Public Health Association in 1872. Nonetheless, they adamantly opposed any competition from public health activists. One of the major focuses of conflict, as discussed by Paul Starr in *The Social Transformation of American Medicine,* was the New York City Health Department, headed by Herman Biggs. The health department pioneered work in bacteriology in terms of both diagnosis and treatment.[61] Biggs's success with containing the spread of diphtheria was, however, criticized by physicians and pharmacists as socialistic. Their political clout was such that the health department had to cease the commercial sale of diphtheria antitoxin.

The same story can be told of school health programs. In New York, where the health department remained acutely aware of the dangers of usurping doctors' business, school inspectors were reminded to avoid any sort of treatment for ill children.[62] Health centers, conceived of as an auxiliary to private practice for the poor, were also steadfastly opposed by the medical profession. The most fully developed plans for such centers, Biggs's concept of rural health centers, were sharply criticized.

Public health advocates were not the only enemy seen by the medical profession. Company doctors and health plans were also targets of criticism and political opposition. Led by railroad and lumber interests, many industries had attempted to set up contracts with local practitioners to care for workers.[63] But doctors who agreed to such contracts suffered the condemnation of their peers and were threatened with exclusion from the medical societies. Yet another development opposed by the AMA was the concept of health clubs or lodges, in which fraternal societies, organized as lodges, incorporated medical coverage for its members—especially among immigrants. This was in essence a form of health insurance for working poor people. The AMA "could see 'no economic excuse or justification' for lodge practice, objecting to the unlimited service for limited pay and the 'ruinous competition' it 'invariably' introduced."[64]

In its opposition to these developments, the AMA, speaking for the profession, was consistent. The organized profession opposed all institutions that asserted control over the doctor-patient relationship. Fee for practice was the only economic relationship acceptable. This can, of course, be interpreted two ways. On the one hand, the profession was in a struggle to ensure the welfare of the patient by eliminating any mixed loyalties, especially loyalty to institutional requirements. This then enabled the development of a true duty-based relationship between doctor and patient, insulating the therapeutic encounter from the market and the public morality of liberalism. On the other hand, the profession's protection of its territory can be seen as monopolization of the means of practice, a way to maintain the doctors' authority vis-á-vis patients.

This tension was not resolved as the scientific basis of medicine, as well as the profession's internal organization, were evolving. In the early part of the twentieth century, the AMA abandoned its old organizational framework. Previously, it had been difficult for the association to formulate policies. There was no procedure for reaching agreement on controversial matters, no mechanism for creating and proclaiming an official policy. After 1901, however, the House of Delegates began to act as a locus of power. Its members were chosen by the constituent medical societies, thus interlocking these organizations with the AMA. As a result, the structure of the modern organized medical profession was readied for the twentieth century.

The AMA's development was enhanced by the reaction to the Flexner Report, which was published in 1910 following an investigation of medical schools by the Carnegie Foundation and the AMA's Council on Medical Education. The report recommended that the AMA grade medical schools. Those with substandard grades were left with the choice of improving or closing. Schools were to reorganize "largely along the lines of the Johns Hopkins Medical School and [reorganization] was based on the new developments in science, the teaching hospitals, the laboratory, and basic and clinical research."[65] As a result of this reform, the number of medical schools decreased from 154 in 1904 to 66 in 1933.[66]

The reform of medical teaching allowed with great efficiency the incorporation of biological and scientific advances into the clinical area. Medical science began to experience rapid growth both in depth and breadth. Clinical practice could only absorb all the new information through increased specialization. By 1915 the profession was already becoming a heterogeneous collection of specialists, and medicine was rooted in scientific research.

This period also saw the emergence of carefully prescribed training programs for specialists. After completing medical school, physicians would spend several years at a hospital training in their chosen field. Working long hours for little pay, physicians would learn first hand that care of the patient was their immediate and sole function.

By the time these changes had defined a revolution in the scientific basis of medicine, the medical profession had largely eliminated competition through the AMA's insistence on a certain organization of health care. Starr has summarized five developments that the profession took advantage of, or contributed to, in a significant fashion.[67] First, doctors controlled the labor market in medicine through licensing laws. Second, commercialism in medicine was not tolerated, and much capital investment in the profession was philanthropical. Third, all countervailing powers were eliminated so that doctors had no one to answer to other than their peers. Fourth, the boundaries of medicine and public health were clearly demarcated—care would be the province of doctors. Finally, the growth of specialization and hospital-based care would increase the strength of professional organization. Thus after 1915, the profession was well placed to exercise its control over practice.[68] In 1920, the AMA's convention passed the following resolution:

Resolved: That the American Medical Association declares its opposition to the institution of any plan embodying the system of compulsory contributory insurance against illness, or any other plan of compulsory insurance against illness which provides for medical service to be rendered through contributors controlled and regulated by the federal government.[69]

The AMA's opposition to outside control of medical care was also illustrated by the reaction to the report of the Committee on Costs of Medical Care (CCMC), which was commissioned by eight medical foundations to study health care and medical practice. In 1932, it noted five great needs in American health care:

1. Better organization of personal health services, especially through comprehensive practice incorporating various specialties.
2. Stronger public health services.
3. Group payment of steadily increasing costs, through nonprofit insurance, taxation, or combinations of both.
4. More effective centralization and coordination of services.
5. Improvement of professional education, with increasing emphasis on the teaching of health and the prevention of disease.[70]

The AMA immediately rejected these proposals. An article in the *Journal of the American Medical Association* went even further, claiming that the majority responsible for the committee report was composed of "the forces representing the grant foundations, public health officialdom, social theory—even socialism and communism—inciting to revolution."[71] The AMA clearly feared that any government involvement would send American health care down the slippery slope to socialized medicine.

In summary, American medicine in the late 1920s had developed a political structure that isolated the doctor-patient relationship from oversight by, or interference from, any outside body. The physician was extraordinarily free to operate as he saw fit within the confines of the "patient comes first" moral posture. Of course, the physician, placed as he was in a position of control over another human being, accepted moral risks foreign to the public morality of the liberal state. The medical institutions supported not only an ethic but an ideology that only doctors armed with a special code of ethics should be involved in the care of patients and only they could be expected to resist a profit motive in health care. Over the next thirty years, this ethic was modified to allow others to pay for health care, so long as they did not interfere with patient care.

The Golden Years

The reaction of the organized medical profession to the CCMC Report convinced Franklin Roosevelt that direct national health legislation was politically impossible. Nonetheless, as the Depression brought a drop in doctors' salaries, physicians became more accepting of governmental benefit programs that paid medical bills.[72] Certain reform movements within the AMA began to clamor for a national health insurance.[73] The hierarchy at the AMA remained adamantly opposed to any government role in medicine even as a new class of urban specialists gained more power in the organization throughout the late 1930s.

The old hierarchy realized that it had less than total support for its fee-for-practice gospel. As a result, the AMA proved willing to compromise when the Roosevelt administration, led by I. S. Falk, proposed a new round of health benefits in 1938. In order to isolate health insurance from other issues, the AMA House of Delegates "approved protection of loss of income during illness, as well as cash indemnity insurance . . . endorsed the expansion of public health services and even recognized that federal aid might be required for care of the medically indigent."[74] The profession had come to realize that the public demand for some government-sponsored health benefit system could not be ignored.

The political power of the AMA leadership was not seriously diluted, even though compromises had to be accepted at times. Indeed, by the end of the 1930s, the hierarchy seemed to have regained the firm support of its membership. Attorney General Thurman Arnold acknowledged the strength of the AMA's position at the same time he opposed it: "Organized medicine should not be allowed to extend its necessary and proper control over standards to include control over methods of payment for services involving the economic freedom and welfare for consumers and the legal rights of individual doctors."[75] A short time later, the association was charged with violations of the Sherman Antitrust Act after certain physicians were blacklisted by the District of Columbia's Medical Society. Although the United States Circuit Court of Appeals ruled that the AMA was acting as a trade, not a profession, no structural reforms were ordered.[76]

Following the Second World War, liberal senators continuously submitted bills to Congress that contained various national health insurance proposals—proposals consistently opposed by the AMA. The AMA imposed a twenty-five dollar assessment on all its members for a special contingency fund, which was to be used to employ public relations firms to design an effective media campaign against any compulsory health insurance scheme. In 1945 and 1946, the AMA again braced for battle as Harry S. Truman submitted his own national health plans. The new president's proposals, however, met with only lukewarm support in Congress, probably as a result of AMA lobbying.[77] Moreover, in the early 1950s the AMA public relations firm successfully characterized national health plans as socialistic—strengthening public opposition to them.

While national health plan legislation was falling before AMA opposition, private health plans were allowed in the back door. Such health plans were of two types: indemnity plans that paid subscribers for medical expenses, and service benefit plans that reimbursed hospitals and doctors directly: Both required a third-party organization to administer the plan. Many such plans were established and flourished during the period in which the AMA concentrated its efforts against government health plans, as Starr has discussed at length.

Blue Cross, a service-benefit organization, established its first health plan in 1929, just as the Depression made private, out-of-pocket payment for health care an impossibility for many Americans. Underwriting support for small Blue Cross plans originally came from the voluntary hospitals.[78] In order to overcome certain insurance regulations, special enabling laws had to be passed to allow hospital participation. The popularity of the plans was such that by 1939, twenty-five states had passed enabling legislation.[79]

The AMA embraced these programs with some warmth. In 1934, ten principles setting out the AMA requirements of physician participation in health plans were published in the *Journal of the American Medical Association*.[80] These required the maintenance of all doctor prerogatives, and opposed any restrictions of doctor control over practice. The principles also supported indemnity, as opposed to benefit, plans. "In short, the AMA insisted that all health insurance plans accept the private physicians' monopoly control of the medical market and complete authority over all aspects of medical institutions."[81] These principles were obviously violated by group health plans, which controlled doctors' incomes and work places. The clash between advocates of such plans and the AMA was eventually won by the AMA, although only after it had defended itself against several antitrust suits.[82]

The Blue Cross programs escaped professional opposition because they were indemnity plans and did not threaten doctor-patient relations. Blue Shield plans were also allowed by the profession to proliferate once it became clear that physician control of such plans was possible. Blue Cross and Blue Shield plans then began to cooperate in administrative matters—both were careful to maintain doctor prerogatives in treatment matters. Both were provider controlled and operated. Hospitals refused to deal with plans other than Blue Cross and physicians boycotted service-benefit plans not operated by Blue Shield. As Starr states, "As of 1945, the structure of private health plans was basically an accommodation to provider interests."[83]

After the war, commercial insurance plans of the indemnity form preferred by the AMA had expanded greatly. Their growth was such that by 1953, they provided more hospital insurance than did the Blues. Their expansion was a result not only of the cohesiveness of service offered by the huge life insurance companies, but also their ability to give healthy young people better premiums.[84] This practice, called experience rating, was eventually mimicked by the Blues. Thus the Blues and commercial insurance tended to imitate one another. Moreover, neither group disturbed the doctor control over the doctor-patient relationship or the fee-for-service method of reimbursement.

They were acceptable third parties. The physician-patient relationship remained free of outside control.

Beginning in the early 1960s, national health insurance again made Congress's political agenda, this time largely because of a grassroots movement on behalf of the elderly.[85] The Democrats lacked the votes to extend the Kerr-Mills program of federal support for welfare medicine programs until the landslide of 1964. In 1965, Representative Mills put together a package that included health insurance with social security, government subsidized health insurance, and expanded welfare and health benefits for the poor.

All the AMA public relations weapons could not halt the passage of this Medicare/Medicaid legislation during the Great Society initiative. Many reformers hoped that this legislation (Titles 19 and 20) would change the character of health care within the United States. In the words of an HEW handbook of policies:

The potential for this new Title [19] can hardly be overestimated as its ultimate goal is the assurance of complete, continuous, family-centered medical care of high quality to persons who are unable to pay for it themselves. The law aims much higher than the mere paying of medical bills, and states, in order to achieve its high purpose, will need to assume the responsibility for planning and establishing systems of quality medical care comprehensive in scope and wide in coverage.[86]

A variety of mechanisms were to make this quality care possible: certification of care by state health agencies; state assurances that there would be enough practitioners available to provide such care; an adequate fee structure developed to ensure practitioner participation; prohibitions on limitations of services such that care for the needy would not be impeded; and establishment of early and periodic screening diagnosis and treatment programs (EPSDT).

These high hopes were not fulfilled. The programs did provide care for some who had never had access to it, but broad public health measures have never been fully instituted. One astute observer has argued that the federal programs were doomed from the start because of two erroneous assumptions: "(1) the assumption that supplying governmental money to the private market will make good medical care available to those who need it; (2) the congressional mandate, reiterated again and again, that governmental action to assure medical care should not interfere with existing patterns of medical practice."[87] In essence, then, Medicaid and Medicare represented victories for the

AMA and the medical profession. The fee-for-practice system was not really modified. Instead, the federal government simply joined the other third-party payers, which the profession had already accepted.

As Starr has noted, Congress was aware of the need for the support of hospitals and the medical profession to implement its programs. The legislation therefore established go-betweens that separated the federal bureaucracy from the providers of health care. Most hospitals nominated Blue Cross as the "fiscal intermediary" under Part A, and Blue Cross an the intermediary under Part B of Medicare. "As a result, the administration of Medicare was lodged in the private insurance systems originally established to suit provider interests. And the federal government surrendered direct control of the program and its costs."[88] Moreover, the administration agreed to pay hospital costs for Medicare and calculated such costs in a manner very favorable to hospitals. Finally, an extremely liberal policy with regard to capital cost reimbursement provided hospitals with the means to purchase new technology.[89]

The result was a new influx of money into health care, without any real changes in the physician prerogatives. The fee-for-service system was left intact. Physicians did not have to answer to any administrators about the decisions they made in a clinical setting. Patient control was in no way increased. If anything, the distance of the third-party reimbursement mechanisms removed even the control the patient might have claimed as a consumer. Medicare/Medicaid turned out to be another triumph for the organized profession. Third parties continued to pay for health care and yet exercised no control. The doctor-patient relationship remained isolated from the public morality of the liberal state. Through the early 1970s, American medicine had become a thoroughly peculiar set of political and economic institutions.

The Mature Fee-for-Practice System

In general terms, the economic model for the practice of medicine is a simple enterprise market. As Friedson notes, "In the case of medicine in the recent past of the United States, the marketplace has been organized as a fee-for-service basis, practitioners being entrepreneurs, nominally competing with each other for the fees of prospective patients. The merchant-customer relationship has been emphasized."[90] In theory, patients were free to shop around, and would do so if they believed that they were not receiving the kind of care they desired.[91] In reality, however, the institutions of health care were arranged such that the individual physician retained a majority of the prerogatives, and avoided competition with other physicians.[92]

Consumers of health care were expected to compensate physicians for their services in one of two ways. The first was simple out-of-pocket payment according to the services provided by the physician. This was becoming an increasingly minor part of the physician compensation scheme. Consumers paid only 39 percent of physician costs in 1979.[93] In the second form of compensation, the physician billed a third-party insurer of the consumer: Medicare, Medicaid, Blue Shield, or a private insurance company. Especially with regard to the Blue Shield program, physicians attempted to retain control even over the reimbursement agency. In 1976, the Federal Trade Commission launched an investigation of Blue Shield plans. As Clark Havighurst has noted, "The theory underlying this investigation in its early stages was that a Blue Shield plan is a kind of joint selling agency, through which competing doctors indirectly fix prices and determine their own incomes."[94] After the investigation, a staff report recommended broad changes in the Blue Shield structure.

These antitrust concerns suggest that the market, the mechanism of equality in the liberal state, was excluded from medical arrangements to prevent outside interference in the doctor-patient relationship. But while the liberal state accepts modifications of the market that increase equality, there is no evidence that the modifications of the medical market did so; indeed, there is some suspicion they mainly benefited providers.

Perhaps more important than the issue of antitrust violation was that of the moral hazard created by the third party reimbursement system. In any insurance scheme, there exists a set of "moral hazards," incentives and constraints experienced by the different actors involved. With regard to consumers, there is the risk of becoming a free rider. Kenneth Arrow has pointed out that the consumer is more likely to try to get something for free out of an arrangement when a distant third party suffers the consequences.[95] In the case at hand, the medical consumer would overuse the system because an insurance company foots the bill. There are also moral risks resulting from the complex role of the physician-provider: "He acts (1) as the agent of the insurer, constraining consumer moral hazard, (2) as agent for the consumer who is largely responsible for determining what the consumer demands, and (3) as agent for himself and other providers (for example, hospitals) who are, among other things, interested in making money. These three roles are not mutually reinforcing. Provider income can be increased by downplaying the first two roles."[96]

The insurance method of payment for health care could thus be abused by physicians. The physician did not need to weigh the question "How much can my patient afford?" against "How much treatment would be ideal?" Physicians would argue, as I have suggested, that this system of financing brings patient and physician closer because it avoids the need to consider the cost of treatment. The consumer realizes of course that sooner or later there will be bills to pay in the form of an increased insurance premium. But isolating the physician's relationship with the patient from the market provides critical support for the "patient comes first (doctor decides)" attitude because the physician's moral commitment and clinical judgment are not constrained by financial concerns. Moreover, the physician is best suited to withstand moral hazard because of the special nature of duty-based medical ethics: the physician puts the patient first.

In summary, the central problem of the doctor-patient relationship is the inequality of knowledge, and thus of power. The doctor understands the complicated biological events that cause ill health; the patient who lacks the doctor's specialist training, cannot. The patient may also be emotionally weakened by ill health.

To resolve this inequality and create a relationship in which the patient can talk freely and openly with the doctor, a particular medical morality has developed. The physician is duty bound to treat the patient with greatest respect. The physician must maintain a loyalty to the patient and engender the patient's trust. The patient must "come first" even if this requires some self-effacement and sacrifice on the part of the physician, although in fact, "the patient comes first" ethic is synonymous with physician authority. Other concerns should not intrude on this relationship. The moral code of beneficence works best if it is isolated from the usual concerns of the liberal state, especially the competitive market. The doctor's moral code, not civil law, provides the foundation for the doctor-patient relationship. The dutiful doctor can withstand the pressures of moral hazard because of his ethical commitment. Other possible players in a medical care market would not be as immunized from profit. Thus fee-for-service dominates, and only conditionless insurance is allowed.

As a result, medical morality is estranged from the public morality that guides the liberal state. The notion of patient liberties and the justice provided by the public morality through law had little impact on medical morality. The patient's negative freedom is rather unimportant in the healing process described by Parsons and others. Contractual models of the doctor-patient relationship are overruled. A true market cannot operate.

The ethical theory of medicine was thus integral to, and sustained by, the economic and political structure of medical practice. Government officials and other professionals were excluded from the care of patients. The regulation of doctors was confined to the medical profession itself. A system of third-party payers was allowed so that economic constraints would not play a role in doctors' care of patients. In short, the doctor-patient relationship was insulated from the constraints of the market, the chief arbiter in the liberal state. Medical institutions thus meshed neatly with the ideology of medical ethics.

The notion of the symbiotic relationship of medical ethics and the medical enterprise is largely conceptual. There are a number of other possible explanations for the growth of institutions of medical care. The symbiotic relationship also assumes that certain aspects of the social morality (for instance, medical ethics) can remain relatively detached from the public morality of the liberal state. In the next chapter, we will look at some of the competing explanations for the peculiar structure of medical care, review the changes of the past fifteen years in that structure, and suggest that the public morality of the liberal state has asserted itself and, with changes in the nature of the medical enterprise, made the "patient comes first" brand of medical morality obsolete.

3

Medicine in the Liberal State

In the last chapter, I suggested that medical ethics has been conceptually at odds with liberalism. In this chapter, we further explore this conceptual dissonance, and the changes that have brought the medical enterprise more in step with our market-based, pluralist society.

Much of the discussion necessarily will proceed at a rather theoretical level. Physician behavior itself does not overtly evince many of the moral overtones we discuss here. Indeed, observers have noted that the typical practitioner pays little attention to the role of an ethical code in his daily work. Friedson's empirical study led him to the following conclusion:

Curiously enough, we could raise little interest among physicians by interview questions about the problem of ethics in medical work. Ethics seemed to be unproblematic to them and rather less related to being a doctor than to being a properly brought up (middle-class) human being. Ethicality was "pretty much common sense," . . . was learned "when you are brought up by your mother." . . . To most physicians the word seemed to refer to the norms of decency and honesty that were expected of all proper middle-class people and that had not and need not [have] been taught to students in medical school.[1]

Nonetheless, for the moment, a certain theoretical purity must be maintained to illustrate medical ethics in the liberal state.[2]

Medical Ethics and Paternalism

The central theme of medical ethics, from the perspective of the beneficence model, is the doctor and patient partnership. The physician is in a sense a friend who has a commitment, a duty, to the patient and is bound to treat the patient as an end in himself and, if necessary, to make sacrifices to help the patient return to health. The doctor and patient thus work together, but under the physician's leadership, for mutual ends. More accurately, the physician uses her specialized knowledge on behalf of the patient.

The problem with this model of medical ethics is that it overlooks pluralism, one of the primary virtues of the liberal state. Alasdair MacIntyre has argued quite convincingly that the liberal state allows and encourages a number of different moral points of view.[3] This pluralism creates the diversity that enriches the social morality. But it also eliminates the grounds one would use to justify action on behalf of another.

As MacIntyre relates, previous societies did not celebrate pluralism; rather, they encouraged conformity with a single moral point of view. But our society eschews such shared values. Instead we have only the minimal glue provided by the public morality of liberalism. More important, that public morality emphasizes the importance of individual choice and negative freedom, not shared values. Pluralism makes no effort to shape shared assumptions.

The medical ethics of "the patient comes first" model assumes that physicians can act on behalf of the patient simply because the physician is duty bound to help the patient place his welfare first. The problem for such a theory is that in a liberal state only the individual can define his or her own personal welfare. Thus the "patient comes first" model must conflict with liberalism. Specifically, the liberal state cannot accept the paternalism inherent in medical ethics.

Paternalism can be defined as interference with or failure to respect affairs normally designated as matters within an individual's sphere of liberty for the sake of that individual. Dworkin offers a more technical definition of paternalism as "roughly the interference with a person's liberty of action justified by reasons referring exclusively to the welfare, food, happiness, needs, interests or values of the person being coerced."[4] Paternalism thus represents a decrease in personal liberty by interfering with another's behavior, choice, or opportunity for choice for that person's well-being, though that interference need not be actual or physical, and indeed may simply be a failure to seek consent.

While that interference may be justified on the basis of a higher good, it is viewed in the liberal state with a great deal of suspicion. The liberal state maximizes the amount of negative freedom granted individuals so as to minimize the possibility of the abuses that can occur under the name of positive freedom. Liberalism assumes that the individual citizen typically knows what is best for himself; thus the rationale for paternalism is undercut, and individual autonomy is accorded the widest respect possible.

Times and situations occur even in the most liberal of states in which paternalism may be justified. For example, in our society parents are allowed and encouraged to restrict their children's freedom and to make decisions on their behalf. The close, affective ties between parents and children are the justification for paternalism. We do not fear, as a rule, that parents will take advantage of paternalism and exploit their children because parents usually behave in a dutiful and self-effacing manner. The ends of child welfare then are central to parental decision making.

To a certain degree, the analysis of the "patient comes first" medical ethics is analogous to familial love, in which the doctor (the parent) and the patient (the child) work together for a common good—the patient's welfare. This commitment justifies the doctor's decisions on behalf of the patient, and also justifies an institutional framework that isolates doctor and patient from the oversight of the liberal state. To the extent that these institutions flourish, we can assume that society is convinced that the medical profession's paternalism is not exploitive.

Others have taken a narrower position that paternalism is justified "only when the person's choice is different from what it would be given his or her normal character and decision-making abilities, and more specifically, only when the impairments in these abilities are such that they result in the person withholding consent to paternalistic interference to which he or she would have given consent."[5] By twisting or exaggerating the notion of impairments, however, a physician could justify paternalism every time her patient disagrees with a prescribed course of therapy (which leads Childress to argue that medical paternalism is much broader than mere coercion[6]). Believing that the expert knows best, the physician pushes ahead with a program of her own design in order to benefit the patient. Medical institutions nurture this endeavor, protecting the doctor's decisions from public judgment.

In a liberal state, in particular our liberal state, however, such broad physician prerogatives cannot be sustained. The medical enterprise, and the overly broad paternalism it sanctions, inevitably must be addressed. That is what occurred around 1970 when the American public's perception of medicine began to change. In a variety of ways, the public became convinced that physician paternalism was really physician exploitation and that medicine was set up not to nurture the patient but to benefit the physician. This led to an assertion of patient autonomy and liberty and restriction of physician power. In the following section, we will review evidence of how the American liberal state began to rein in the powers of the medical profession and to reintegrate it with the principles of liberalism. In the process, physician paternalism was limited and the "patient comes first" ethic was discredited.

The End of the Golden Years

In the early 1970s both politicians and business leaders became alarmed about health care in the United States. Starr details evidence of this concern:

President Nixon told a press conference in July 1969, "We face a massive crisis in this area. Unless action is taken within the next two or three years, we will have a breakdown of our medical system." In January 1970 *Business Week* ran a cover story on the "$60 Billion Crisis" that compared medical care in America unfavorably to national health programs in Western Europe. That same month, editors of *Fortune*, in a special issue on medical care, declared that American medicine stood on "the brink of chaos."[7]

This sense of crisis was a result of the staggering rise in health costs initiated by the operation of Medicare and Medicaid. The average annual rise in health costs more than doubled to 8 percent in the five years after the legislation passed, as compared to the five years before enactment.[8] Health costs more than doubled to $336 per capita from 1960 to 1970.[9]

Nor did cost escalations moderate in the 1970s. Total health costs rose from $61 billion in 1969 to nearly $200 billion in 1981,[10] and grew throughout the 1970s at a rate 50 to 100 percent higher than that of inflation.[11] By 1980 the U.S. government was contributing $59.8 billion to the total health care bill,[12] while the rest was paid by consumers or by third parties, including Blue Cross, Blue Shield, and private insurance companies. This system proved quite lucrative to the medical profession; throughout the 1970s physicians ranked first among all professional groups in total income. By 1981, Americans spent $1,225 per capita on health care.[13]

This phenomenon was the result of the economic structure of medical care. Incentives under the third-party system maximized reimbursement instead of saving money. As Alain Enthoven has noted, "Third party reimbursement leaves the consumer with, at most, a weak financial incentive to question the need for or value of services or to seek out a less costly provider or style of care."[14] The physician was, of course, seen as an integral part of medical hyperinflation. "Physicians receive only about 20 percent of the health-care dollar, but they control or influence most of the rest. . . . Their professional values combine with the financial incentives and other factors, such as malpractice threat, to minimize concern over cost and to foster cost-increasing behavior."[15]

Most physicians chose to ignore this aspect of practice. Those few who reflected on it, however, realized the significance of unrestricted cost increases. For example, Benson Roe, a cardiothoracic surgeon, wrote in 1981 that the need for controls on medical practice was in large part a result of doctors' abuse of the system.[16] He noted that AMA pressure had managed to integrate customary-and-reasonable fee reimbursement patterns into third-party payment plans, and he argued that this had led to an explosion of fees by young doctors unable to steer themselves away from the "moral hazard."[17] Moreover, he detailed his charge with evidence from California Blue Shield that fees for coronary artery bypass surgery had risen to $9,000 for four to five hours of work. The impact of such reports on the public's perception of physicians cannot be doubted.[18] Both the public and government began to see medical practice only in terms of the great and lucrative power exercised by doctors. Medical paternalism no longer seemed justified in the 1970s.

To control physicians and hospitals, states began to pass laws that regulated hospital reimbursement rates. Led by New York and New Jersey, many states by 1976 had some system for oversight of costs.[19]

These were the first efforts to control medical costs and to limit the physician's role as sole arbiter in the medical market.

Even more radical in terms of its intended impact on physician independence was a federal initiative involving facility-use review. Most hospitals had utilization review committees by 1975 that were intended to prevent inappropriate practices. Yet, as the Senate Committee on Finance noted, "Utilization review activities have, generally speaking, been of a token nature and ineffective as a curb to unnecessary use of institutional care and services. Utilization review in Medicare can be characterized as more form than substance."[20] In an attempt to rectify this, Congress in 1972 enacted legislation that instituted Professional Standard Review Organizations (PSROs). PSROs were to be independent of hospitals and medical societies and were to develop standards of care.[21] Unfortunately, these organizations were prematurely instituted and never really overcame the collegial attitudes of the medical profession. Yet as a challenge to physician hegemony over the consumers of medical care, they marked a milestone.

Another reform effort in the 1970s was the National Health Planning and Resource Development Act. This act set up two hundred regional health system agencies (HSAs), with boards that had consumer majorities. The HSAs were to coordinate health care services within regions. As Starr has noted, "The law seemed to be a decisive rejection of the view that the market could correct itself, and that the doctors and hospitals had the last word on how medical care ought to be organized."[22] But the HSAs never managed to free themselves from professional control and have had little impact in most areas. The concept of the need for social control of health care was, however, a significant development.

The third reform movement of the 1970s had as its goal a national health insurance. In 1976 the Carter administration renewed the government's attempt to provide wider access to medical care. The president was willing to, at least rhetorically, emphasize the great importance of a national health plan: "One of the highest goals of the 96th Congress should be taking action to provide all Americans with the opportunity to lead a more healthy life. This opportunity has been denied to many in our country because of health care services which are unaffordable, inaccessible, and inefficient."[23] The federal government finally seemed to have realized that intervention was necessary if the United States was to have a more equitable health system.

   Thus several legislative proposals on national health insurance were
made by Congress during the late 1970s. B. Mitchell and J. Schwartz
have analyzed these proposals and have arrived at the following conclusions:

Continued controversy over national health insurance financing revolves
around two major issues. The first involves the extent to which additional
national resources should be expended on the health care of families above the
lowest income levels. . . . Among the four prototypical proposals, the Long-
Ribicoff bill produces the smallest increase in national expenditure ($3 billion)
and the Kennedy-Cormon the largest ($13 billion). The second issue concerns
the extent to which, for any given level of spending on health care, a national
health insurance program should redistribute income. Here controversy is
sharpest between advocates of a premium based program (Administration)
who wish to minimize redistribution of income, and advocates of a payroll tax
approach (Kennedy-Mills), who seek to shift income toward those at lower
earning levels.[24]

   The Long-Ribicoff Bill, on the one hand, proposed coverage only
for those who had contracted a catastrophic illness; the federal government was to step in once a family had spent a large amount of their
own money. Kennedy-Cormon, on the other hand, was a step toward
a real national health system.
   The Kennedy-Corman Bill was always perceived as the most radical
of the health care system proposals and was also recognized as the one
that most assertively incorporated the concept of a right: "At one end
of the spectrum, as exemplified by the full coverage provisions of the
Kennedy-Corman bill, are those who feel that 'health care is a right'—
that access to health services should neither be limited or rationed by
price."[25]
   The Kennedy-Corman plan explicitly brought the notion of right
into the debate over a national health care system/national health insurance. This is clear from the sources of revenue for the plan. A
payroll tax was relied upon to generate about half the total revenues
needed to operate the plan. This was seen as the best way to spread the
cost of the system throughout the society. In addition, there was no
cost-sharing requirement. In cost-sharing arrangements, the patient
must pay as much as the third-party source, in this case the government, up to a certain total. Cost-sharing tends to penalize those with
limited resources. The Kennedy-Corman plan's avoidance of this device demonstrated its full-fledged commitment to free access for all to
health care. The tax burden resulting from the plan would thus fall on

those more able to pay: "Although it raises approximately 50 percent more total revenue than the other bills, [it] places a much smaller burden on lower income families."[26]

The set of principles embodied by the bill was very clear. Health care was treated as a right.[27] Proponents of this type of plan were most concerned about redressing the inequality of the health care system; they wanted equal access for all. They also chose the language of rights to express this valuation of equality because they recognized that they must confront the power of the medical profession. Implicit within such proposals was the criticism that the existing system was "tailor made to maximize the income of the providers."[28] The legislative initiative thus had to be organized as a direct challenge to medical exploitation and paternalism. The Kennedy-Corman plan would have greatly constrained the fee-for-practice system with restrictions that were seen as essential to an equitable health care system.

But the Kennedy staff and the Carter administration could never reach a compromise position. Carter wanted a much less radical restructuring of health care. Moreover, by 1979 the Democratic House did not even want a bill on national health insurance submitted.[29] Soon Kennedy opposed Carter in the primaries, Carter won, and then lost to Reagan. National health insurance faded from the political agenda.

Despite this series of failures in the late 1970s to reform health care in the United States, several important themes had become clear. There was significant political pressure to change the existing structure of medical practice, and reform proposals were offered that centered on the need to limit doctors' prerogatives as a way to bring down costs. Thus many politicians were ready to reject the profession's claims that a proper doctor-patient relationship depended on a fee-for-service system and its attendant undivided loyalty of physician to patient. They were ready to end the isolation that the profession had defended as necessary to medical morality. The liberal public morality was reasserting itself. The rise in health costs had convinced many that medical ethics, and the motivations upon which it depended, masked professional economic advantage.

Brave New World

With the 1980s came the first modifications in the health care system inserting liberal imperatives into the doctor-patient relationship. The new modifications were really three different developments, but all combined to produce a new kind of doctor-patient interaction. The new relationship, as we shall see, became more like others found in the liberal state—one in which rights, rather than duties, are the appropriate form of moral discourse.

The first and by far most important development was the institution of competitive market values in health care. It involved several initiatives, beginning modestly with a set of suggestions about how to incorporate the market into health care in order to control costs. In 1978, Enthoven wrote what was to become a very influential article in the *New England Journal of Medicine*,[30] noting that there was "very little competition among providers of care to produce services more efficiently or to offer a less costly style of care, and to pass the savings on to consumers."[31] He recommended expanding health maintenance organizations (HMOs) to provide large third-party health care purchasers with a choice of providers.

The HMO concept had been discussed for years.[32] Its advocates saw in it the answer to the failures of the American health care system. As Saward and Sorenson argued in 1982, "The new [procompetition] effort hinges on HMO-like concepts. Organized medical-care systems can enroll populations for a predetermined price to deliver defined services for which they will be at risk. The hypothesis is that there will be a number of such organizations competing in each area of the medical movement."[33] Moreover, the HMOs of the future were encouraged to be "for profit," in order to assure greater efficiency. Employee/physicians would thus bear a responsibility to shareholders to return a profit. The physicians would be employed by, and owe loyalty to, the institution rather than to the patient alone.

But reliance on HMOs was not enough for many businesspeople, who increasingly felt the pinch of costs associated with financing health plans.[34] In the Reagan administration, business found a welcome ear with regard to cost-saving and increased economic competition. Indeed the administration threw its support wholeheartedly behind the Gephardt-Stockman Bill, which would have deregulated much of hospital administration and emphasized profit-making by hospitals.[35] The AMA, as one might expect, opposed this bill. As Iglehart noted, the organization took "strong exception to provisions in the Gephardt-Stockman Bill that the AMA feared would lead to federal preemptions of state laws, to more corporate involvement in the direct provision of health care, to open hospital staffing and to broad authority for the HHS secretary."[36] As usual, the AMA opposed any innovation that might have diluted the physician's control over the delivery of health care. The AMA's political base within the profession had weakened over the 1970s, however, and its opposition to the Gephardt-Stockman Bill was not well organized. Nor was the AMA prepared for the next development coming down the congressional pike.

Spurred by an increasing number of academic voices in favor of competition,[37] Congress moved to make Medicare reimbursement a competitive issue. Faced with gaping budget deficits, the Reagan White House and the Republican Senate decided that it was time to develop prospective payment policies that would put a ceiling on Medicare reimbursement.[38] The hospital and medical professional lobbies had largely lost their influence by the early 1980s as a result of the ineffectiveness of their voluntary efforts to control costs. Thus in the fall of 1982, Congress amended section 223 of the Social Security Act, instructing the Department of Health and Human Services (DHHS) to work out a prospective payment plan.

The conference report attached to the bill instructed DHHS to rely upon the diagnostically related group (DRG) case classification system developed by Professors Robert Fetter and John Thompson of Yale University.[39] Used by the state of New Jersey since 1980, the DRG concept based reimbursement on diagnosis. A hospital is reimbursed according to the classification into which a patient's diagnosis fits; that is, not according to costs, but according to the preset amount for each diagnosis. The DRG concept assumed that every patient's condition could be fit into a discrete diagnostic category, an assumption that some have criticized.[40]

The DRG scheme created new incentives for hospital administrators. They realized that they would be receiving only one sum for each patient with a given diagnosis. As a result, a premium was put on moving the patient through a care program as quickly as possible.[41]

This meant that hospital executives placed pressure on physicians to minimize care programs and eliminate needless testing. These pressures were formalized into hospital policy, to which doctors were expected to adhere.[42] Thus the doctor-patient relationship was no longer isolated from institutional pressures—the fiscal health of the hospital now intruded as a factor under prospective payment plans.

The new situation was exemplified by the fact that while DRGs were being considered in Congress, the main political players were the American Hospital Association and the American Association of Medical Colleges (AAMC).[43] The AMA, on behalf of the organized profession, did not play a significant lobbying role. There are several possible explanations for this change of professional posture in the early 1980s. Perhaps doctors accepted that intervention was a foregone conclusion, given the public opposition to rising medical costs. Perhaps the organized profession no longer believed that the ethical duty to put the patient first required an independent doctor-patient relationship. In any case, the development of DRGs and the profession's acceptance of them signaled a departure from the traditional scheme of the medical enterprise and medical ethics. It indicated that physicians had acknowledged that medicine, like any other industry, could not continue to operate outside the imperatives of the liberal state and market economy.[44]

The DRG initiative applied only to federal reimbursement. Iglehart noted that a plan as comprehensive as this could create incentives to shift costs to the Blues and private insurers. He added, however, that "commercial insurers [were] active at the state level, pushing legislation that [required] equalization of payment among public and private payers."[45] Thus private insurers moved quickly to avoid cost shifting by physicians and hospitals eager to retain some semblance of the previous set of economic relationships.

The new reimbursement system for Medicare was signed by President Reagan on April 20, 1983. The DHHS report to Congress signaled how different the new system would be:

Within each hospital, staff physicians can be expected to compete with each other for available resources as the hospital budget is constrained. This competitive atmosphere will encourage recognition of the costs as well as the benefits of existing treatments and new technologies as they are developed. Peer pressure should influence physicians with relatively costly and cost ineffective practice patterns to modify their behavior.[46]

The diagnostically related group method of reimbursement is thus revolutionary, at least with regard to its impact on the constellation of ideas that I have argued provided the grounds for the ethical practice of medicine in the decades before 1970. The DRG concept is designed to force doctor and hospital to think about cost-effective care. Moreover, it creates incentives for hospitals to assert control over physician decision making. These changes have been antithetical to medical ethics as we have described it. They are a reflection of the values of the market, the engine of pure procedural justice in the liberal state. Thus DRGs are an outcome of the liberal state's struggle to gain control over the medical enterprise, to use the public morality to constrain physicians. In this struggle, two developments are likely. First, as the virtues of the marketplace, including cost-benefit analysis, efficiency considerations, and competition, are brought to medical care, then all actors—doctors, patients, and administrators—become more likely to utilize the language of rights and liberties, just as other people in a liberal state do.[47] Second, the "patient comes first" ethic becomes obsolete unless it undergoes major modification.

Diagnostically related group reimbursement schemes are not, of course, the only method of cost control that have intruded into health care. States have attempted to halt the rise in medical costs by placing limits on the budgets of hospitals.[48] Among the most important of these were the initiatives in the 1980s in Massachusetts and California. Massachusetts favored an "essentially noncompetitive" economic franchise "because it sustains the sometimes extreme disparities between hospitals in terms of cost and price."[49] Massachusetts, like Connecticut, set prospective budgets for each hospital. As a result of compromise among hospitals, the Massachusetts Medical Society, and the major third-party purchasers, the reimbursement system created "incentives for hospitals to reduce the number of days of care, deliver outpatient services as an alternative to inpatient care, and restrain growth in ancillary services."[50] The impact of such incentives should prove to be much the same as those of DRGs. They tend to render both the traditional medical enterprise and traditional medical ethics obsolete by bringing about cost consciousness.

Even more radical was California's new Medi-Cal reimbursement program. California decided that government and private insurance companies should "negotiate prepaid contracts with hospitals and providers as a 'tool' to contain costs."[51] The negotiated contracts were designed to bring hospitals into competition with one another for care contracts. Both hospitals and care providers were to be designated as policyholders. The California legislature thus hoped to confine fee-for-practice reimbursement; to promote management consulting in hospitals; to encourage physicians to create diagnostic protocols and standard treatment plans; to further health education and preventive practices; and to foster competition among hospitals and doctors.

David Kinzer predicted that the new California system would result in a two-tier system of care for indigent and affluent[52] and there is evidence that he is correct.[53] All the intricacies of the California program are but a chapter in the long volume on hospital cost control. For our purposes, it is important to note that the competitive structure in California probably will bring provider competition, management consulting techniques, and standard treatment protocols to health care. All of this cuts in the same direction that the DRG concept did: the doctor-patient relationship will no longer take place in a context isolated from the demands of the market-based liberal state.

The second major development that will draw the medical enterprise into the liberal state is the change in medical manpower demographics. In 1980 the *Report of the Graduate Medical Education National Advisory Committee* (GMENAC Report) suggested that there would be a physician surplus in most subspecialty fields by 1990.[54] Concern about the limited supply of physicians in the 1950s and 1960s had produced a massive increase in the number of people graduating from medical schools. Between 1959 and 1978 the number of medical schools increased from 85 to 126.

Now at the beginning of the 1990s, we know that there are definitely more physicians available, but it does not appear that there is a surplus now, nor that there will be in the next twenty years.[55] New research suggests that GMENAC overestimated the growth of physician supply and underestimated demand because it failed to take into account the decreased amount of time most female physicians work, the aging of the general population, and the relatively sluggish growth of HMOs. Nonetheless, there is little doubt that for many areas there is no lack of physicians.

The expanding numbers of physicians should have at least two effects. First, medically underserved areas will finally begin to have physicians available. There are signs that this is happening already, with a general relocation of physicians to once underserved rural areas.[56] Second, physicians will undoubtedly attempt to increase demand to keep step with supply, leading to more unnecessary operations and procedures.[57] Even so, there will still be greater competition among doctors for a smaller health care pie.

Alvan Tarlov and his former group at the University of Chicago discussed the repercussions of increased competition in the early 1980s.[58] First, Tarlov argued, "Salaried positions are becoming increasingly attractive to newly trained physicians in an increasingly competitive environment as they demonstrate willingness to sacrifice income flexibility in favor of income security and fewer work hours."[59] Tarlov predicted that more doctors will be willing to practice in HMOs; in addition, professional autonomy will be sacrificed for collective bargaining. Second, he foresaw a general movement to more entrepreneurship in medicine, with growth of prepaid group practices. With aggressive marketing, "the trusting covenantal relationship between doctors and patients, which has characterized medical practice for hundreds of years, will react to the contractual structures' interest in organized medical plans."[60]

Third, in Tarlov's analysis, competition will dovetail with new prospective payment plans to make doctors much more aware of costs. As a result, there will be greater incentives to adopt a corporate approach to efficient practice, including the use of organizational schemes and diagnostic algorithms.[61] Fourth, there will be more choices for the patient as consumer. Patients will change physicians more frequently and become effective shoppers in the medical marketplace. Tarlov very effectively summarized the results of these changes:

Formerly, a physician and a patient developed a covenantal relationship in which the patient's well-being was supposed to be the dominant consideration. Multiple accountabilities will soon distract from that simple relationship. The physician will be accountable to the underwriting plans, to restrain costs; to the hospital, to help make it financially viable; to the health-services corporation, of which he or she may be a partial owner; and to governments. These accountabilities will be reinforced by preset quantitative expectations of physician productivity and regular feedback on performance data, and perhaps by penalties. Working agreements, such as a 40-hour week and weekend coverage, may further contribute to the erosion of the traditional sense of the physician's personal responsibility for the patient. The patient will become a client of the corporation. The physician's attentiveness to the patient could become an effort to maintain good business.[62]

Thus the changes in medical demography will parallel and in some ways complement those changes rooted in reimbursement patterns.

The old "patient comes first" duty, which required a doctor-patient relationship isolated from the liberal economy, seems increasingly inappropriate. Ethical relations will thus have to be redeveloped to resemble more those of the liberal state—negative freedoms guaranteed by rights will have to be balanced against mutual duties. But before developing this argument, there is a third major health care issue to be considered.

This third issue is the growth in investor-owned for-profit hospitals. The term "growth" must be explained. In 1928 there were 2,435 proprietary hospitals, which made up 36 percent of the total number of hospitals. By 1969 this number was down to 769, 11 percent of the total, and by 1979 down to 727.[63] These numbers reflect the decline of the small family-owned hospital in rural America. But the decline from 1970 to 1979 in the number of proprietary hospitals is deceiving. Many proprietary hospitals were replaced by small for-profit hospitals owned by corporate hospital chains.[64] As a result, the percentage of hospital beds that were for-profit rose in the 1970s. Moreover, these beds were concentrated in high-growth areas such as in California and Florida.[65]

By 1979 "there were 35 investor-owned corporations directly owning or holding contracts for the operation of two or more general hospitals."[66] These chains also owned a number of psychiatric hospitals.[67] The gross income of the proprietary hospitals was between $12 billion and $13 billion in 1984. The largest chains, Humana and Hospital Corporation of America, each gross about $1 billion annually. Thus the proprietary hospital chains carry massive financial and political clout. Moreover, hospitals are only a part of the corporate push; a large number of imaging centers, dialysis facilities, and especially nursing homes are operated for profit.

The growth of for-profit hospitals is startling only in light of the fact that the hospital sector has traditionally been nonprofit. Some would play down the differences in profit versus not-for-profit hospitals. For instance, R. M. Cunningham argues that "the two systems are not that far apart in their interest in providing high quality patient care in their communities. Moreover, many nonprofit institutions and systems are now pursuing the kind of aggressive marketing and merchandising of their services for which they criticized for-profit hospitals just a few years ago."[68] Good management is good management, runs this argument. Others are not so sure. Edmund Pellegrino has asked whether the ethic of a "proprietary hospital" is the ethic of business, a minimalist ethic always indelibly stamped by the need to make a profit. . . . In a competitive ethos, price becomes the criterion, and the canons of ethics can be submerged in the canons of economics. When costs and finances come into conflict with needs of those who are sick and who come in the expectation of help, how shall the conflict be resolved?[69]

Advocates of proprietary hospitals answer this question by saying that nonprofits run into management problems as well; neither type of hospital can afford to run deficits for long. In addition, the for-profit boosters roll out typical liberal economic arguments to make their point: for example, investor-owned hospitals stimulate competition among hospitals and thus hold down inflation in health costs.[70] These nicely complement other "competition" arguments noted above. It is not, however, entirely clear that for-profit hospitals are the paradigms of efficiency they pretend to be.[71] Indeed, in one study for-profit hospitals did not appear to be any more efficient than not-for-profit hospitals.[72]

Yet they continue to grow, although the rate of growth has dropped off.[73] Bruce Steinwald has argued that much of the impetus for the growth of for-profits is that proprietaries "skim"—in other words, they selectively admit "patients who are likely to generate the greatest profit."[74] These patients are patients who require uncomplicated nursing care and who use operating rooms, intensive care units, and other services that generate a good deal of hospital revenue. Another aspect of skimming is that for-profits are accused of taking only patients with high reimbursement medical plans—Medicaid patients are excluded. Thus some argue that investor-owned growth is discriminatory.

None of this, however, answers the question posed by Pellegrino, when he points out that health care is not usually thought of as a commodity. Moreover, as Arnold Relman notes, most patients are not perfect consumers of health care.[75] Relman feels that physician investment in for-profits should be prohibited to avoid the conflict of interest:

What I am suggesting is that the medical profession would be in a stronger position, and its voice would carry more moral authority with the public and government, if it adopted the principle that practicing physicians should derive no financial benefit from the health care market except from their own professional services.[76]

It is doubtful that this kind of prohibition is politically viable. Indeed, recent efforts by Congressman Pete Stark to limit physician self-referral have not met with much interest in Congress.[77] Nonetheless, Relman's proposals reflect an interest on the part of at least some leaders in medicine in addressing the ethical dilemmas raised by the new institutional setting of health care. Thoughtful reformulations of medical ethics in light of the changes in the medical enterprise have not, unfortunately, been the rule.

Professional Reaction to the Liberal Market

The American Medical Association's *Principles of Medical Ethics* reflect the profession's increasing awareness of the changes in medical practice. Principle 4 clearly states: "A physician shall respect the rights of patients, of colleagues, and of other health professionals, and shall safeguard patient confidences within the constraints of the law."[78] The rest of the AMA's judicial opinions are peppered with similar acknowledgments noting that market issues and liberal rights are part of medical practice. The AMA defers to the government to work out equitable allocation of health care. The doctor must be conscious of costs, although patient care is the first consideration. Patients' choices are to be primary, especially in life and death situations.

Doctors are allowed to own or "have a financial interest in a for-profit hospital, nursing home, or other health facility. However if a conflict arises, it must be resolved for the patient's benefit." Physicians may advertise with few restrictions. Physicians may also contract freely with hospitals or other health care units. Division of income in a group practice is allowed. The AMA determines that "competition between and among physicians and other health care practitioners on the basis of . . . factors such as quality services, skill, experience, miscellaneous conveniences offered to patients . . . is not only ethical, but [should be] encouraged."[79] Finally, the profession notes that "the patient's right of self-decision can be effectively exercised only if the patient possesses enough information to enable an intelligent choice. The patient should make his own determination of treatment."[80]

Thus the organized medical profession has accepted the increasing role of the liberal marketplace in health care, and it has abandoned in many ways the duty-based medical ethics that justified physician paternalism. This development is viewed as sad, if not entirely destructive, by some observers. Mark Siegler, for instance, describes three ages of medicine. The first he calls the age of paternalism, from the time of Hippocrates to 1965. Next came the age of autonomy from 1965 until October 1983. Since that time, he notes with some regret, we have been in the age of "bureaucratic parsimony," in which the good of the patient must be weighed against other goods including the needs of society and the rights of patients. Siegler argues that the core trust between doctors and patients has been lost because of the intrusion of liberal notions of rights into their relationships. In other work, he states that the "imposition of rights language may supplant the traditional model of medicine, a covenant model premised on promise keeping, indebtedness to society, justice and fidelity, and replace it with a narrowly contractual model based on libertarian principles of self-determination."[81] I would argue that this contractual model has already supplanted the "patient comes first" ethic.[82]

Other physicians have reacted to the changes of the past decade by emphasizing the importance of negative freedom in the liberal state. One of the most consistent of these arguments is that of Robert Sade, who has written a number of articles in response to demands for national health insurance. Sade assumes that "the concept of rights has its roots in the moral nature of man and its practical expression in the political system he creates."[83] The rights he speaks of are not, however, those of the patient, but those of the physician, and they are concerned largely with physician autonomy.

Sade's argument takes the following course. He states that the moral foundation of liberal rights are traceable to the most sublime fact of existence: "The moral foundation of the rights of man begins with the fact that he is a living creature: he has the right to his own life."[84] From this foundation, Sade deduces that since man as a being is capable of action, he must be granted unbridled choice in order to express his humanity. Sade, of course, values the free choice of man and individual expression of humanness just as Mill and Nozick would. Rights guarantee that the individual will retain personal prerogatives, what we have called a large sphere of personal liberty.

The right to life implies three corollaries: First, the right to select those values one deems necessary to guide one's own life; second, the right to exercise one's own judgment of the best course of action to achieve the chosen values; and third, the right to dispose of those values, once gained, in the way one chooses, without coercion by other men.[85]

It is clear that Sade draws heavily on Nozick. Sade would support a negative rather than a positive sense of freedom and would not compromise the values of liberties for those of equality.

Sade then applies his political philosophy to the practice of medicine. The physician is the bearer of the rights he has discussed.

The concept of medical care as the patient's right is immoral because it denies the most fundamental of all rights, that of a man to his own life and the freedom of action to support it. . . . Health care cannot morally be granted to anyone. It is a service: it must be purchased by those who wish to buy it, or given as a gift to the sick by the only human beings who are competent to give that gift; the health care professionals themselves.[86]

This is a classic interpretation of rights as the guarantees of personal liberty. Sade's thesis is straight out of the contractual rights tradition that Nozick has summarized. The core of this tradition is that one has a right over the products of one's labor. Just as Wilt Chamberlain should be allowed those dollars he earned by playing basketball, so too should the physician have control over and be paid for the treatment he produces. As Sade puts it, "The economic values produced, however, are not given as gifts by nature, but exist by virtue of the thought and effort of individual men. Goods and services are thus owned as a consequence of the right to sustain life by one's own physical and mental effort."[87] Thus Sade sees the doctor as being in much the same position as a baker: he has a right to sell or give what he has produced, whether it is medical knowledge or a loaf of bread.

Sade's support for liberty is obviously at odds with government intervention. Such intervention puts "immoral" limits on the individual's free choice. Government regulation of reimbursement or of standards review limits the physician's prerogatives. Sade believes that "the only proper function of government is to provide for the defense of individuals against those who would take their property by force."[88] Sade, with Nozick, accepts only negative freedom, certified by a set of rights, as the means through which one expresses one's autonomy. For Sade, justice prohibits government intervention in the form of the removal of obstacles to health care.

His argument against a right to health care is not so interesting, in that it is based on the conception of the right *in personam* against a physician. Most would conceive of a right to health care as *in rem* against society (an issue discussed later in his book). What is of interest is Sade's rendition of the rights of doctors. His conception of doctors' rights has been roundly criticized. He conveniently seems to forget that the doctor is not the only rights bearer in the doctor-patient relationship. The patient, too, has rights, as George Annas has pointed out: "Not being able to recognize the difference between medical care and the baking industry, Sade is completely incapable of going on to consider the human rights of his patients while they are under his care."[89] Annas's message is that rights are not solely the accoutrements of those who can afford them; rather, they are borne by every person in the liberal state. This is not his only point. He also makes a statement about the specialness of the caring occupations. Gene Outka also speaks of this: "To assume that doctors autonomously produce goods and services in a fashion akin to a baker is grossly oversimplified."[90] Outka and Annas thus balk at Sade's defense of the practice of medicine with liberties that emphasize the individual and his privileges in dealing with other people.

Outka's criticism is more limited than one that challenges Sade's entire conception of society. It is based on the observation that doctor-patient interchanges are unlike most other interchanges, and that they therefore deserve special rules. Outka admits that Sade's "stress on a free exchange of goods and services reflects one historically influential rationale for much of medical practice."[91] Nevertheless, Outka will not accept that the notion of contract, which is the paradigm Sade uses to characterize encounters with his doctor-baker, is appropriate in the field of medicine: "When lumps appear on someone's neck, it makes little sense to talk of choosing whether to buy a doctor's service rather than a color television set."[92] To Outka, it simply does not seem right that a doctor should approach his patient's situation assuming that the patient has a choice similar to those that might be made in commercial matters.

Masters presents this argument very clearly:

(1) The "interest" of the buyer of health services in his own life is not comparable to the "interest" or concern of the purchaser of ordinary economic goods; (2) the knowledge of the health care buyer is limited, unlike that of the partner in a paradigmatic contract; (3) the purchase of health care cannot be deferred until options in the market have been surveyed; (4) the institutional context of medical practice determines the kind of treatments offered, not a free negotiation between equals.[93]

These points represent the salient differences between a doctor-patient relationship and a true contract. The contract is indeed the ideal relationship in the liberal society that Sade envisions. Nevertheless, doctors cannot hope to elaborate the same set of rights in dealing with a patient as would a baker in dealing with a customer. In short, Kass has put it, it is only "loose talk" to refer to health as a commodity. Sade's characterization of medical practice is inappropriate even in a society that highly values liberties guaranteed by rights, even in a society that believes the contract model is the best way for people to deal with one another, and even in a society that insists that medical enterprise should be directed by the public morality of the liberal state.

For the better part of this century, doctors thought in terms of duties when considering their responsibilities to patients. The choice of the language of obligation was significant, given our society's emphasis on rights. The medical emphasis on duties and the sanctity of the doctor-patient relationship were closely associated with, and nurtured by, a system of health care that relied on fee-for-practice reimbursement. The doctor's decisions were thus unfettered by economic or organizational influences—only the patient's best interest was to be considered. Supervision of professional conduct was limited to the profession itself. This set of relationships created great moral hazards for the physician, who was placed in control of both the supply and demand of medical care.

The moral hazard, and the costs associated with it, proved to be too great. Over the past twenty years society has come to realize it cannot afford a medical care system completely controlled by doctors. A competitive marketplace has been encouraged and is taking shape. In many ways the doctor's role is being redefined. Doctors increasingly experience competing loyalties in their interactions with patients. Because of the demand for cost efficiency, medicine is becoming more bureaucratic as it is reintegrated into the liberal marketplace.

Of course this is not the only explanation for the changes that are occurring in medical care. Pellegrino, for instance, cities the growth of participatory democracy, the increasing education of patients and the increasing moral diversity of our country. All of these factors no doubt play a role.

In light of these changes, however they are explained, doctors and patients are going to have to become accustomed to thinking in terms of negative rights and autonomy. Doctors cannot be offended when a patient claims a right to something. Nor should patients be offended by the doctor's assertion of her own rights. Traditional ethical notions must be modified because doctors can no longer say the "patient comes first," for they must also consider the hospital, the group practice, and the publicly approved reimbursement scheme. This is not to say that the language of rights exhausts the set of concepts that defines ethical relations. Indeed, the doctor-patient relationship can likely never be purely contractual nor should a contract be the goal.

In light of the evolution of medical care, a new notion of medical ethics is needed which must take into account the virtues of the institutions of the liberal state. The doctor-patient relationship can no longer operate outside institutional considerations. In other words, justice, as instantiated by laws, must become part of the fabric of medical morality. Patients' rights must be considered, but without losing the sense of service that has been central to the traditions of the profession. The potential for exploitation of the patient through a set of noncompetitive economic relationships must also be avoided. In the following chapter, we will formulate such a medical morality, and then specify it further in succeeding chapters as we consider the relationship of medical morality to law and justice.

4

Just Doctoring: Medical Ethics for the 1990s

In the last chapter, I may have created an impression that I perceived doctors as monopolists, interested in defending their power over patients at any expense. I may have also created the impression that there was concerted and conscious action on the part of the profession to maintain a set of prerogatives at odds with the normal principles of the liberal state. In my focus on the political context of medical practice, I may have alienated readers who are confident of the good intentions of their physicians, as well as physicians who feel the characterization of them as being concerned as much with power and profits as with their patients is deeply unfair.

I intend now to counter these negative impressions and to begin the constructive portion of the book. Having elaborated the conceptual framework that I believe is the necessary foundation for thinking about medical ethics in our society, I would like to move forward with some proposals, which will only be as helpful as they are concrete. To maintain a sense of the real world, I will use examples from my own medical practice, and from the experiences of my colleagues.

My colleagues are fairly representative of the kind of physicians who have become commonplace in the last twenty years. We are all employees of one hospital, with no direct fee-for-service relationships with our patients. We provide the primary internal medicine practice for our medical center. We share the responsibility of being on call and teach residents and medical students. Many of my colleagues are women. My colleagues' research interests are in such areas as the conduct of the medical interview and the education of medical students. They are committed to providing excellent primary care to their patients, and would readily respond that they owe their patients special duties, including respect for the patient's autonomy. They practice medicine not out of an interest in profit, although we are well paid, but because it is a challenging and enriching occupation. They are not the power-hungry, self-centered individuals I may have portrayed in the previous chapter.

Nonetheless, many of my colleagues are wary of state influence over medical practice. They think a patient is best treated if the physician follows her personal and ethical code in dealing with sensitive issues. The division between law and ethics is carefully drawn; there is no sense of the "law as integrity" or as having a moral purpose in itself. Nor do most of my colleagues think that medical ethics should define a public role for physicians, or that health law and policy should represent moral challenges for physicians.

Rather, they tend to think, as do most physicians, that medical morality is restricted to the doctor-patient interaction. My colleagues would never lie to patients, or consciously treat them in a paternalistic fashion. They make every effort to be honest and to help their patients cope with illness. Most are far more adept at this aspect of medical practice than am I. In other words, they respect the patient's autonomy.

Yet I am sure they feel, as I do, that this respect for autonomy is not the same as respect for the autonomy of other individuals in the liberal state. For example, I occasionally do some consulting on hazardous substance litigation. I respect the autonomy of the person who hires me, and I deal with him honestly and openly. I rarely have a contract, but he and I respect the efficiency of the market and the constraints it imposes. In other words, I am paid appropriately and he gets the work he expects.

This is not the relationship my colleagues have with most of their patients. Recently one of my colleagues took care of a lawyer in his late thirties, Mr. Z., a very intelligent gentleman with a job at a respected firm. His girlfriend and his father are both physicians. He came to see my colleague, Dr. A., for a well-patient visit, "just needing a physical." On examination, he was fine and Dr. A. said she would see him in one year. Several weeks later, however, Mr. Z. called somewhat concerned. He was having dark diarrhea and felt weak when he stood. Dr. A. recommended he come to see her at the office that day. As Dr. A suspected, Mr. Z. was suffering from gastrointestinal bleeding, and he was hospitalized.

The story does not end there. Mr. Z. did not want to come to the hospital that first night. Dr. A. pointed out that Mr. Z. would be endangering himself if he went home, although his blood counts had not dropped very much. Because Dr. A. wanted him to stay in the hospital, she painted a fairly grim picture for Mr. Z., but she was willing to accommodate him if he wished to go home. He consulted relatives and friends and decided to stay.

The next day there was another similar discussion. The gastroen-terologists had been consulted and recommended endoscopy, in which a small device is passed into the stomach to look for ulcers. The patient was hesitant. Dr. A. did not feel strongly, as her understanding of the medical literature was that endoscopy at this point would be optional. Dr. A. said she would respect his decision, although she felt the slight uneasiness that comes with disagreeing with subspecialists (presum-ably they know best). In addition, she would have been more confi-dent about treatment if they could confirm what they all expected, a small ulcer.

Over the night, Mr. Z. changed his mind and agreed to have the endoscopy. His decision was the product of his own careful reasoning. But he also expressed his fears, and sought Dr. A.'s advice. He told her that the illness had made him feel vulnerable and that he did not like hospitals. She gently reassured him, revealing she felt the same way when sick. After a long, somewhat personal conversation about Mr. Z.'s fears, he felt much better. Neither patient nor doctor understood their relationship as being similar to one in which Mr. Z. had hired Dr. A. to consult about a case!

The endoscopy surprisingly revealed an ulcer with a bleeding artery in its crater. Mr. Z.'s counts dropped still lower, and Dr. A. consulted the surgical staff. It was necessary that Mr. Z.'s counts had to be stabilized before surgery, but they showed no sign of increasing over the course of several days, indicating some bleeding still at the site of the ulcer. A special X-ray of the stomach, called an air contrast upper GI series, did not reveal any bleeding. Yet Mr. Z.'s blood counts remained low.

As might be expected, these clinical issues caused some changes in the attitudes of both patient and doctor. The patient, while not in-timidated by medical authority, seemed to want to take a less active role in the decision making. Feeling more vulnerable, he wanted medical expertise to guide the decision making.[1] However, as he recovered, he became frustrated with the conflicting diagnostic reports, and with the physicians' inability to pinpoint the nature of the bleeding and to treat it. He had many questions, and Dr. A. and others labored to answer them.

Mr. Z. maintained his autonomy. He forced doctors to share their uncertainty with him by asking difficult questions that probed the doubts doctors prefer to keep to themselves. Dr. A. wanted to maintain Mr. Z.'s confidence in her medical knowledge, but she knew she could do this only by being honest with him. Indeed, his care was made less difficult because he was willing to help make decisions, and to take some authority and responsibility for his treatment. To this extent, the relationship approximated a typical relationship in a liberal state, approaching the norm encouraged by advocates of patient autonomy. Having said this, we still see in the case of Mr. Z. how the relationship of doctor and patient defies such definition.

Just after his first endoscopy, Mr. Z.'s blood counts had stabilized. One Saturday night, they fell again. He was concerned and called Dr. A. Dr. A. reassured him this was common and told him not to worry. Mr. Z. was uncertain when the blood counts would be checked again, and was quite anxious. To allay his fears, and to ensure the counts were being checked properly, Dr. A. drove over to the hospital, excusing herself from a dinner party. Mr. Z. was very happy to see her, and the counts were checked appropriately.

This kind of visit is one of the most gratifying aspects of medical practice. But it is not really part of relations between citizens in the liberal state. Dr. A. could have called the house officer physicians and ensured that the blood counts were to be checked. That would have been adequate. Yet it would not have fulfilled the sense of duty and affection Dr. A. and other doctors have for their patients. Dr. A. knew quite well the patient would be reassured to see her and to know someone was watching out for him. This visit did not decrease his autonomy. It did not remove the relationship from the liberal state or help maintain Dr. A.'s power over Mr. Z. Rather it involved moving beyond the relationship required by the liberal state. While I would hardly call a simple visit like this one a virtuous or altruistic act, it does represent a morality in which more than a simple "contract" between two autonomous people is expected.

Perhaps this is the best way to think of medical ethics in the liberal state of the 1990s. The patient is owed all the respect due any other person in the liberal state. The fact that he bears rights as a citizen should preclude any form of medical paternalism. Moreover, the doctor-patient relationship should remain firmly within the public morality of the liberal state, and the market should provide procedural justice in health care. This will eliminate the physician influence that created a health care system centered on, and highly profitable for, doctors. But the physician's ethical code should still comprise duties to patients that go beyond those normally owed other citizens in the liberal state. Altruistic behavior should be expected of physicians in their vocation as caregivers. So long as the justice provided by liberal laws and the public morality of the state are respected, the patient should come first.

Of course, this means the patient should come first not only in the intimate dealings between doctor and patient, but also in the relations the physician has with the institutions of medical care. As noted in chapter 3, one of the most debilitating aspects of medical ethics in this country in the first three-quarters of this century was the proposition that the doctor should consider only the patient, and that institutional aspects of medical care should be ignored. This code isolated doctor and patient from market and governmental control, creating an enormously expensive system of care. This kind of isolation was wrong, as I have argued. Medicine must heed the public morality of liberalism.

Ending the isolation of the doctor-patient relationship requires not only respect for patients' rights but also concern for the institutions in which medical practice occurs. In the liberal state, a medical ethics that respects rights but expects altruism in the case of the individual must also provide guidance for action in the realm of politics and economics.

Fortunately, these political and economic issues do not arise in the care of every sick patient. Returning to Mr. Z.'s case, for instance, there is little in his care that would raise larger social issues. One could, however, imagine circumstances in which his case might do so. For example, suppose that instead of working for the hospital and medical group, Dr. A. worked for an aggressively for-profit health maintenance organization. Say the HMO allowed only ten days for treatment of an acute gastrointestinal hemorrhage. As the tenth day approached, Dr. A. knew that she would face personal economic penalties if Mr. Z. stayed in the hospital past that deadline. The HMO would only be guilty of integrating some marketplace concepts into health care. But Dr. A. would suffer economically, and she might be induced to send the patient home earlier than we would prefer. Perhaps this example only shows the personal ethical dilemmas that arise in for-profit medicine, but perhaps it also raises questions about the extent to which we should regulate the market in health care.

Consider a more poignant if not tragic example. Later when I go to my office, I will be seeing Mrs. J. She is always several minutes early for her appointment, delightfully polite to the people in the office, yet painfully shy. She carries herself with a great deal of dignity. She likes early afternoon appointments, from which she can leave directly for work at an electronics plant where she assembles microchip boards. She does not earn much there, and she is routinely laid off every couple of months so that the employer does not have to pay for health insurance. She is one of the working poor that our fiscally embattled state is committed to helping.

Her medical problems are chronic and fairly severe. She suffers from hypertension (high blood pressure) and diabetes. She also has very high cholesterol levels in her blood. Her high blood pressure has been difficult to control, and she is now on three medications. Diet alone has done little to help her high cholesterol. Given that she has a family history of heart disease and is fifty-five years old, she has a very high risk for developing a heart problem. I would like to use a new medication to bring her cholesterol down, but she cannot afford it.

During each visit, she takes out her medicines and we go over the cost of each. We try to decide what to add, and then figure out what to subtract in order to bring the total cost down. Right now, we have controlled her blood pressure and lowered her cholesterol with a less effective medication than the one I would like to use. At first, this process seemed to me to be a challenge, especially in working out the details of the antihypertensive regimen, which became more and more peculiar because of Mrs. J.'s inability to pay for the typical medications. Now it saddens me. To make matters worse, Mrs. J. was laid off for four weeks owing to poor demand for her company's products. Her regimen of medications will have to be narrowed. In the meantime, someone has left a copy of *Automobile* magazine in our waiting room. Paging absentmindedly through it, I notice that Ferrari is selling over a thousand cars costing $160,000 each in the United States this year. This raises questions in my mind regarding the distribution of goods in our society.

I have to ask, do not I as a physician who believes in a fundamental responsibility to patients have some duty to help people like Mrs. J. obtain medications at a lower cost? Once I have cast aside the isolation of medical ethics of the past, do I not have to address the social and economic issues that harm my patients' health? Do I not have duties to address policy issues?

We live in a liberal state, and the public morality of the liberal state provides important parameters, guaranteeing justice as fairness and essential liberties. The particulars of the governance of that state are not, however, cast in stone. The liberal state is flexible. If enough citizens believe that the market should be regulated to create a cooperative polity, this is done. Citizen participation creates reform in the liberal state.

Thus while physicians should welcome integration of the principles of liberalism into medical care, with their focus on patient rights, decreased physician hegemony, and market efficiency, physicians should also be expected to modify those principles wherever necessary to protect patients. Just as we are willing to visit sick patients late at night, physicians should be willing to address political and legal issues to help our patients. In the rest of this chapter, I will discuss the nature of this public medical ethics that accepts liberalism yet still puts the patient first.

The Idea of Professional Ethics

Since I am now preparing to develop a theory of professional medical ethics, it is necessary to return briefly to a more conceptual discussion. First, it is important to specify my understanding of the nature of a profession, and its relationship to an ethical code. As discussed in chapter 2, sociologists have long been interested in professions, and especially in medicine. Weber, as interpreted by Parsons and the functionalism school of American sociology, has had great influence on our conception of a profession.

Michael Bayles has elaborated and summarized the Weberian view.[2] He notes that a profession has three aspects. First, the profession must provide important, if not essential, services. Thus lawyers, teachers, and physicians are seen as playing especially important roles or functions in our society. Second, a profession should have monopoly control over a certain body of information. Again, lawyers' knowledge of legal matters and doctors' knowledge of medicine are the best examples. The lay person would not claim to understand to any great extent the knowledge of the physician. Moreover, professions maintain this monopoly by controlling access to it; they accredit the schools where students learn the trade. This highlights the third aspect of professions for Bayles: there is no public control over them. Society expects the professions to police themselves.

What Bayles does not discuss at the time he defines the professions (although it is the topic of his book) is that they all possess a self-assumed ethical code. Society grants such extraordinary authority to professions because society trusts in the professions' adherence to codes. These codes, and the moral intent they reflect, are meant to regulate the relations between professions and the public, especially the client.

Bayles characterizes five models of relations between clients and professionals. They include agency, contract, friendship, paternalism, and fiduciary models. The agency and contract models are similar to what I have called the formal relations between citizens in the liberal state. Both sets of relations involve highly formalized expectations that bind the parties overtly. The friendship and paternalism models draw closer to the nature of medical ethics found in this country before 1975. The physician acted as a friend, but was prepared to act paternalistically and overlook the patient's autonomy, whereas the fiduciary relationship involves trust without usurpation of autonomy. The professional in a fiduciary relationship acts on behalf of the patient but respects the patient's rights. It is this kind of relationship that I would argue doctors should advocate as the norm of medical ethics.

Others would say that I am mistaken even before I start, on the premise that the liberal state itself, not physicians, should dictate the nature of professional ethics. Veatch, for instance, believes that any efforts by physicians to dictate the nature of medical ethics will lead to usurpation of patient rights.[3] Bayles takes the same position. He argues that professions are meant to serve society, and thus society should develop a set of expectations for professions.[4] Many observers have called for a decrease in the power of doctors to monopolize the means of entry into the profession. The lack of public trust in the profession and the attendant decrease in prestige have been noted by many sociologists.[5] That trust and prestige are now sorely missed by many physicians, who often have failed to see their own part in the loss.

While acknowledging the causes of the "deprofessionalization of medicine" and the good intentions of those who advocate further erosion of the professional model and its monopolization of power, I would like to offer a model of an ethical medical profession that defines for itself the nature of ethical practice. I do not see medical ethics as a mere pledge or a matter of group loyalty.[6] Nor do I see medical ethics as the consensus that the profession develops.

Rather, I understand professional ethics in medicine as an evolving set of principles. Physicians participate in this evolution, as do all members of the liberal state. The primary principles in medical ethics are the special needs of the patient and the commitment physicians have to the patient's well-being. With this commitment, there must be a capacity for altruistic behavior beyond that which the liberal state can expect of citizens generally. In addition, however, there must be respect for the public morality of liberalism, especially respect for patients' rights, their liberty, the integrity of the law and the sense of justice it reflects, and the pure procedural justice of the market. This sense of medical ethics calls for debate within the profession and active efforts by its members to make rational arguments that convince their peers of the necessity of certain ethical duties.

For example, many people are quite concerned about the problem of physicians' refusals to care for patients infected with the human immunodeficiency virus (HIV).[7] One could argue that health care professionals have a duty to treat all patients, including those with HIV infection, despite personal risk. Some physicians have stated unequivocally that any theory of medical ethics requires that physicians provide care for AIDS patients.[8] Indeed, both the American Medical Association and the American College of Physicians maintain that physicians are ethically required to care for those with HIV-related illnesses.

Do these assertions by some physicians and organizations of physicians necessarily mean that there is an ethical obligation for physicians to care for people with HIV-related disease? The answer is no. Individual physicians' opinions about ethical duties are helpful as a form of encouragement, but they carry no more intellectual force than do opinions that doctors have no ethical responsibilities. Professional societies' ethical guidelines are at best codifications of a professional censensus. They do not themselves create obligations of an ethical nature. Indeed, many physicians deny they have any duty to care for AIDS patients.

To understand the scope of the debate over the duty to treat every patient, one must understand the fluid nature of medical ethics and the difference between *individual* and *professional* ethical obligations. The critical elements of an individual's ethical obligations are that the obligations are self-assumed and that they derive from a set of rational principles. Professional ethical obligations are those that exist because the rational principles that give rise to them are closely related to the enterprise of the profession. Professional ethical obligations are related to individual ethical obligations in that both are self-assumed and both involve reasoning from principles to actions.

Professional ethical obligations are meant to bind the members of the profession. Of course, there is a possibility of disagreement within the profession about those obligations. Anyone can assert that members of a profession should recognize a certain ethical obligation. Someone else may assert that the ethical obligation does not follow rationally from principles of ethical action and thus should not be recognized. In this case, the second individual asserts that the profession will not recognize the obligation asserted by the first because the obligation is not reasonable. Thus any single assertion about professional ethical obligations does not mean there is an accord about those obligations.

Indeed, there is a dynamic relationship between individual assertions about professional ethics and an accord about professional ethical obligations. This dynamic relationship creates the fluid nature of medical ethics. Individuals may put forth their own interpretations about professional obligations. They will try to convince other members of the profession that they are correct in their choice of principles, and in their reasoning from those principles to action. Others will counter these assertions and disagree both about principles and the reasoning from those principles to action. This lively debate can and often does lead to an accord about ethical obligations.

Of course, not all ethical obligations are the subject of controversy. The paradigm of the debate can also explain ethical obligations upon which there is agreement. For example, physicians have argued that one principle is to do no harm to their patients. Understanding that sick patients are especially vulnerable both emotionally and physically, and that the patient's sharing of intimate life details is necessary for optimal therapy, doctors recognize an ethical obligation not to engage in sexual relations with patients. Since most physicians agree with these principles and reasoning, there is professional accord about this obligation.

I call these ethical obligations upon which there is professional accord or consensus "mature professional ethics." The public can and does rely on these obligations. They are the resolutions, at least in a theoretical sense, of debate. Issues that still provoke lively debate are not yet mature professional ethics. In addition, professional ethical propositions once thought to be mature can come under new scrutiny, the subject of active reflection.

Indeed, I have argued that the mature (in the sense of being settled, not particularly well-reasoned) professional ethics of the early 1970s has come under intense scrutiny over the past ten or fifteen years. As we have seen, there are many reasons for this. Foremost, the incredible costs of health care awakened society to the need for change in our medical system. The marketplace has as a result become a more dominant force in medical care. But as the medical profession has been drawn closer to the values of the liberal economy, there has been less and less agreement possible about the fundamental principles that should guide decisions about right and wrong. This is perhaps the great weakness of the liberal state. Liberalism, which celebrates individual choice, tends to disrupt the consensus that leads to mature professional ethics. The social morality of our society is incredibly diverse. For these reasons, many moral philosophers have begun to focus on contextual decisions, and to forego efforts to identify fundamental concepts of duty and obligation.

Where does this leave us with regard to the ethical obligation to treat AIDS patients? We cannot easily re-create a time in which there was less pluralism in medicine. Indeed, there are many reasons to prefer the changing social context of medicine and physician's freedom to partake in, and be guided by, the overlapping consensus that defines the liberal state. However, as we shall see in a later discussion, medicine imbued only with the marketplace concepts and the principles of liberalism may prove to be quite hostile to the idea of an ethical obligation to treat all patients, including those with HIV-related disease. At this point, however, we can only say that the dynamic process is ongoing, and that there is still disagreement within the profession about a duty to treat all patients.

I will return to this issue later in the book. Indeed, most of the remaining chapters will present a series of arguments about particular subjects I would like to submit to the ongoing medical ethics debate. I will be arguing that a new medical ethics should embrace certain propositions, given that medical ethics must accept the liberal public morality, yet move beyond that morality in the direction of altruism. Before delving into these specific arguments, however, I will indicate in more detail the broader role I see for medical ethics in the liberal state.

The Cooperative Liberal State

In previous chapters we noted the difference between negative and positive freedom. In the liberal state, these two types of freedom are in tension. The liberal state, as I have defined it, cannot be wholly libertarian (as conservatives like Nozick would suggest). As Rawls notes, there must be a sense of cooperation among citizens for a polity to exist. In Rawlsian terms, the rules of liberalism are converted from a mere modus vivendi to an overlapping consensus by the cooperation between citizens.[9]

Indeed Rawls and other liberals have arrived at such conclusions only after becoming the targets of political philosophers who believe that the concept of liberalism, defined for example in *A Theory of Justice*, is too individualistic to constitute the grounds for a community. The "communitarian" critics of liberalism are many. A review of one such critic's work can help highlight the deficiencies of the theory of classic liberalism and also suggest some different aspects of the modern liberal state as I have defined it. Moreover, notions of community in liberalism can help define the appropriate place of medical ethics.

Throughout much of his influential book, *Liberalism and the Limits of Justice*, Michael Sandel disagrees with Rawls and other liberals. He begins his critique by defining what he calls deontological liberalism, whose core thesis he describes as follows:

Society, being composed of a plurality of persons, each with his own aims, interests, and conceptions of the good, is best arranged when it is governed by principles that do not themselves presuppose any particular conception of the good; what justifies these regulative principles is . . . that they conform to the concept of right.[10]

For the liberal the primary good is justice, along with the neutrality of rights, that guarantees liberty.

In deontological liberalism, a nonempirical foundation justifies the primacy of justice. As Kant asserts, the basis for primacy of justice and the importance of rights is the autonomous will of a rational man.[11] The bearer of rights is the deontological self, or what Kant calls the noumenal self. Rights are therefore secured not by social interest or desires, but by the nature of relations between autonomous beings. This foundation of the notion of rights in individual persons provides the primacy for negative freedom secured by rights. Thus the public morality of the liberal state, justice as fairness, outweighs any other collection of social moralities; negative freedom takes precedence over positive freedom.

Sandel has two objections to this foundational role for rights and justice. We can call them sociological and philosophical objections. The sociological objection is that the neutrality of the public morality of the liberal state is untrue. As Sandel puts it: "All political orders thus embody some values; the question is whose values prevail and who gains and loses as a result. The vaunted independence of the deontological subject is a liberal illusion. It misunderstands the fundamentally social nature of man."[12]

Sandel argues that the neutrality of liberal rule, of the primacy of negative freedom, is not neutrality at all, but an endorsement of a particular social order brought about by the market. Sandel never moves from this argument to one concerning the class nature of society or the profit certain classes extort from others. Rather than pursuing a Marxist path, he shifts grounds slightly to emphasize that human beings do not have neutral relations with one another, but instead enjoy relations imbued with a variety of social meanings. The example he uses is the family, and he endorses the rich relations between family members as a model that makes greater sense for society than the proto-contractual models of market liberalism.

Sandel's philosophical objections to a foundational role of rights continues in this vein. He argues that modern liberals have had to recast Kant in order to move Kantian political and moral philosophy away from Kant's noumenal world. Sandel argues that Rawls and others have recognized that deontological liberalism must have empirical grounds. The original position is not—it cannot be—a completely and essentially idealistic world in which there are no needs and desires. Understanding this, Rawls addresses the primary goods that individuals would want to apportion in the original position and tries to create a balance between a "thin" and a "thick" theory of the good. But in so doing, Sandel believes, Rawls irretrievably harms the justifications for the emphasis on liberty and justice and neutrality that issue from Kant's synthesis. As he notes, Rawls cannot find the proper balance between Kantian metaphysics and an empirical basis; that is, Rawls fails to achieve "a standpoint neither compromised by its implication in the world nor dissociated and so disqualified by detachment."[13]

Throughout *Liberalism and the Limits of Justice* Sandel employs these arguments to undermine the liberal insistence that neutral justice and negative freedom define relations between citizens. He argues that once one descends, even thinly, to the empirical world, it is no longer clear why justice should be the primary means for ordering relations between individuals. Sandel, for one, can imagine a number of associations in which brother- or sisterhood, or a sense of allegiance to a common cause, would provide the means for ordering relations. He sees no reason why individual virtues and group solidarity should not provide grounds for a real community, in which justice is secondary. Again, however, he does not elaborate a Marxist utopia; he only suggests that communitarian values are also important. Liberalism is not exhaustive.

Sandel does allow that Rawls sees nothing wrong with communitarian values.[14] Sandel also suggests that some communitarian values are alive in the liberal state. For instance, he argues that affirmative action is sensible only as a communitarian project; it cannot be understood as a portion of a truly liberal state.[15] However, since he refuses to step toward Marxism, and yet appears to reject liberalism, it is never clear what Sandel thinks communitarianism should be. Is it a philosophy of a new state or is it an adjunct to liberalism? What Sandel seems to be saying is that liberalism has certain limits, and that the best community would be one that moved beyond these limits to establish some grounds for communitarian ideals.

Amy Gutman has made this notion explicit in an article in which she criticizes Sandel and other communitarians.[16] Gutman argues that Sandel has underestimated Rawls's theory. She notes that "Rawls need not claim that 'justice is the first virtue of social institutions' in all societies in order to show that the priority of justice obtains absolutely in those societies in which people disagree about the good life and consider their freedom to choose a good life an important good."[17] For liberals, justice is absolutely necessary in a state that favors pluralism. It is my thesis, as well as that of Gutman, that modern liberalism can accommodate some of the virtues of communitarianism within its commitment to equal concern and respect for each individual.

The liberal need not, however, exchange the emphasis on personal liberty for a poorly defined sense of communal needs, as the more radical communitarian may require. For example, Gutman objects to Sandel's either/or classification of political theories: "Either our identities are independent of our ends, leaving us totally free to choose our life plans, or they are constituted by community, leaving us totally encumbered by socially given ends."[18] Gutman's point is that there is no need to choose just one approach. She argues that communitarian policies do have a place within the liberal state. While justice provides the primary virtue for the public morality of the liberal state, communitarian virtues and an ethics of social cooperation can flourish. The social morality of the state has plenty of room for communitarian enterprise, so long as individual freedom is respected.

The modern liberal, unlike the classic liberal, realizes that an equal concern and respect for each human being is the key to a just polity. This requires personal liberty, but it need not be unfettered personal liberty. At times personal liberty must be constrained in order to decrease substantive inequalities in society. Thus the market, the preferred distributional mechanism in the ideal liberal world, may have to be modified in a manner that obstructs some individuals' choices, so that others may enjoy equal opportunities. These modifications of the law may well reflect what Sandel calls communitarian values. For example, affirmative action binds some people's liberty so that others may enjoy opportunities traditionally denied them. The modern liberal accepts these modifications, many of which can be characterized as communitarian. Communitarian reforms need not threaten the essentially liberal nature of the state. While justice is the first virtue of the state, cooperation and community are encouraged. Communitarianism helps to define the cooperative aspects of the modern liberal state and reminds liberals of the importance of community, of the importance of monitoring the antiegalitarian aspects of the market.

Some may argue, however, that the emphasis on equality and the

acceptance of communitarian values make what I call modern liberalism into a form of socialism. I counter by reminding these critics that
the guiding prescriptions of this state are negative freedom and the
market for purposes of distribution. Restrictions on the market, and
on negative freedom, may be necessary at times to reiterate the equal
concern for and respect of the individual. Modern liberals will not
accept a community definition of rules that restricts individuals'
choice.

I will use communitarianism as a model for the function of medical
ethics in the liberal state. I would propose that we physicians think of
medical ethics as a communitarian project that respects the public morality of the liberal state, as well as the procedural justice of the market,
yet strains to improve liberalism by helping create a community for
health care. This builds a foundation for a medical morality based on
physicians' altruism whereby the patient indeed "comes first," but also
keeps his autonomy. It also encourages a social ethic for physicians
that enables them to understand the law and policies of health care and
to strive for a form of health care that benefits patients in a just manner.

Michael Walzer's notion of spheres of justice enriches this theory of
medical ethics. Walzer, searching for a means to guarantee the virtues
of egalitarianism, suggests that there are different spheres of justice
within a state,[19] corresponding to the fact that there are different
goods, each implying different distributional concepts. Thus a medical
sphere might be partially detached from the usual market sphere because one would want to distribute health care differently from the
way one distributes other goods. The sphere of justice for health care
would thus be somewhat independent of the procedural justice of the
market, yet the values of the liberal state would remain primary.

This does not mean that physicians can be free to set up a distributional pattern that benefits physicians. Walzer is very clear that in
the state he envisions, the power of professions would be carefully
constrained. Indeed, Walzer notes that "any fully developed system of
medical provision will require constraint of the guild of physicians."[20]
I would argue that one aspect of medical ethics should devote attention to political and economic issues, but that attention should be
driven by concern for one's patients and should voluntarily constrain
any power-maximizing aspects of the profession.

In this theory of medical ethics in the liberal state, physicians should
accept the market as the prime means for obtaining procedural justice

in the liberal state, but they should also be willing to modify it when good medical care requires distributional patterns that the market cannot fully provide. Physicians must respect the integrity of the law, but also be willing to work democratically to modify the law when it unnecessarily constrains the communitarian aspects of medical care. An altruistic medical ethics, both in direct relations with patients and in the development of a just system of health care, will then contribute to a sense of social cooperation in the liberal state.

This is how I believe medical ethics should function. But I will be successful in defining a new medical ethics only insofar as I can convince others it is sensible, and I will only convince people if I can show more clearly the shape of medical ethics as a form of social cooperation in the modern liberal state. Indeed, it will be important to begin to move, in the next few chapters, from my reified notion of modern liberalism, to particular liberal states—especially the American one.

Doctor-Patient Relations in the Liberal Community

I have argued that medical ethics in the future must have two not entirely separable aspects. One retains a focus on relations between doctors and patients. The other moves beyond that focus to address economic and political issues in health care. Traditional ethics allowed physicians to ignore the overall social repercussions of medical ethics. This is no longer possible, even if it were desirable. In accepting the public morality of the liberal state, physicians must develop a medical morality that combines selfless action with the goal of promoting social cooperation and a sense of community within the liberal state. We must now see how my notion of medical ethics takes shape in the setting of the doctor-patient relationship.

While not employing the same theoretical framework I have, many other commentators have addressed the problems of combining traditional notions of medical ethics with respect for individual liberty. In the medical ethics literature, these problems usually take the form of a debate over the relative merits of an autonomy-based medical ethics versus a beneficence-based one. The supporters of the latter, almost always doctors and their collaborators, argue that medical ethics must be motivated by the best interests of the patient. On the other hand, proponents of autonomy-based ethics demand that patients' choices be respected.

At first glance, there would appear to be little real debate between the opposing factions: will not patients usually make decisions that are in their own best interests? The answer is yes, but medical ethics thrives on tough cases. The doctor may decide in a difficult case that the patient's decision is wrong, that the patient is incapable of making the decision he would make if he were healthy. The beneficence model therefore calls for different action than would autonomy-based ethics.

Respect for beneficent practice runs deep in medical traditions. Veatch has noted that the Hippocratic oath itself is paternalistic and consequentialistic.[21] The physician is instructed by Hippocrates to follow the system that according to her own judgment will benefit the sick. Such paternalism raises deep suspicion in a liberal state and has caused many ethicists to create defenses against it on behalf of patients. These defenses usually center on covenant models, in which respect for patient autonomy is formally integrated into the moral relationship.[22]

In at least partial recognition that traditional medical ethics was out of step with the liberal state—leaving aside my claim that the liberal state has been actively seeking to reintegrate the practice of medicine into its broader public morality—new models of beneficence that include greater respect for autonomy have been developed. Pellegrino and Thomasma have led the way in this regard.[23] They argue that medicine is beneficent at root because patient problems are the primary concern of medicine, harm to patients must be avoided, and both patient autonomy and physician paternalism must be superseded by a focus on the patient's best interests. They elaborate on this basic proposition by noting that the patient's existential experience is the basis for any moral reasoning in medicine, that doctors and patients must negotiate when difficult situations arise, that any medical decision should be based on the consensus of doctor and patient, and that the moral values of both parties must be respected.[24] In short, Pellegrino and Thomasma understand medical ethics as a moral relationship between two individuals, each of whom is worthy of respect.

But we have seen how a singular focus on the doctor-patient relationship has been associated with a set of beliefs that legitimated the moral and economic power of physicians over patients. This is not to say that Pellegrino and Thomasma have bad intentions. To the contrary, much of their argument is fueled by a belief in, and insistence on, an altruistic medical ethics. Indeed, they argue forcefully that sick-ness and disease weaken patients' capacities and that doctors' devotion to care is a part of the healing process.[25] Health is not a relative value for physicians, but a primary one.

Most patient-rights advocates are unconvinced even by this com-promised beneficence model that Pellegrino and Thomasma outline. Their major objection is that the role of physician in this model has great potential for abuse. Jay Katz has outlined the reasons why well-meaning physicians could abuse the authority granted them by the beneficence model. In his careful analysis of the doctor-patient rela-tionship, *The Silent World of Doctor and Patient*, Katz explores the relation of doctor to patient through historical and legal research and from a psychoanalytic perspective. His conclusion is that doctors have never placed a premium on communicating with their patients and in fact have significant psychological and professional obstacles to over-come before such communication will be possible.

Without attempting to do justice to the texture of his arguments, I would like to summarize some aspects of Katz's book that explore the reasons underlying many observers' fears regarding "beneficent" phy-sicians. In particular, Katz has formulated three key insights. The first of these is the historical point that there has never been any emphasis in medical ethics on open discussion with the patient. Katz notes that "from the decline of the Greek city states to the eighteenth century no major primary or secondary documents on medical ethics . . . reveal even a remote awareness of a need to discuss anything with patients that relates to their participation in decision making."[26] Moreover, as modern professional ethics was developing in this country, physicians chose to emphasize the lonely role of the doctor as decision maker, thus precluding patient participation. While some may differ with Katz on certain points of this analysis,[27] it is difficult to escape his conclusion that the historical relation of doctor to patient is one of silent authority.

The second and third points I have culled from Katz's book concern the psychoanalytic notions that underlie physicians' opposition to open communication and patient decision making. Katz introduces his psychoanalytic perspective by instructing us about the importance of the rational and irrational in any relationship. Autonomy itself, he argues, relies on the "simultaneous operation of rationality and irra-tionality."[28] One of the most troubling parts of the doctor-patient relationship is that doctors assume they are completely rational, and that patients are generally irrational. This tends to preclude self-examination on the part of physicians and closes off the possibility of real communication with their patients.

The obstacle to open communication represented by the physician's failure to consider his or her own irrationality is buttressed by the manner in which physicians cope with uncertainty. Katz argues that uncertainty places a psychological burden on the doctor, and this burden is typically relieved by denying the existence of uncertainty. "Physicians' denial of awareness of uncertainty . . . makes matters seem clearer, more understandable, and more certain than they are."[29] Even more disconcerting is Katz's statement that "professing certainty serves purposes of maintaining professional power and control over the medical decision-making process as well as maintaining an aura of infallibility."[30] Thus physicians are motivated to profess certainty and to overlook the interplay of rationality and irrationality in their interactions with patients.

Certainly, Katz's insights here are fundamental. In the example I used previously of Mr. Z., the lawyer with gastrointestinal bleeding, one can uncover exactly the motives Katz discusses. Dr. A. really wanted to be certain, and she had to resist constantly the desire to appear certain to the patient. Moreover, Dr. A. wanted to view the patient as irrational when he balked at being tested, but on reflection Dr. A. could see she was the one who was irrationally "digging in" and refusing to consider options.

Viewed in this light, it is easier to understand the suspicion many harbor regarding physician beneficence. Dr. A. wanted what was best for Mr. Z. and was even willing to go far beyond any contract in her dutiful approach to his care; but Dr. A. also wanted some authority. She wanted to exercise some control, given her greater knowledge and experience in dealing with sickness. Mr. Z.'s desire to control matters thus appeared irrational to her. Katz's argument, that the dynamic of the doctor-patient relationship pushes even the most beneficent relation toward paternalistic behavior, is therefore of extreme importance.

Given the psychodynamics of the doctor-patient relationship, it seems that medical ethics must first guarantee autonomy. The patient's liberty and negative freedom must be overtly recognized and respected. Any beneficent components of medical ethics must be added onto, and constrained by, respect for individual autonomy. Physicians should be encouraged to act in a beneficent manner, but they should never expect that in return the patient's liberty will be diminished.

Pellegrino and Thomasma have offered a series of possible models for the doctor-patient relationship.[31] Included among these are business, contractual, covenant, preventive, and beneficent models. The authors defend, on the one hand, the beneficent relationship in which trust and the good of the patient, who is in a state of "wounded humanity," are central. The covenant model, on the other hand, explicitly involves respect for patient autonomy and also patient trust.[32]

The best model seems to me to lie somewhere in between. I believe that autonomy of the patient must be central. The patient must be treated and should expect to be treated without condescension. Issues should be aired openly and alternatives discussed in a rational fashion. Those patients who have difficulty understanding must be accorded the respect of further discussion. The patient should maintain his realm of negative freedom, and the physician should not trespass this barrier.

In addition, the physician must be willing to move beyond the behavior expected of members of the liberal state and act for the good of the patient. The physician should make sure the "patient comes first." The way in which the physician accomplishes this "moving beyond" is not only to respect patient autonomy, but to help the patient maintain autonomy. The physician must deal with the sick patient's wounded humanity by doing everything necessary to restore that humanity.

Consider again Mr. Z. The night Dr. A. drove over to the hospital to discuss his decreasing hematocrit with him, he was greatly concerned. He was young, but his body was failing him and he felt vulnerable. Dr. A.'s reassurances helped him to begin to think clearly about the options before him. He could shake his depression, if not completely, at least enough to think rationally about the treatment plan. This kind of action would not necessarily be expected in the classic liberal state. It requires respect for liberty, not efforts to promote it or restore it. Medical ethics should thus provide a sense of cooperation and "other regardedness" often lacking in classic liberalism. Yet it should not subvert the public morality.

I am not, by any stretch of the imagination, the first to suggest this kind of interpretation of medical ethics. But others who do so go further. Pellegrino and Thomasma, for instance, develop the theory of beneficence in a way that leads to a discussion of virtue. They note that a virtuous physician, like Aristotle's virtuous person, has special knowledge, chooses acts for their own sake, and has a secure and confident character.[33] Physician altruism in this model leads to truly selfless activity on behalf of patients. Aristotlean virtue thus seems the model for the moral action of physicians.

For reasons already stated, I do not condone such reliance on virtue, for fear it may lead physicians to disrespect, in some ways, negative freedom. The physician altruism I posit is simply an other-regardness that goes beyond what is expected of liberal citizens, but in no way trespasses autonomy. If you like, it is a *thin* theory of altruism that fits well with liberalism. In the following chapters, I will illustrate it further.

For now, the point I want to make is fairly simple. Medical morality or ethics must involve both respect for patient autonomy and altruistic efforts on the part of physicians to maintain patient autonomy. Physicians must be willing to act in an other-regarding manner while carefully considering the constraints of liberalism. Indeed, there should be little conflict between physician altruism and liberal morality. Physician altruism is based on patient autonomy; without asserting any "right" to act on behalf of the patient, it adds the warmth of cooperative relations to the somewhat colder exchanges between citizens of the liberal state. We can say, then, that the ethics of the doctor-patient relationship involve the following principles: (1) rejection of physician paternalism and professional efforts to usurp authority; (2) endorsement of the altruistic "patient comes first" ethic; (3) actualization of patient autonomy through reassurance and careful, mutual negotiation of a treatment plan.

These principles cannot be restricted to the doctor-patient relationship, at least in its narrow meaning as a personal relation between two people. As I have argued in previous chapters, the great mistake of medical ethics and the medical profession was the failure to understand the economic and political repercussions of the structural organization of medical care. The "patient comes first" attitude created a "physician profits most" system that eventually called into question physician altruism. Since I am now advocating physician altruism in the liberal state, that altruism must also be applied within the structure of medical care.

Physician altruism should help nourish a Walzerian health care sphere. The public morality of liberalism garners respect in the sphere of health care, but certain compromises in the particulars of a market economy may be necessary to create the proto-communitarian atmosphere necessary for maintaining patient autonomy. The market should be taken as a given, not as a foreign interloper in medical care. Where necessary, however, the procedural justice of the market may need to be replaced by just regulatory devices.

The same is true of the law. Legal rulings should be understood as representing the integrity of the law, as renditions of the justice inherent in the public morality of the state (while recognizing that not all laws, in even the most liberal of states, reflect the principles of liberalism). Legal imperatives should not necessarily be rejected as secondary to ethical considerations; rather, they should be viewed as efforts to maintain and respect patient autonomy. Nevertheless, legal mandates must be examined from the vantage point of medical ethics. The health care sphere, for example, may call for different mandates than that of the securities trading sphere.

Physicians should play a role in this scrutiny of market relation and legal imperatives. As patient advocates, and as people who are altruistically committed to patient autonomy, physicians should be willing to question whether the unregulated market is the best organizational device, both for financing and delivering medical care (a distinction that will assume some prominence in subsequent chapters). If the answer is no, then physicians should offer solutions in the form of regulations that support patient autonomy without subverting the market to physician control. Physicians should also scrutinize laws carefully to ensure the integrity they represent is truly appropriate for medical care.

Others disagree that physicians should play this institutional role. Pellegrino and Thomasma would argue that health is an absolute value for physicians and that other goods are beyond the ken of medical ethics.[34] Veatch argues that physicians must be committed to individual patients, and this commitment precludes a physician role in policy decisions.[35]

I reject these positions without hesitation. To create a health care sphere, a sense of medical care imbued with cooperation and community, and thus a set of institutions in which physicians' altruistic behavior can operate without transgressing the public morality of liberalism, physicians must be willing to address policy issues. The same other-regardedness that drives medical ethics in the doctor-patient relationship must be directed toward consideration of health law and economics. Medical ethics in the liberal state must address not only interpersonal relations, but also institutional relations. The communitarianism of medical care must benefit the liberal state at both the human and institutional level.

Returning to the examples I outlined above, Dr. A. is committed as a physician who behaves ethically to go the extra step necessary to maintain Mr. Z.'s autonomy. She must reassure him, yet be willing to share her uncertainty. She must make sure he "comes first" by acting on his behalf, and yet she must recognize that his irrationality is matched by her own.

In the case of Mrs. J., the same rules must hold. I cannot simply stand by and see her autonomy and health diminished by the fact that she cannot pay for her prescription medicine. I must respect the market in most cases and the procedural justice it brings to relations, but I must also be willing to regulate the market to maintain human dignity. I must therefore try to help find solutions to situations like Mrs. J.'s, and in so doing restore a sense of community to health care and indeed to the liberal state. I cannot focus, as an ethical physician, on a narrow definition of doctor and patient. I must be willing to pursue efforts to overcome institutional arrangements that diminish autonomy.

Thus medical ethics in the liberal state involves a number of principles beyond those mentioned above. A complete list would include:

1. rejection of physicians' paternalism and efforts to usurp authority;
2. endorsement of the altruistic "patient comes first" ethic;
3. actualization of patient autonomy through reassurance and careful, mutual negotiation of a treatment plan;
4. careful attention to the institutional setting for the practice of medicine;
5. respect for the public morality of the liberal state and its reliance on individual liberty and market justice;
6. conscientious efforts to mold the health care sphere so that it conforms to the liberal state yet evinces a spirit of cooperation and community that nurtures the "patient comes first" ethic.

Admittedly these principles are quite abstract. To outline my view of the medical ethics as a moral enterprise within liberalism, not as an alternative to liberalism, I would like to review a series of developments in the law and governmental regulation of health care. I will then propose the manner in which a just physician should act with regard to such initiatives. This is not to say that my positions will be a reflection of how physicians do act; my aim is prescriptive, not descriptive. Given the model of professional ethics I outlined above, I seek to stir debate within the profession as we develop a set of ethical norms appropriate to liberal medicine.

Since the theory of medical ethics I envision overtly recognizes principles of liberalism, as well as the institutions of medical care, it centers more on justice than do traditional medical ethics. Nonetheless, I seek to retain the traditional virtues of altruism and selflessness that characterized the art of patient care, or doctoring. Hence I term this characterization of medical ethics, "just doctoring." In the following chapters I hope to specify what just doctoring means.

5

Informed Consent

Medicine has changed, in many respects radically, over the last twenty-five years. These changes have occurred not only in health policy but also in the conceptual underpinnings of the relations of physicians to their patients and to the institutions of medical practice. These changes in health law and policy have created a demand for a new theory of ethics in medicine that I have called just doctoring. Just doctoring properly should concern not only ideal relations between two individuals but also determinations of the best possible shape for new health policy initiatives. From the physician's ethical viewpoint, new policies should conform to a liberal public morality and yet reaffirm the cooperation and egalitarianism central to the best possible liberal state and essential to the practice of medicine. Physicians must abandon their distrust of (indeed hostility toward) matters of law and politics—a posture that has belied their continuous efforts to maintain control over the practice of medicine—and now become activists. They must speak on behalf of patients when legal or policy reforms are introduced.

In this chapter, we will examine the issue of informed consent in medical care, a subject of great concern for medical ethics. Reviewing informed consent will allow us to trace the evolution of a legal initiative that has helped to reintegrate medicine within the liberal state, laying the foundation for just doctoring.

The history of informed consent in this country is one of patients attempting to overcome the paternalistic attitudes of doctors generated by the inequality of knowledge that exists between them. The demand for informed consent has been justified in terms of rights. Patients want to maintain their right to refuse treatment, and they do not want to have their liberty usurped by physicians.

Consider again the case of Mr. Z., the patient who was suffering from a bleeding duodenal ulcer. When he was first admitted to the hospital, Dr. A. was uncertain about the source of his bleeding. She recommended that he undergo endoscopic examination. This procedure entails passing a long tube of fiberoptic equipment down the esophagus and into the stomach. Its risks are generally minor, but it could potentially cause perforation of the stomach, necessitating emergency surgical intervention.

Mr. Z. was hesitant; he did not want to stay in the hospital. He did not like the idea of seeing doctors, and he felt he would forfeit personal autonomy once he entered the hospital. Dr. A. did not want to cause him further anxiety, but she did want the endoscopy performed. Therefore Dr. A. was reluctant to detail all the potential risks of the procedure.

One route Dr. A. might have chosen would have been to withhold some information concerning the risks of endoscopy, her justification being that sick people often act irrationally and that she had to take this irrationality into account. This is called "therapeutic privilege," an expression of physicians' paternalism toward sick patients. Dr. A. could have invoked therapeutic privilege and withheld information.

I would argue that physicians are less likely to invoke therapeutic privilege now than they were twenty-five years ago. Patients have defended their rights by suing physicians who have failed to inform them fully of the risks and benefits of a treatment. A review of the legal history of informed consent reveals the manner in which the law has reasserted control over medicine, overcoming physicians' resistance to supervision. It also reveals that physicians have an ethical duty to pursue further efforts to inform patients fully.

While there are many functions of informed consent suits, my attention is restricted to the patient's assertion that her negative freedom be respected, in keeping with the values of the liberal state.[1] In addition, I will continue to assert that the law reflects the public morality that underlies the modern liberal state.[2] Following Alan Donagan, I concentrate on suits that ensure that the "physician proposes and the patient decides" in a manner that is consistent with the liberal principles of society and health care institutions.[3,4]

Typically, a suit by a patient to whom a physician has failed to give adequate information when seeking consent to an operation is part of torts, or personal injury law. More precisely, such suits are usually tried as cases of negligence; the patient asserts that the physician failed to meet the standard of care expected of the profession. In such cases, courts expect to hear professionals' expert testimony on the quality of the information provided to the patient in order to evaluate the consent given by the patient.[5]

Not all informed consent suits are framed this way. Some are heard as cases of battery. In these suits, the plaintiffs claim that they were victims of unconsented touching. There is no need in such suits for expert testimony, as there is no determination of a standard of care. Battery suits in effect state that the physician is liable even if she can find other physicians who agree that the amount of information she provided was appropriate. (In the real world, most plaintiffs will raise both points when they sue, and the court has some prerogatives over the grounds it thinks are best considered.) The tension between battery and negligence cases informs much of the recent history of informed consent suits. Analyzing cases from this perspective can help to reveal the manner in which courts have thought about informed consent and the rights of patients vis-à-vis doctors' ethical duties.

The Early Evolution of Legal Principles of Informed Consent

Anglo-American common law holds that no medical procedure can be performed on a person unless that person has given her informed consent. This prohibition is based on the respect that the law accords one's body, a respect that coincides with the concern for negative freedom, which lies at the heart of liberalism. The prohibition is an ancient one, as well.[6] Until the early part of this century, it was usually expressed in terms of battery. As noted above, a battery is an intentional touching to which no consent has been given.[7] As Fowler Harper and Fleming James have related, the battery doctrine is the patient's interest "in the physical integrity of the body, that it be free from physical contact," and "the purely dignitary interest in the body, that it be free from offensive contact."[8] Katz has discussed the implications of the battery standard:

Battery, which evokes frightening visions of physical violence, is an uncompromising remedy, allowing few defenses. Only a very restricted question is asked: Did the patient know and agree to what was going to be done to him?

If the answer is no, law does not require the patient be physically damaged by the intervention. . . . Nor is proof required that the patient's probable conduct in submitting to the touching would have been different, had the doctor fulfilled his duty to disclose the nature of the operation.[9]

Thus the battery doctrine provides unmitigated protection of the patient's exercise of free choice in line with the tenets of negative freedom.

Since the 1930s, courts have largely abandoned the battery standard in informed consent suits—and have adopted in its place the standard of negligence. This standard incorporates principles of medical professional negligence, treating failure to inform as negligent nondisclosure.[10] The negligence standard differs from the battery standard in several important ways. First of all, it ties informed consent to professional norms. Often practitioners must testify as experts in order for the court to discern what negligent nondisclosure is. As Arnold Rosoff has noted, the important question is whether the physician has told the patient everything that an "average reasonable practitioner" would have revealed in a set of similar circumstances (as we shall see, the reasonable practitioner has been replaced, in some jurisdictions, by the reasonable patient).[11] The second difference is that there is no purely dignitary damage in negligence: physical injury must be demonstrated. The informed consent suit that is tried as a case of negligence is thus much more dependent on professional standards and expertise than one that is tried as a case of battery.

The laws regarding battery and negligence are substantially different. The former directly protects the patient's person from interference; it guarantees negative freedom. The latter turns on the customs of a profession, with less of an emphasis on the patient's liberty. Battery concentrates on interference with a person's liberty without consent; negligence concentrates on a professional's transgression of professional norms. These differences should not be minimized by characterizing battery and negligence as two points on the same spectrum. Marcus Plante for example, has suggested that negligence applies to failure to warn about a collateral hazard of a procedure, while battery applies to a more central hazard.[12] This analysis, however, misses the key tension within informed consent suits: the conflict between the patient's negative freedom and the prerogatives the physician seeks to maintain.

The decision of *Pratt* v. *Davis* in 1905 is representative of the judiciary's use of the battery standard when physicians fail to inform patients.[13] In this decision, Justice Brown of the Illinois Appellate Court affirmed that damages should be awarded to Mrs. Davis as a result of Dr. Pratt's failure to get her consent to a hysterectomy. Mrs. Davis had been afflicted by epilepsy and consulted Dr. Pratt, who told her that her lacerated womb would have to be repaired. He then proceeded to remove both ovaries and uterus, sterilizing the plaintiff and causing her great emotional pain.[14]

Pratt, the appellant, argued that "when a patient places herself in the care of a surgeon for treatment without instructions or limitations, upon his authority, she thereby in law consents that he may perform such operation as in his best judgment is proper and essential to her welfare."[15] The court refused to accept this definition of the physician's prerogatives. Justice Brown's reasoning is worthy of lengthy quotation:

On the contrary, under a free government at least, the citizen's first and greatest right, which underlies all others—the right to the inviolability of his person, in other words, his right to himself is the subject of universal acquiescence, and this right necessarily forbids a physician or surgeon, however skillful or eminent, who has been asked to examine, diagnose, advise and prescribe (which are at least the necessary first steps in treatment and care) to violate without permission the bodily integrity of his patient.[16]

In this decision, then, we see the juxtaposition of opposing sets of values. Pratt's defense is the medical ethical principle of mutual partnership, reformulated such that the doctor's autonomy is emphasized. Mrs. Davis's suit is based on her right to her self, the negative freedom guaranteed to all in a liberal state. The suit itself was tried as a case of battery, and Mrs. Davis's rights were upheld accordingly.

The *Pratt* v. *Davis* decision appears to have assumed that the grounds for a battery suit were self-evident. In another case that year, a Minnesota court was forced to consider explicitly whether the battery rubric applied to consent suits. In *Mohr* v. *Williams*, defendant had decided that the plaintiff's right ear was more diseased than his left and operated accordingly. The plaintiff had, before undergoing anesthesia, agreed only to an operation on the left ear. The court allowed that "the operation was in every way successfully and skillfully performed."[17] The defendant argued that "under the facts, an action for assault and battery will not lie. . . . There is a total lack of evidence showing or tending to show malice or an evil intent on the part of defendant, or that the operation was negligently performed."[18]

The court addressed this contention directly: "Every person has a right to complete immunity of his person from physical interference of others . . . and any unlawful or unauthorized touching of another . . . constitutes assault and battery."[19] Judge Brown was not swayed by the argument that the right ear was diseased and the operation a success. The plaintiff's liberty to choose the operation had been infringed—a battery had occurred. Typical notions of negligence did not apply.

Benjamin Cardozo reemphasized this point nearly ten years later in the case of *Schloendorff* v. *New York Hospital*.[20] The trial court had found that Mrs. Schloendorff was operated on without her consent by Drs. Stimson and Bartlett. Cardozo noted that "in the case at hand, the wrong complained of is not merely negligence. It is trespass. Every human being of adult years and sound mind has a right to determine what shall be done with his own body; and a surgeon who performs an operation without his partner's consent commits an assault, for which he is liable in damages."[21] The court emphasized that the issue was battery, and that physicians must get a patient's full consent before operating.

The underlying principle in all these decisions was that the patient's negative freedom must be protected, in accordance with the principles of a liberal state. It is notable that all of these cases occurred just before the AMA began to consolidate the position of the medical profession in health care.[22]

This is not, however, to say that courts during this period were unanimous in their support of a battery standard and individual patient's rights. In *Bennan* v. *Parsonnet*, an appellate court reversed a jury verdict that awarded damages to the plaintiff after Dr. Parsonnet operated on his right groin.[23] Dr. Parsonnet was to operate on the other groin, but decided after the patient was anesthetized that the right hernia was more serious. The court thought that the employment of anesthesia was critical and that

when a person has selected a surgeon to operate upon him and has appointed no other person to represent him during the period of unconsciousness that constitutes a part of an operation, the law will by implication constitute such surgeon the representative pro haec vice of his patient and will, within the scope to which such implication applies, cast upon him the responsibility of so acting in the interest of the patient that the latter will receive the full benefit of that professional knowledge and skill.[24]

In this case, the situation was quite similar to that of *Mohr* v. *Williams*, yet the outcome was directly opposite. Here Judge Garrison appeared to focus on the inequity of the knowledge and introduction of technology into the doctor-patient relationship. As a result, he asserted that the patient was to trust his physician, and the physician was to act on the patient's behalf. The reasonable expectation that the patient would so trust the surgeon was not addressed in the decision.

There are several unargued assumptions within the decision. Judge Garrison also seemed to believe that the doctor's actions would be guided by an ethical code that prohibited abuse of the patient's trust. Moreover, this code was protected and endorsed by the court, which found that a doctor's ethical code was not to be threatened by suits asserting a patient's negative freedom, especially when no physical damages occurred. This proposition was formulated somewhat unclearly in the court's decision:

This concluding suggestion may perhaps be ethical rather than legal, but it does not seem in good morals a patient ought not, in his efforts to obtain a money verdict, be permitted to repudiate the sound judgment exercised in his behalf by the surgeon of his choice in whose judgment, had he been capable of consulting, he would have unquestionably concurred.[25]

In other words, instead of protecting the patient's liberty to choose, as in *Mohr*, the court here exhorts the patient not to abuse the trust relationship with the physician.[26] The influence of traditional medical ethics on the judge's interpretation of the tortious act is apparent.

Although there are few cases to support any specific propositions, it seems that battery claims were slowly abandoned over the period from 1920 to 1960. A typical case is that of *Hunt* v. *Bradshaw*, decided in 1955.[27] Hunt was the victim of an occupational accident in which a piece of steel lodged in his brachial plexus, a large set of nerves in the shoulder and chest. He was told by Dr. Bradshaw that a simple operation could remove the metal and prevent its migration toward the heart. Hunt agreed, but as a result of the operation, he was partially paralyzed for life. Hunt charged that he had not been warned of the risks involved in the operation. The appeals court's decision does not mention battery, but drily notes that "the plaintiff's case fails because of lack of expert testimony that the defendant failed, either to exercise due care in the operation, or to use his best judgment in advising it."[28] The decision is based on the fact that there was no expert testimony that labeled Dr. Bradshaw as negligent. The judicial emphasis on patient liberty and self-determination witnessed in the earlier cases that were tried as battery was absent entirely in this decision.[29]

The trends noted in the cases above were consolidated in *Salgo* v. *Leland Stanford University Board of Trustees*.[30] In this case, the California appellate court considered the relationship of Salgo's paraplegia to an abdominal aortography performed by Dr. Gerbode. Salgo sued for malpractice and also claimed that he was not informed of the serious risks of aortography. Judge Bray's decision consisted in large part of a discussion of the trial court's mishandling of the *res ipsa locquitar* instruction. (*Res ipsa locquitar* means literally "the thing speaks for itself"—no testimony is needed as to how negligence occurred if the outcome is in fact the product of negligence.)

The court then turned to the informed consent issue. While criticizing the trial court's broad instruction on the duty to disclose, Judge Bray nonetheless suggested that "a physician violates his duty to his patient and subjects himself to liability if he withholds any facts which are necessary to form the basis of an intelligent consent by the patient to the proposed treatment."[31] This language would suggest that the court planned to embrace again the battery standard rather than negligence. Yet Bray tied the mandate to inform to the physician's sense of duty and self-imposed ethics: "At the same time, the physician must place the welfare of his patient above all else and this very fact places him in a position in which he must choose between two alternative courses of action."[32] As the court outlined, one course of action was to explain every risk that may attend a procedure; the other was to recognize that each patient is different, and "that in discussing the element of risk a certain amount of discretion must be employed consistent with the full disclosure of facts necessary to an informed consent."[33]

Judge Bray had hopelessly intermixed opposing positions. First of all, he stated what sounded like a strict battery standard, one that would respect the negative freedom of the patient. As Katz has noted, "The court appeared to recognize for the first time that physicians might be held liable for failure to disclose important information beyond the ancient requirement of revealing the nature of the operation."[34] However, Bray went on to pay tribute to the "patient comes first" core of medical ethics and appears to have made the bottom line that patients have to trust doctors' discretion. Thus, instead of advocating the patient's self-determination, he ceded authority to the physician, largely because of the physician's duty to place the patient's welfare above all else. In its initial use, as the expression was coined by the *Salgo* court, the term "informed consent" was thus tied to the physician's discretion at the core of medical ethics, rather than to a battery standard that would better protect the patient's liberty. But this case also signaled to many lawyers that courts were willing to hear the patient's claims so long as there was expert testimony available to support the plaintiff's position. The *Salgo* decision, with its willingness to hear rights claims and yet accept the role of medical ethics, revolutionized informed consent law.

The notion of informed consent was further transformed by the decision of the Kansas Supreme Court in *Natanson* v. *Kline*.[35] Justice Schroeder, writing in 1960, considered the plight of Mrs. Natanson, who had received a large amount of cobalt radiation while being treated for breast cancer by Dr. Kline. Among Mrs. Natanson's claims was Dr. Kline's alleged failure to warn her about the treatment. Schroeder's survey of the law led him to conclude that the difference between battery and negligence was that the former is intentional, the latter unintentional. As a result, he concluded that negligence was the proper standard for an informed consent case.[36]

Schroeder described the dilemma he faced. On the one hand he allowed that "there is probably a privilege, on therapeutic grounds, to withhold the specific diagnosis where the disclosure of cancer or some dread disease would seriously jeopardize the recovery of an unstable, temperamental or severely depressed patient."[37] In other words, the doctors must have some discretion to employ their ethical reasoning regarding the good of the patient. On the other hand, he paid tribute to the negative freedom of the citizen in the liberal state:

Anglo-American law starts with the premise of thorough-going self-determination. It follows that each man is considered to be master of his own body and he may, if he be of sound mind, expressly prohibit the performance of lifesaving surgery or other medical treatment. A doctor might well believe that an operation or form of treatment is desirable or necessary, but the law does not permit him to substitute his own judgment for that of the patient by any form of artifice or deception.[38]

Justice Schroeder's solution was to quote extensively from *Salgo*, and to accept the deference to the physician's ethical code that Justice Bray had set forth: "In our opinion the proper rule of law to determine whether a patient has given an intelligent consent to a proposed form of treatment by a physician was stated and applied in *Salgo* v. *Leland Stanford University Board of Trustees*."[39] Yet Justice Schroeder went a step further and stated that the extent of an informed consent was to be determined by expert testimony. The duty to disclose "is limited to those disclosures which a reasonable medical practitioner would make under the same or similar circumstances. How the physician may best discharge his obligation in this difficult situation involves primarily a question of medical judgment."[40] In effect, this meant that physicians were to tell courts of the extent of their "patient comes first" (doctor decides) ethics, and that courts were to accept this as expert testimony. Justice Schroeder thus sanctioned a more complete deference to medical ethics than did Justice Bray, in that he defined revelation of ethics as a matter of expert testimony.

Natanson v. *Kline* rationalized informed consent to a certain extent. Informed consent suits were, according to Schroeder, to be strictly analogous to malpractice suits. The difference between the two types of suits was that malpractice involved expert testimony on what was medically prudent and reasonable, whereas informed consent involved expert testimony on what was ethically prudent and reasonable. The profession was to decide what it would countenance in terms of the amount of information a patient needed to make a decision about a procedure. Thus Justice Schroeder significantly consolidated the power of the physician in the doctor-patient relationship by ruling that the ethical code that legitimated physician authority in the relationship was to be interpreted only by physicians.

It is ironic that two suits, *Salgo* and *Natanson*, that attempted to frame the doctor-patient relationship in terms of an encounter between right-bearing individuals resulted in an exaggeration of the physician's authority within that relationship. Following *Natanson*, doctors alone were to determine the extent of the duties shared by the doctor and patient. In addition, however, these cases enabled courts to hear patients' complaints about lack of informed consent without challenging the profession too directly. Cases tried as battery tended to make judges nervous, in that any battery claim could be countered by the physicians' assertion that lay people (and judges) should not tell doctors how to practice medicine. Use of the battery standard would have forced judges to challenge the contentions that if physicians told the whole truth, patients would act irrationally. Thus *Salgo* and *Natanson* allowed patients' rights claims but subordinated those claims to the powerful defense of medical ethics and doctor's therapeutic privilege. Paternalism was alive and well.

Informed Consent Suits in the Liberal State

According to Katz, *Natanson* v. *Kline* defined the law in almost all jurisdictions for twelve years.[41] There were, however, some decisions that provided new refinements. In *Shetter* v. *Rochelle*, for instance, Judge Molloy more firmly tied the notion of informed consent to a physician's ethical duty: "[Courts] have reasoned from the fact that the relationship between a physician and his patient is one of trust and confidence [to] the conclusion that there is a duty to disclose all facts relative to the treatment prescribed. . . . This seems to this court to be a non sequitur."[42] The patient's informed consent suit, demanding treatment as a free person with personal liberties, was thus turned away with a reminder that informed consent was a matter of the physician's duty. The patient's claim to negative freedom, to do as he wishes with his own body in accordance with the tenets of liberalism, is turned on its head: "The doctor's loyalty to the best interests of the patient must be given consideration in the formulation of a rule of law pertaining to disclosures and . . . a breach of duty on the part of the physician is not made out by merely establishing a nondisclosure of possible failures inherent in a contemplated surgical procedure."[43]

Not all jurisdictions minimized the critical role of patients' rights. In the case of *Mason* v. *Ellsworth*, the court argued that "the basis of the theory of informed consent is both the patient's right to be reasonably informed of all material elements, including risks, which may affect his consent to the procedure, and the physician's duty to inform his patient in a medically sound fashion."[44] The problem was that expert testimony determined the extent of the physician's duty, and this testimony usually sealed the decision. As Katz put it, "Since physicians . . . are generally not committed to patients' participation in the medical decision-making process, recourse to a professional standard of disclosure had to stifle the . . . call for self-determination."[45] But *Mason* was the first major indication that courts might be willing to overturn physicians' therapeutic privilege and to provide greater respect for patient autonomy.

Indeed, *Canterbury* v. *Spence* explicitly reasserted patient rights. The decision by Judge Spottswood Robinson can be seen as a direct challenge to physicians' desire to maintain their positive freedom and professional prerogatives.[46] The case concerned a patient who was not warned of the possibility of paraplegia following back surgery. Judge Robinson began by citing Cardozo's self-determination quotation in *Schloendorff* as his root premise.[47] From this premise, he argued that a patient's cause of action should not be dependent on a professional standard. "Respect for a patient's right of self-determination on particular therapy demands a standard set by law for physicians rather than one which physicians may or may not impose upon themselves."[48] He recognized, moreover, that the ethical standard upon which the physician's duties were based was not inherently medical. Evaluation of behavior in line with an ethical code does not require special knowledge. "The decision to unveil the patient's condition and the chances to use mediation, as we shall see, is oft times a nonmedical judgment and, if so, is a decision outside the ambit of the special standard."[49] Judge Robinson's point was that lay people can decide whether or not the "patient comes first," or whether the doctor treated the patient with due respect. Since all citizens are right-bearers in the liberal state, each should be able to recognize respect for autonomy. It follows that special medical knowledge has nothing to do with ethical duty. This was, of course, a radical departure from the *Salgo-Natanson* line.

There is some reason to believe that Judge Robinson feared his decision went too far. He was concerned that ethics might be confused with medical knowledge and that physicians would be abused by lay decisions. So he hedged his decision: "When medical judgment enters the picture and for that reason the special standard controls, prevailing medical practice must be given its due."[50] Moreover, Judge Robinson refused to draw any sharp lines with regard to situations in which medical expert testimony would be required. "There is no bright line separating significant from insignificant; the answer in any case must abide a rule of reason."[51] Thus, while recognizing that the ethical relationship that exists between doctor and patient can be grasped by the nonexpert, Robinson refused to prohibit medical testimony and, in effect, moved away from the *Natanson* disposition of informed consent suits less radically than he might have.

Nonetheless, Robinson's decision did significantly diminish the physician-centric approach to informed consent. First of all, as noted above, Justice Robinson attempted to differentiate between ethical and medical decisions to disclose, arguing that the former was not a matter over which physicians had the final say. Medical ethics, insofar as it is ethics, could properly be considered by judges and jurors, reflecting on the public morality of the liberal state. Only when esoteric medical facts came to the fore was the decision on disclosure to be solely in the hands of medical experts. Second, Robinson dealt with the question of the extent of disclosure from the point of view of the patient. Rather than relying on a standard based on what a prudent physician would have told a patient, Judge Robinson's standard is based on the reasonable patient, and what that patient is likely to need to know and what significance the patient is likely to attach to certain risks.[52]

Both of these points approach the key problem of informed consent suits: the power of the physician vis-à-vis the patient and the role of professional medical ethics. As we have seen, the ends of traditional medical ethics were to generate patient trust in a physician. An informed consent suit asserts that this trust was breached and that a patient's rights must be respected. Judge Robinson's description was thus quite insightful. By separating ethical and technical expertise, he teased out the role of medical ethics in informed consent suits. His emphasis on the patient's viewpoint in deciding what is to be disclosed served the same purpose: it denied reliance on physicians' ethical expertise and on their habits of disclosure that were steeped in notions of paternalism, which are antithetical to the liberal state.

The medical profession, like all professions, has a monopoly over a critical body of knowledge. Physicians must thus explain some technical issues to patients, especially when they are proposing therapy alternatives. To the extent that these proposals are incomplete, the traditional notion of the "patient comes first" ethic held that physicians would always act in the best interest of the patient. Indeed, many physicians believed that it was better to act on behalf of the patient than to discuss matters with him.

When a patient determines that medical paternalism has led to therapy he would not have chosen, the plaintiff-patient must act as a liberal citizen acts, and assert his rights, which protect his negative freedom. Canterbury, for example, argued that even though Dr. Spence may have believed he was acting ethically by withholding certain critical information from him, the doctor should not have failed to warn him of the risks of a laminectomy. Canterbury himself would have preferred to have made an informed decision about the laminectomy. He felt that Spence should have made an effort to get past the issue of authority in their relationship—an issue based on the inequity of knowledge between doctor and patient. When this did not occur, he believed that his only course was to assert his rights and the negative freedom they guarantee. He, like the plaintiff in any informed consent suit, sought a redefinition of the doctor-patient relationship in terms of an encounter between two rights-bearing citizens, each with a sphere of negative freedom that must be respected. The court agreed.

In lieu of a battery standard, however, it is not possible to completely prohibit the paternalistic aspects of the doctor-patient relationship. This is clear in *Canterbury* v. *Spence*. Despite Judge Robinson's intentions, the medical community retains some control with regard to the extent of informed consent. As noted, the decision allowed that medical expert testimony was still necessary to determine the physician's duty to disclose. In essence, this meant that a doctor may justify his actions by arguing he was duty bound to do the best for the patient, and that he determined that the best for this patient was less than informed consent. Moreover, *Canterbury* held that the physician was still to decide what a reasonable patient needed to know before consenting to a procedure. This allowed a doctor to continue to assume a paternalistic posture that is atypical in the liberal state—and to justify this in terms of a special relationship with the patient. The individual whose negative freedom has been violated is thus given less than total regard throughout a trial based on the *Canterbury* v. *Spence* paradigm, Judge Robinson's dicta notwithstanding.[53] Nevertheless, decisions like Judge Robinson's do restrict physician prerogatives. *Canterbury* v. *Spence* greatly expanded the notion of informed consent and signaled to the medical profession that patient autonomy was to be respected and that physician paternalism was not to be tolerated. Informed consent decisions of this sort point to a new understanding of doctor-patient relationships—they demonstrate an evolution of patients' rights and a reintegration of medical practice into the liberal state.

Since *Canterbury* v. *Spence*, courts have been forced to consider the lay standard and judge its worth compared to the professional standard. The *Canterbury* decision thus pervades legal reasoning on informed consent, even if it is not wholly embraced by every court. Indeed, there is a great deal of inconsistency in rulings about informed consent. Consider, for example, the case of *Haven* v. *Randolph*. This case involved a malpractice suit to which was appended an informed consent claim.[54] The plaintiffs alleged that the risks of an aortogram were not fully explained to the patient's parents. The District of Columbia Federal District Court decision, handed down one day prior to Judge Robinson's *Canterbury* v. *Spence* decision, emphasized the importance of expert medical testimony to determine the limits of disclosure.[55] There was no mention of lay testimony with regard to the duty to disclose. The decision was thus fundamentally at odds with *Canterbury* v. *Spence*. Moreover, the district court decision was approved on appeal by the same federal circuit court of appeals that had ruled on *Canterbury*.[56] In a later decision in the D.C. Circuit Court, Judge Robinson noted, "We think it clear that nothing in *Haven* undercuts *Canterbury* in the least."[57] Thus the courts appeared to be willing to countenance some ambiguity in decisions regarding informed consent.

The sometimes schizophrenic posture of the courts is well demonstrated by the decision of *Cobb* v. *Grant*.[58] Justice Mosk, writing for the California Supreme Court, penned the first half of a classic informed consent decision—negligence based on and dominated by the testimony of medical experts. He noted that "battery theory should be reserved for those circumstances when a doctor performs an operation to which a patient has not consented."[59] He then went on to consider the extent of the physician's duty to disclose. Justice Mosk allowed that "even if there can be said to be a medical community standard as to the disclosure requirement for any prescribed treatment, it appears so nebulous that doctors become, in effect, vested with absolute discretion."[60] Be this as it may, Justice Mosk could not limit the physician's discretion, having accepted a negligence standard. Negligence claims require expert testimony. Justice Mosk could only advocate "full disclosure, tempered by the fact that 'a mini-course in medical science is not required,' "[61] and note that there was no duty to disclose "when it is common knowledge that such risks inherent in the procedure are of very low incidence."[62] Justice Mosk's decision thus further reflects judicial willingness to hear patients' rights claims, and to compromise the positive rights claimed by physicians. It also reflects courts' hesitance to force physicians into a position in which they must reveal every possible hazard of every therapy.

It would be an exaggeration to suggest that physicians' positive rights have been totally removed by recent court decisions on informed consent. Nonetheless, courts have straightforwardly asserted that doctors must inform patients of alternative treatments.[63] In similar development, a federal circuit court has ruled that a hospital must

inform patients of the limits of the care offered by an institution.[64]
The momentum of patients' rights is slowed only by the courts' questions about how to deal with the intricacies of medical technology:

> The matters involved in the disclosure syndrome, more often than not, are
> complicated and highly technical. To leave the establishment of such matters
> to lay witnesses, in our opinion, would pose dangers and disadvantages which
> far outweigh the benefits and advantages a "modern trend" rule would bestow
> upon patient-plaintiffs. In effect, the relaxed modern trend rule permits lay
> witnesses to express, when all is said and done, what amounts to medical
> opinion.[65]

Despite this caveat, the modern trend is that the medical profession's
prerogatives no longer totally determine the parameters of the doctor-
patient relationship. Courts have asserted that patients' autonomy
must be respected.

The final rebuilding of patient autonomy must be left to the profession itself. Up to this point, the interest of many medical ethicists
in an autonomy-based standard has no doubt been secondary to the
influence courts have had. But courts cannot and will not usurp the
professional role of physicians as healers. They are too afraid that they
might get the technical aspects of medical practice wrong and cause
great harm. They have initiated and pushed along the task of reinte-
grating the doctor-patient relationship into the liberal state by insisting
on informed consent. Now physicians must complete the task by supporting a set of ethical principles that reiterate patient rights and that
seek to maintain the autonomy of the patient (principles that I argue
are embodied in the theory of medical ethics as just doctoring). Physicians have slowly come to realize that there is no role for paternalism
in medicine, even when it is employed in the name of the patient's best
interest.

Over the last ten years, informed consent rulings by courts have
become murkier.[66] This is largely attributable to the fact that informed
consent suits were perceived by the profession as a major contributor
to what it felt was a malpractice crisis (an issue to which we will return
in chapter 6). Organized medicine has put pressure on state legislatures to reinstate the professional standard. According to A. Meisel,
most of the resulting statutes have been specifically designed to pro-
scribe action by plaintiffs,[67] and there is evidence that attorneys for
medical societies have actually drafted laws in some states. In any case,

fourteen state legislatures have adopted a professional standard for evaluating disclosure, while only two allow lay evaluation.

At the same time, state courts have continued to endorse the patient perspective as the best legal standard to guide disclosure.[68] Moreover, some courts may now be willing to grant remedies, including money damages, to patients when the only harm suffered is failure to receive full disclosure.[69] In essence, this is equivalent to compensating for infringement on negative freedom. Perhaps most important, there is evidence that physicians are remarkably less likely to mislead or misinform patients now than they were twenty years ago.[70] Informed consent is now the rule, rather than the exception, and is a central tenet of medical ethics as just doctoring (the one exception perhaps being resuscitation status,[71] a matter we return to in chapter 8).

In summary, the judiciary's insistence that informed consent suits be considered as part of the doctrine of negligence is best seen as a tacit understanding of the role of medical ethics. Yielding to medical expertise meant not only technical expertise, but also ethical expertise. When courts asked doctors to testify as to the extent of a plaintiff's informed consent, they were asking those doctors to comment on the defendant's fulfillment of his duty. Thus physicians were deemed to be experts on the depth of a mutual trust relationship, and suits were possible only when other physicians were willing to say that medical ethics had been violated.

The patient, of course, wanted his negative freedom preserved. Perhaps the most direct way to have accomplished this goal would have been to return to the battery standard. This standard, as applied in *Pratt* v. *Davis* and *Schloendorff* v. *New York Hospital*, effectively protected the patient's right to self-determination. As I have argued, the battery standard is uncompromising in its protection of the individual from unconsented touching. It also prohibits the use of professional testimony, the vehicle through which the patient's purest demands for negative freedom have been so effectively blunted. Thus, with a forceful simplicity, the battery standard enforces the patient's claim to autonomy, in keeping with the tenets of the liberal state.

Courts were, however, generally loath to embrace the battery standard, especially since physicians so often thought they were acting ethically in keeping frightening information from patients. The battery standard even strikes some rights advocates as inappropriate for determinations of doctor-patient relations. The reasons for this were

summarized in the case of *Trogun* v. *Fruchtman*.[72] Justice Wilkie noted
first that informed consent suits do not "fit comfortably within the
traditional concepts of battery or the intent to unlawfully touch the
person of another."[73] Second he noted that "the failure to inform is
probably not an intentional act. . . . Third, the act complained of is
not within the traditional idea of contract or touching."[74] Each of
these propositions underscores the fact that the doctor-patient relationship is rarely considered a setting for a battery. Nondisclosure—
intentional or not—does not deserve this charge.

The compromise approach, as championed by Judge Robinson in
the *Canterbury* case, used the negligence standard but tied it to the
opinion of the layperson. This approach required integrated consideration of the patient's wishes and blunted physician paternalism. It
acted, in effect, as a method for introducing liberal assumptions into
the patient-physician relationship. Rights advocates like Judge Robinson have forcefully insisted that doctors are not the sole judges in
that relationship. Patients' rights must be considered and their judgment respected by truly informed consent.

Decisions like *Canterbury*, handed down by a prestigious court like
the District of Columbia Circuit Court of Appeals, cannot help but
promote informed consent suits in other courts. The law, as a reflection of the public morality of the state, thus has sought to reintegrate
the doctor-patient relationship into the liberal state. Patients who sue
for informed consent downplay the role of medical ethics in generating
patient-doctor trust. Courts that rule in favor of plaintiffs acknowledge
that professional ethics cannot replace public morality. When patients
perceive that the political and economic setting of medical practice is
at odds with a "patient comes first" attitude, they will be less inclined
to give up autonomy in deference to the physician's self-assumed moral
code.

This reintegration process has prompted the revisions in medical
ethics outlined in previous chapters. Medical ethicists, and indeed
many physicians, insist that paternalism cannot be acceptable to any
theory of medical ethics, and that patient autonomy must be paramount. These values are enshrined in the principles of ethics of the
American Medical Association and American College of Physicians.
The patient as rights-bearer is a central concept in most recent theories
of ethics. Indeed, physicians today are much more likely to try to gain
truly informed consent from patients, discussing the risks of treatment
and the course of disease. Medical ethics, prompted by the liberal state,

now encourages informed consent; certainly medical ethics as just doctoring does.

This is not, however, the final word on the subject. Much of the
discussion of informed consent, and especially the case law, emphasizes
the importance of informing the patient of the risks of a procedure.
But cases of informed consent usually are tried not only on risks but
on benefits.

I would argue that if we accept an ethical code that centers on
maintaining patient autonomy and repudiating the restriction of ethical thinking to the personal encounter between doctors and patients,
then we cannot restrict ourselves to a discussion of the risks of a
procedure to the patient. In a theory of medical ethics as just doctoring, we must also try to share with patients the likelihood of the
benefits of the procedure. In medical terminology, a test or procedure
that holds the "promise of great benefit" for the patient is an appropriate test. Thus informed consent must include a focus on appropriateness.

Appropriateness Research as a Form of Informed Consent

Typically, informed consent has centered on the physi-
cian's description of the possible detrimental side effects of a therapy,
and of the possible alternatives to that therapy. Far less attention has
been paid to those cases in which the patient has undergone therapy
that has not been rigorously proven to be beneficial. Such cases, which
must be brought under an implied warranty rubric, or negligence, are
notoriously difficult. When good data are lacking that suggest that a
treatment is efficacious, each party to the litigation will be able to
present experts who will testify to the benefits, or drawbacks, of the
procedure. Thus a plaintiff can rarely win this kind of suit.

But plaintiffs' failure to win such suits does not mean that all forms
of therapy are efficacious. In fact, there is good reason to believe that
many procedures are done unnecessarily. Most of our insight into this
problem is provided by research into variations in rates of procedures
between geographic areas. The pioneer of this research is John E.
Wennberg, and a review of some of his writings is informative.

Wennberg has been studying the variation in rates of procedures between geographic regions for the past fifteen years. Examining various regions that are well matched demographically, Wennberg has demonstrated that procedure rates for simple surgical techniques can vary by a factor of four to five.[75] Operations with very high rates of variation include knee operations, transurethral prostate resections, tonsillectomies, hysterectomies, and dilation and curettage (DNC) operations. Wennberg and colleagues have produced data demonstrating that these variations are a universal phenomenon. The procedures with highest variation all appear to share one characteristic: they deal primarily with common problems of aging.

Wennberg has hypothesized that there are many reasons for practice variations. These include specialty training, clinical experience, and personal characteristics of the patient and physician. Variation is especially prevalent when there is little consensus about the best way to handle a problem. Presumably, one rate for a procedure is optimal in a given population. When some region has a very low rate, this suggests the procedure is not being done often enough. When the rate of the procedure is much higher than expected, it suggests inappropriate procedures are being done.

Wennberg and B. A. Barnes have argued that supplier induced demand may be playing a large role in creating inordinately high rates of procedures.[76] As our analysis has made clear, physicians have traditionally controlled both supply and demand of medical care. This creates the temptation to provide more services than are strictly necessary. The patient is not a rational consumer, given his deficit of information. Given as well a lack of consensus among physicians about the appropriateness of many procedures, the pressure of economic reimbursement for doing the procedure will push rates up. Thus the decision-making process between doctor and patient is isolated from the values of the liberal market, which will presumably increase rates of unnecessary procedures.

How does one go about defining which procedures are necessary? Wennberg and his collaborators have begun to address this problem. They have recently published a comprehensive review of their attempt to define appropriateness for one procedure, the resection of prostates.[77] Many elderly men develop benign enlargement of the prostate gland. This hypertrophy can become great enough that urinating becomes difficult. As these symptoms develop, patients are often referred to urologists, who often recommend resection of the prostate. The preferred method of resection is the transurethral procedure (TURP) as opposed to an open procedure. Unfortunately, the procedure is often accompanied by bleeding, and it sometimes fails to relieve symptoms. The optimal timing of the operation as the disease advances is also difficult to discern. Procedure rates vary greatly for the TURP from region to region.

Wennberg and collaborators have attacked this problem with a fourfold research approach. First they reviewed and carefully evaluated all published reports on the natural history and treatment of prostatic hypertrophy. Second, they obtained large data bases of claims information from insurers. Since many patients have some form of insurance, and since their treatment leads to claims for payment, this is an excellent way to obtain information on the number and types of procedures. These data also provided information on complications, and on the efficacy of various forms of alternative treatment. Next, Wennberg's team interviewed patients and physicians to assess patients' symptoms as well as functional status. The interviews also provided data on complication rates. Finally, the researchers entered much of this information into a set of algorithms called decision analysis. Using data on outcomes and alternatives, the decision analysis allows the researchers to test a series of hypotheses.

Some of their conclusions were quite surprising. First, they found that the frequency of complications following prostatectomy was higher than that reported in the literature. The patient interviews proved to be most helpful in this assessment. They also found that surgery actually decreases the average life expectancy of those operated on, although it improves their quality of life somewhat.

The researchers concluded that in the case of prostatectomy, and presumably in a number of other high variability procedures, patient choice was the critical factor in determining the efficacy of the treatment. Some patients may wish to trade a few days of life, overall, for higher quality days while alive. Others may choose to avoid procedures that pose any risk, however small. Only full information for the patient will allow an optimal outcome in such procedures. Wennberg and his colleagues propose an interactive, computer-driven, video presentation to help patients choose between prostatectomy and watchful waiting. The video device presents information on the probabilities of outcomes associated with watchful waiting and operation. Videotaped interviews made of actual patients who have opted for or against the operation help the patient understand the significance of the various outcomes.[78]

This seems to be a straightforward approach to the problems of informed consent when the advantages of a procedure are not clear. In essence, the video helps inform the patient about his options. It helps create a relationship between doctor and patient that is more akin to one between individuals in the liberal state than the one that was the model for traditional medical ethics. Allowing the patient to make an informed decision is a matter of maintaining his autonomy. Thus this innovation is one that ethical physicians should support.

The importance of Wennberg's research agenda for medical ethics does not, however, stop here. Wennberg has proposed that in order to develop rational patient choice in a significant manner, it will be necessary to monitor and distribute information on procedure rates to hospital markets.[79] Using insurer records and information from hospitals, Wennberg would feed back to providers information on: (1) the status of health resources allocation to specific communities; (2) the utilization of surgical services and diagnostic procedures, as well as causes for admissions; and (3) reports on outcomes from insurance data and interviews.

To whom would this information be transmitted? Wennberg asserts that medical societies, specialty societies, and hospital staffs should be the target. He believes that educating providers can bring about changes in the indications for procedures and will also lead to the best possible education of patients.

Again, Wennberg's proposals have an ethical dimension, at least in my vision of medical ethics as just doctoring. Patients should be accorded the full respect due rights-bearers in the liberal state. To maintain their negative freedom, it is necessary that they be informed. They can only be informed about the appropriateness of procedures insofar as physicians undertake the kind of programs Wennberg has outlined. Thus there is an ethical imperative for physicians to participate in programs that help define appropriate procedures and allow the most informed decisions by patients. Medical societies, hospital staffs, and individual physicians must take the lead in developing and responding to research initiatives on appropriateness.

This will strike those schooled in traditional medical ethics as odd. Medical ethics has historically focused on the relation between a doctor and her patient. What I propose is an ethics that involves research and concerted action by many physicians. These efforts will not affect or involve the individual patient I am now treating. Physicians must act on their concern for, not only the individual patient, but the class of patients. This does not demean or belittle the commitment to the individual patient; it does add new ethical importance to the larger issues of health care. It is precisely what must occur once we conceive of medical ethics as part of the liberal state.

So what am I asking of physicians? Let me return to the case of Mr. Z. Suppose that instead of an obvious bleeding ulcer, he had had only peptic symptoms. Given these symptoms, Dr. A. might have referred him to a gastroenterologist, who in turn might have argued that such a young patient should undergo endoscopy to discern the cause of his symptoms. Some would have suggested that this endoscopy was inappropriate.[80] Others might have thought it was indicated.[81] As an ethical physician, what should Dr. A. do?

In this situation, Dr. A. should give Mr. Z. the best rendition of the facts she can muster, as well as her recommendation. With this information, he can decide. In addition, however, she and the other physicians in our hospital or community should take an active interest in the issue of appropriateness. In this sense, we have an ethical duty to determine whether procedures are being done appropriately and to regulate our practice if they are not. This will require careful record keeping and also significant amounts of time reviewing data and developing criteria. All physicians should participate in the gathering of data and the feedback process, as well as in the development of educational devices so that patients like Mr. Z. can make informed decisions. While this may sound bureaucratic and unexciting, it is as integral a part of medical ethics as just doctoring.

I have argued that the shape of medical ethics in the liberal state should be different from traditional medical ethics. Most important, I have argued that the maintenance of, and respect for, patient autonomy should be paramount. Others have agreed. I have also argued that medical ethics as just doctoring should have a public role and that physicians should reform medical institutions to fit with the sense of altruism that informs the attitude that the "patient comes first."

The law of informed consent has allowed us to specify the nature of the model I have suggested. First, the evolution of the law demonstrates the manner in which the state has sought to reintegrate medicine and require respect for the public morality of liberalism. The law has stated that patients are to be fully informed. The profession has

responded and informed consent is now enshrined in principles of
ethics as well as in the mind-set of physicians. Second, evolution of
informed consent indicates new ethical requirements for physicians.
We must now begin to struggle to define the appropriateness of procedures and to develop new and better ways to inform patients about
the utility of our therapies. Thus medical ethics as just doctoring sets
forth a public role for physicians in the liberal state. To formulate a
medical enterprise that respects patient autonomy, but also incorporates altruistic behavior by physicians and a concern for the social
implications of our action, we must consider, as a profession, new
policy initiatives. The development of information for patients on the
appropriateness of our procedures is one such initiative.

6

Physicians and Quality of Medical Care

As we noted in chapter 3, any profession must have as a high priority the provision of the best possible service. Since clients can rarely judge the quality of professional service, professions must police themselves. Indeed, such self-regulation is the hallmark of professions. The highest quality service is a universal professional ethical imperative.

The medical profession meets these standards, or at least seems to do so in the abstract. It places a high premium on excellent and conscientious care. Physicians are recruited from the brightest college students and then rigorously trained in biomedical and clinical sciences. Arduous postgraduate training with rigid supervision by attending physicians reinforces the importance of quality medical care. Physician error is carefully reproached by other members of the profession.

The professional orientation toward quality medical care fits neatly with the traditional ethics of medicine. Since the patient's well-being is the primary objective of the ethical physician, provision of good quality care is a salient concern of the profession.

This rendition of the relationship of traditional medical ethics to quality medical care is an ideal. It also reflects the same attributes of the profession we have noted in previous chapters. Ethics provides a guarantee, this time of good quality care. Yet the patient and the public are unable to evaluate the extent of the physician's fulfillment of her professional duty. The public is in effect again asked to trust the profession, because the profession is duty bound to provide excellent care. There is no regulation other than decentralized oversight by physicians themselves.

As medicine is drawn into the liberal state, will this societal attitude toward good quality care persist? The answer is no. Indeed, the law concerning patients' reactions to the quality of medical care, medical malpractice law, reveals that over the last thirty years, patients have become less and less willing to accept doctors' offers of trust.[1] Injured patients have increasingly sought relief from the courts for care that has been substandard. Under the theory of tort law, this creates incentives for physicians to provide better-quality care. That judges have been increasingly willing to hear liberal theories of negligence indicates that in medical malpractice, as in informed consent, courts are striving to reintegrate medicine into the liberal state by enforcing the law as integrity rather than accepting physicians' self-regulation. Thus a professional perception of a crisis in malpractice litigation can be interpreted, at least in part, as physician resistance to the changes demanded by society.

Medical ethics as just doctoring must consider the role of medical malpractice law in quality assurance. Rather than merely resisting changes in malpractice law, physicians must recognize increased litigation as a given. The liberal state requires evidence of good quality care. Therefore ethical physicians must think about new methods for providing high quality care as an answer to rising rates of malpractice litigation. More important, this quality assessment must be made public, in keeping with the assumptions of the liberal state. In this chapter I explore physicians' reactions to malpractice and the notion of quality assurance as a priority for medical ethics today. Of note, in this chapter, as in the last, we move from discussions about a theoretical liberal state, into analysis of our particular American liberal state.

The (Short) History of Quality Assurance

While the professional commitment to good quality care is as old as physicians' codes, the history of organized efforts at quality assurance is quite short. Ernest Codman is now celebrated as the pioneer of quality assurance. As early as 1914, this Boston surgeon proposed evaluating the end results of therapy to improve the quality of care.[2] His views were not, however, acceptable to the majority of surgeons at the Massachusetts General Hospital, and he had to leave that institution to start his own hospital. His work was somewhat ignored, as was that of other pioneers such as R. I. Lee and L. W. Jones.[3] When A. Donabedian and others began to undertake a systematic assessment of the quality of care in the mid-1960s, they moved in largely uncharted waters.[4] Indeed, the last twenty years have seen several false starts in the quality assurance movement.[5]

A good deal of the blame for the stunted growth of serious and systematic quality assurance must lie with the medical profession. Charles Rosenberg and others have carefully documented the manner in which the medical profession gained authority over the administration of hospitals in the early twentieth century.[6] Until that time, hospitals had been controlled, at least to a certain extent, by their lay boards. However, by the 1920s, the overwhelming majority of hospitals in this country were not-for-profit institutions with dual forms of governance. A board of trustees and a hospital administration oversaw the business aspects of the hospital. The medical staff had its own separate governance and controlled the manner in which care was provided.[7]

This dual form of government was countenanced and indeed required by those who regulated health care. Most hospitals were licensed by state agencies, often the state department of health. However, few actually tried to provide oversight or to evaluate the performance of hospitals. Instead they relied on the Joint Commission for the Accreditation of Hospitals (JCAH) to perform this service. The JCAH had been born out of a power struggle between physician organizations. In 1912, the newly founded American College of Surgeons had undertaken to standardize surgical practice. It established the Hospital Standardization Program (HSP), which stressed self-regulation by the medical staff. Timothy Jost relates that between 1918 and 1935 the percentage of hospitals with an organized medical staff increased from 25 percent to 90 percent.[8] By 1950, the complexity of health care had overcome the resources the American College of Surgeons could make available to the HSP. After a great deal of fighting among various professional groups, the American Hospital Association, the American Medical Association, the American College of Surgeons, and the American College of Physicians all coordinated their efforts and the JCAH was organized.

The JCAH adopted the HSP regulations that were in place in most modern teaching institutions in the late 1930s. The JCAH focus, however, was slightly different in its emphasis, for instance on the importance of good medical record keeping. It also stressed that physicians were to control the membership of the hospital staff, and that physicians' were the final authority on decisions regarding quality. The major forums of quality assurance were the clinical conferences, in which physicians gathered together to review pathological findings and assess errors in diagnosis and treatment, and the tissue committee meetings, in which the results of surgical procedures were reviewed by senior surgeons.[9]

These formal evaluations at weekly conferences remained the cornerstone of physician-based quality assurance. Such methods relied overtly on the commitment of physicians to better quality care. Complications and errors were to be discussed openly, but only for the benefit of the medical staff. There was no requirement to make any of the reports at "morbidity and mortality" rounds public, or even to share them with the hospital.

Physicians who erred frequently could be sanctioned, but again this was completed solely by the medical staff itself. The sanctions took the form of restrictions on admitting privileges, or, in the worst cases, expulsion from the hospital staff.[10] Again, the hospital and the state authorities were rarely involved in such cases. Indeed, other hospitals were usually not warned about physicians who had performed poorly enough to be shown the door. Perhaps this was only fair, as many of the expulsions from staff no doubt had less to do with incompetence than they did with perceptions of economic competition.

In any case, these methods of quality assurance were enshrined by the early 1940s, and two generations of physicians matured believing that these were the only real means to achieve high quality care. The JCAH approach was anointed by the federal government when it made JCAH accreditation the major grounds for certifying hospitals as participants in the Medicare program.[11]

The system of informal sanctions and treatment of physician error is well captured in Charles Bosk's *Forgive and Remember*.[12] Bosk documents the manner in which senior attending surgeons at a teaching hospital discussed and evaluated errors made by their house staff. He reveals that the sanctions were informal, and that after a lesson was learned, the error was forgiven by the other physicians. The trainees were encouraged to do everything possible for the patient, and this kind of effort made error forgivable. Perhaps most important, the surgeons were trained to refer those cases beyond their own individual level of skill to more senior physicians. Physicians' ethical codes regarding quality of care was to "put the patient first" and to recognize one's own limits.

From Bosk's point of view, this informal system is rational and defensible. His study, however, centered on top surgeons at an academic medical center. One can imagine that not all medical institutions are populated by such conscientious individuals. In hospitals where the skill level is not so high, and the "patient comes first" ethic not quite so established, one can imagine that quality might be ignored completely, for the system puts all the prerogatives in the physicians' hands.

Indeed, this system of informal sanctioning by physicians is another example of their power. Physicians had demanded and hospitals conceded total control over quality assurance. Rather than adopt the statistical methods of Codman, featuring hard endpoints and publicly available information, physicians chose a more private approach. Again, patients were asked to trust physicians, for physicians' paternalism would assure that their colleagues who made mistakes would be sanctioned. The negative freedom of the patient was sharply circumscribed. The patient could not become a rational consumer of medical care because evaluations of physicians by their peers were hidden from view. Thus medical ethics was again to play a critical conceptual role as justification for the lack of social oversight; physicians would provide good quality care because they were devoted to the patient.

The ethics of commitment to good quality care is in many ways rational, for it often brings about better care. Its peculiarity becomes clear only when one considers its lack of openness. An episode from my own training illustrates my point. A patient I had followed in my clinic for several years, and who was very healthy except for a history of diabetes mellitus, was brought to the emergency room in a semi-comatose state. His diabetes appeared to be under control, but many of his blood chemicals were abnormal. He began to suffer from shock while in the emergency room. The physicians on duty called me, and together we puzzled about the cause of the shock. We could not define the etiology, and although we employed all possible supports, the patient died.

As he neared death, a laboratory test, sent off inadvertently, demonstrated that he had taken an aspirin overdose. Indeed, upon receipt of this information, it became clear that the patient's state was well explained by the aspirin overdose. While he had no history either of aspirin use or of suicidal intention, we all felt we should have made the diagnosis more promptly. We felt this even though a very fast diagnosis probably would not have made any difference, as the patient's state was well advanced by the time he was brought to the emergency room.

The case was reviewed at our weekly morbidity and mortality conference in which we went over the deaths for the previous week. Several of the senior physicians asserted the diagnosis should have been made more quickly and pointed out the salient features of aspirin poisoning. The entire staff could learn from the case. Although no one stated this, all of us involved felt we had made an error in judgment. We wished we had made the diagnosis more quickly. Indeed, those of us involved in the case, and many of our colleagues, learned a great deal about salicylate poisoning, and I doubt I will fail to consider it with similar patients in the future. Therefore, my personal experience, as well as that of other physicians, is that this kind of informal quality control can work.

But does this approach always perform well? Do informal sanctions prevent most substandard care in hospitals? There are few good answers to these questions. The most widely quoted estimates of the incidence of adverse events (defined as injuries suffered by patients as a result of medical management rather than of the process of their disease) and negligent care (defined as care that fails to meet the community standard) were developed over twelve years ago in a California study of 20,000 nonrandomly selected medical records.[13] This study revealed that 4.65 percent of hospitalizations resulted in adverse events. Nearly 10 percent of these adverse events resulted in deaths. Negligent care resulted from .79 percent of hospitalizations. These figures would suggest there is a great deal of room for improvement in our approach to quality assurance. Many of these adverse events, and presumably all those arising out of negligence, could theoretically have been prevented. Other reviews of medical records by physicians to identify poor quality care or adverse events have been restricted to nonrandom samples of a few hundred records, but they also suggest there is a great deal of preventable error.[14]

Above and beyond these statistics, and what they suggest about the efficacy of informal reviews, the current approach to quality assurance seems unsatisfactory because of its private nature. Consider again my patient who died of salicylate poisoning. He was one of the most solitary figures I have ever met. He was not born in this country, and he had no family here. None of his neighbors knew him. As near as I could tell, he had no estate. Nonetheless, his case has often caused me to think about the work I do. What if he had been brought to the emergency room sooner, and could have been saved? What if our failure to make the diagnosis had clearly led to his death? And what if he had left a family? Would it have then been appropriate to say nothing to the family, to leave our error in the silent world of doctor and patient? Would not the public expect some discussion of the matter? Does it not serve doctors' interest to keep quiet about these issues? If we are really committed to the patient, should that involve informing the patient when errors are made? Suppose I had not been in training. Would there have been the same kind of attention to the care I and others provided? Or would it have simply been possible for us to forgive each other and forget the episode? Do all hospitals pay as careful attention to these issues as the one in which I trained? Would not more formal mechanisms be appropriate to assure that hospitals and medical staffs are conscientious? Do physicians have some ethical duty to see that this is the case?

Patients might think so. Indeed, just as patients have grown dissatisfied with the traditional handling of information in the doctor-patient relationship, there is good evidence that they have grown skeptical of the profession's reassurances in regard to quality medical care. As with informed consent, the patients have petitioned the courts, this time for supervision of care in the form of medical malpractice litigation.

Tort Law and Quality Assurance

Although the concepts seem foreign to many physicians even today, medical malpractice law has two roles. The first is compensation of victims of accidents. Not all accidents, however, lead to compensation under a tort regime; in fact, only those accidents that were caused by the negligent behavior of another are compensable. Our common law approach ties compensation to negligent behavior. The primary reason for this linkage is the second major function of tort litigation, that of deterrence. The theory of tort law is that the person causing the tort, or the tortfeasor, is deterred from acting in a negligent manner in the future by the economic penalty of the tort award to the successful plaintiff.

Although many of these concepts regarding torts were discussed by Oliver Wendell Holmes over a century ago, they have undergone a reevaluation in the last twenty years.[15] Guido Calabresi's pioneering work on the theory of tort law has spawned a number of economic analyses of tort law, all centering on the value of deterrent and compensation effects.[16] This renewed academic interest in tort law is no doubt related to increases in the amount of tort litigation in the 1960s and 1970s.

Trends in jury awards for malpractice claims and product liability suits indicate that there has been a substantial increase in successful tort litigation in this country in the last thirty years.[17] George Priest has argued fairly persuasively that, at least with regard to product liability, much of the increase in tort litigation can be traced to the ascendance of the theory of enterprise liability, which provides in its simplest form that businesses should be responsible for the injuries caused by their products.[18] Priest suggests that enterprise liability was championed by legal academics who then influenced several powerful courts in the mid-1950s, resulting in a series of landmark legal decisions.[19]

In Priest's view, one of the most influential of the legal academics, along with Fleming James, was Friedrich Kessler,[20] who maintained that the large capitalist enterprises had grown too powerful to be controlled by contract law. Contracts between individuals, the ideal of the nineteenth century liberal state, were no longer possible in the twentieth century. Therefore tort law had to be bolstered by changes in doctrine such that individual plaintiffs could more readily seek redress against concerns like automobile manufacturers or soft drink bottlers. Concepts such as risk spreading and enterprise liability were proposed to restore some balance between litigants and to provide appropriate deterrence signals to industry. Priest argues further that the efforts of academics like Kessler and James were largely successful, and that much of the increase in tort litigation can be traced to the reforms of the common law undertaken at their urging.

This theory of the expansion of tort law bears a great deal of resemblance to our theory about the law as a means to fortify the values of liberalism in relation to those of traditional medical ethics. Just as

I have argued that patients turned to the law when faced with the authoritative claims of physicians, so too can changes in tort law be seen as an attempt by judges, guided by legal academics, to equalize power between plaintiffs and large corporations. Devices such as enterprise liability make defendants fully accountable for injuries sustained by plaintiffs; they reiterate the importance of the individual's negative freedom. Arguments such as those put forth by Kessler are fundamentally liberal.

The increase in tort litigation was not confined to product liability. Medical malpractice became another growth area for personal injury lawyers. The reasons for this are similar to those underlying product liability—judges made it easier for plaintiffs to sue successfully. This resulted, I believe, from the court's perception that the medical profession had grown too powerful, and that the law as integrity in the liberal state demanded change.

There have been a number of explanations for the changes in malpractice litigation that have led to increases in premiums.[21] The overall increase must, however, be laid at the bench of the judges who made it easier to win suits. In the early 1950s plaintiffs faced intolerable barriers to winning a suit against physicians because physicians assumed a code of silence and refused to testify against one another. A plaintiff, who had been unconscious, found it was impossible to develop evidence of operating room mismanagement. Locality rules required that experts testifying against local physicians must be familiar with local standards. This made it all the more difficult to identify appropriate experts. Moreover, courts slavishly applied the rule of medical custom whereby doctors alone were qualified to determine whether care was negligently performed. Courts also refused to find both doctors and hospitals liable simultaneously, nor would they hold a hospital accountable for physicians practicing there.

In essence, the barriers to tort suits kept doctors insulated from outside regulation. Since doctors largely controlled the quality assurance efforts at the hospital, and since there was little state oversight, tort litigation was the only way that patients could demand good quality care. The difficulty of tort litigation and the physicians' control over hospitals consolidated the positive freedom of physicians and removed yet another aspect of medicine from the values of liberalism.

This began to change in the mid-1940s with the California Supreme Court's ruling in *Ybarra* v. *Spangard*.[22] Mr. Ybarra was admitted to a hospital for an appendectomy during an acute attack of appendicitis. After awakening from the anesthesia, he noticed for the first time pain and decreased neurological function in his right arm and shoulder. Any physician would have recognized his symptoms as a brachial plexus injury resulting from poor positioning of the arm during anesthesia. The defendants asserted that there was no evidence of any act of a particular defendant that had caused this problem. None of the defendants would testify as to what happened in the operating room.

To break this deadlock, the plaintiff asserted the doctrine of *res ipsa loquitur*. This ancient doctrine had long stood for a common sense inference from plain facts. The California Supreme Court was willing to adjust this meaning, converting it into a burden-shifting device. Henceforth, the court reasoned, that when a healthy portion of the body was injured during medical care, "such circumstances raise the inference of negligence and call upon the defendant to explain the unusual condition."[23]

The defendants argued vociferously that res ipsa should not be used in medical cases because the doctrine tends to implicate all involved in the care of the patient, without showing that any one in particular was negligent. The court was unyielding. The decision notes that if the court accepted defendants' contentions, there would never be any compensation in medical cases, as patients rarely have access to the evidence of negligence. Thus the *Ybarra* decision was a milestone in malpractice litigation, representing radical use of an old doctrine to empower patients.[24] The code of silence among health professionals was effectively broken and courts proved increasingly willing to allow lay judgments of the quality of care.

The doctrine gained even wider use when the California court decided nearly two decades later that res ipsa loquitur could apply even to cases concerning complex medical issues if an expert testified that a poor outcome would not have happened in the absence of negligence on the part of the physician. In the decision of *Quintal* v. *Laurel Grove Hospital*, the California court ruled that an instruction on conditional use of res ipsa loquitur was appropriate when cardiac arrest occurred during administration of anesthetic agents, even though arrest is a known, but rare complication of such agents.[25] In this case, the expert for the plaintiff testified that arrest rarely occurs in the absence of negligence. The use of res ipsa in such situations further shifted the burden onto defendants to prove they were not negligent.[26] Courts were thus using the doctrine of res ipsa to overcome the patient's lack of medical knowledge and to address "adverse events" that might only tangentially be related to poor quality care. The burden was placed on physicians to prove the high quality of their care.

Courts have not, however, taken the further step of eliminating their reliance on medical custom. Unlike the *Canterbury* decision in the area of informed consent, a layperson standard has not gained ascendance in medical malpractice.[27] At least one court, the Washington Supreme Court has approached this threshold. In its decision of *Helling* v. *Carey*, the court ruled that even though expert testimony revealed that the standard of practice in Washington was not to test patients under forty for glaucoma, a patient who was less than forty who became blind from glaucoma that went undiagnosed for several months, could recover damages.[28] In effect, the court substituted its own lay judgment that the simple test to detect glaucoma should have been employed in this case.

Strong pressure from physician groups caused the Washington legislature to overturn this decision, and no other courts have attempted to abolish medical custom, even though the expert testimony in *Helling* had come under attack.[29] Nonetheless, other changes in doctrine have undercut the rule of medical custom in ways similar to that of the changes in res ipsa loquitur.

For example, courts have largely abandoned the locality rule. As noted above, the locality rule required that experts testify regarding the standard of care in the particular geographic area wherein the injury arose. In cases such as *Brune* v. *Belinkoff*, courts overturned this rule, easing the burden on plaintiffs trying to find experts to testify on their behalf.[30] *Brune* v. *Belinkoff* involved an injury to a patient's nervous system after he received too much anesthetic agent into his spine. The defense claimed the standard of care was different in New Bedford, Massachusetts, than it was in Boston fifty miles away. The Massachusetts Supreme Court protested that there was little sense in "Balkanizing" the medical profession; moreover, the court implied that the burden on plaintiffs in finding an expert within a small geographic area to testify against his peers was too great. Therefore, they overturned the locality rule and allowed plaintiffs to hire experts from other communities. This change in doctrine allowed plaintiffs to overcome a conspiracy of silence by physicians within one community. Again the courts created conditions that led to greater scrutiny of the care provided by physicians.[31]

Yet another blow was dealt to physicians' prerogatives when courts began to apply the notion of corporate liability for care rendered in hospitals. Corporate liability was a relatively old notion in tort law that held that an entire enterprise could be held liable for the negligence of one employee if the corporation was responsible for supervising that employee. It had not been used widely in medical malpractice because most physicians were not employed by hospitals. In 1965, the Illinois Supreme Court ruled that the doctrine of corporate liability could be applied to hospitals, holding them liable for physicians practicing there.[32] This ruling and others like it created incentives for hospitals to supervise their physician staffs more closely, and to consider more thoroughgoing quality assurance than simple reliance on physicians' ethical commitment to patients.[33] While physicians continued to rely on informal review processes and an ethical code that "put the patient first" to regulate the quality of care, changes in doctrine wrought by courts in the two decades between 1944 and 1966 removed quality assurance from the sole control of the physicians.

I believe this greater scrutiny, which can be interpreted as modernity dawning on the medical profession, is perfectly consistent with the theme of reintegration of medicine into the liberal state. As policymakers have become more concerned about injuries arising out of medical care, so has demand for greater accountability increased. Changes in the res ipsa loquitur doctrine and the locality rule have made it far easier for plaintiffs to find experts to review the quality of care rendered and thus to win suits. Changes in corporate liability of hospitals have impelled hospital administrations to provide oversight. These changes in doctrine have stimulated a general social interest in malpractice litigation, creating greater incentives for better quality assurance. In essence, the liberal state has asserted through the courts that physicians will be subject to the oversight of liberal tort law.

Changes in tort doctrine by courts have contributed to an overall increase in the amount and severity of malpractice litigation. This increase in litigation presumably increases the deterrent effect of the law and thus increases the quality of care. Whether or not that can be empirically demonstrated, it seems clear that the motives underlying changes in malpractice doctrine were quite similar to those underlying changes in the doctrine of informed consent.[34] Courts had become convinced that physicians' power was too unrestricted, that the negative freedom of the patients needed better protection. Thus doctrinal changes reintegrate medicine with the public morality of our state.

It is interesting to note that other liberal states have seen the same kind of trends in growth of malpractice claims. Both Britain and Canada have experienced similar increases.[35] These increases have occurred without the same doctrinal reforms as in the United States, but likely, I would speculate, with the same judicial perception that physician prerogatives demand close judicial oversight.

The Profession's Reaction

There are a number of ways in which the medical profession could have reacted to this crisis of tort litigation. It might have engaged in productive self-examination and asked if the informal mechanisms of quality assurance on which it relied were really effective. Alternatively, it could have avoided the quality question and simply tried to decrease the amount of litigation through political means.[36] Indeed, it is arguable that the profession selected the latter strategy.

There are several elements to this "frivolous litigation" strategy, which I will argue has been largely unsuccessful. First, it reflects implicit trust that traditional ethics will ensure that quality care will be rendered by physicians and that the current mechanisms for quality assurance are appropriate. As noted above, throughout the period of increasing litigation since the mid-1970s, there was little evidence that physicians became more interested in quality assurance. Little innovation had taken place in that direction and what was undertaken emanated more frequently from schools of public health than from medical schools.[37] This absence of activity on the part of the medical profession suggests that it believed that quality was being well assured by the commitment of individual physicians to quality (the patient comes first) and by existing informal review mechanisms such as tissue committees and clinicopathological conferences.

Second, the professions' frivolous litigation strategy implies that most suits are without merit, and that rather than being based on errors in medical management and poor quality care, they are prompted by misguided patients and influenced by greedy lawyers. These contentions have been cited time and again by representatives of the organized profession. For example, in an editorial in the *Journal of the American Medical Association*, the general counsel of the American

Medical Association noted that "many patients who file claims have suffered no injury as result of negligence. Even for those patients who do file claims as a result of negligence, there are wide, irrational variations in both findings of liability and the amount of damages."[38] In their report *Professional Liability in the 1980's*, the American Medical Association noted:

Some of the problems lie with the courts; changes in the laws relating to professional liability actions and in some rules of the court could be beneficial. A multitude of other factors also contribute to the professional liability problem—higher public expectations of what medicine can offer, a more litigious society, a greater number of lawyers willing to file suits that may not have merit, and the lure of possible huge awards or settlements.[39]

Nowhere is there consideration that quality of care may be the big problem.

This thesis on the causes of increased liability appears to represent the consensus of the profession. Repeated polls of physicians by the American Medical Association and American College of Obstetrics and Gynecology reveal that physicians find the leading causes of liability to be the litigious society and greedy lawyers. In depth structured interviews recently conducted in the state of New York feature the same themes. Physicians feel victimized by a society that allows so much misdirected litigation.[40] These issues were also reflected in a bill sponsored by the AMA and introduced in the United States Senate in 1985, which included under the section entitled "Findings and Purpose," the following statement: "The number of professional liability claims against health care professionals and health care providers is increasing at disproportionate rates, beyond any relationship to the quality of care provided."[41]

Third, the physicians' frivolous litigation strategy posits that the result of malpractice litigation is not better care, but simply more expensive care, as doctors perform useless tests to decrease the possibility of suits. Thus fear of liability burdens not only doctors, but also society, with the costs of "defensive medicine," which is defined as those medical practices that "are employed explicitly for the purposes either of averting a possible law suit or of providing appropriate documentation that a wide range of tests and treatments has been used in the patient's care."[42] There have been various estimates of these costs, ranging from $3 to $6 billion in 1975 to $15 to $40 billion in 1983.[43] Again, in structured interviews as well as in the official pronouncements of the profession, physicians reiterate that the major effect of litigation pressure is defensive medicine, not better quality care.[44]

Unfortunately, the rhetoric with regard to defensive medicine has not been matched by good empirical research on the subject. Indeed, there are no reliable studies of defensive medicine, and for good reason. The concept itself is very difficult to understand. The provision of medical care lies on a spectrum from care that is reckless to care that is conservative and reduces uncertainty to an appropriate level. We tend to think that the best practitioners leave little to chance and pursue a conservative approach to medical problems. Thus conservative care is often good care, and institutions that provide conservative care are to be encouraged. Defensive medicine is care that is too conservative because it attempts to reduce uncertainty to an inappropriate level, and it is motivated only by fear of litigation. It can also involve not doing things, such as giving up obstetrics to avoid liability. Not all inappropriately conservative care is defensive medicine. Moreover, it is often difficult to define the difference, in particular episodes of care, between defensive medicine and careful medicine. This difficulty is not unexpected; malpractice is defined as substandard practice, and the increase in conservative practices it provokes should, in a perfect system, only bring that practice up to the standard of care.

The existing literature on defensive medicine reflects these conceptual difficulties, and indeed questions the impact of litigation on clinical practice. Nathan Hershey's early interview study suggested that doctors were using some extra diagnostic tests as defensive medicine, but the total cost of these tests was quite small.[45] Another study by the editors of the *Duke Law Journal* also questioned the widespread existence of defensive medicine.[46] L. Tancredi and J. Barondess reached much the same conclusion in their influential review in 1978.[47] Evidence suggests that doctors themselves do not think that defensive medicine plays a large role in their practices. S. Williams and colleagues studied physicians' perceptions about the reasons unnecessary diagnostic tests were ordered and found that less than three percent of practicing internists thought malpractice played a major role.[48] Others have suggested that a major area of defensive medicine is in obstetrics, citing high C-section rates and use of electronic fetal monitoring (EFM). However, these kinds of claims underestimate the complexity of the factors that go into the introduction of technology like EFM and the increases in the use of procedures like C-sections.[49] Indeed, most physicians would probably have a hard time coming up with a list of procedures that are highly influenced by defensive medicine, aside from some uses of radiology, especially in emergency rooms.

In the past few years, estimates of the impact of defensive medicine have been developed through econometric models, most often based on survey information. In a recent study published in the *Journal of the American Medical Association*, R. Reynolds and colleagues used two methods to estimate costs of professional liability.[50] Both methods relied on physicians' responses to mailed questionnaires. There was no way to correlate or evaluate the potential bias in physicians' responses. Moreover, the study defined increased record keeping, increased time spent with patients, and increased follow-up visits as examples of costs of professional liability. It is arguable that these are not defensive medicine costs, but rather examples of better care provoked by the deterrent function of tort law. Thus, as J. E. Harris stated in an editorial that accompanied this study, "We need to probe behind the survey responses analyzed by Reynolds and colleagues to uncover the microanatomic detail of defensive medicine."[51] Nonetheless, defensive medicine remains a potent rallying cry for the profession even though it is very difficult to assess the size of the problem it represents.

Finally, the frivolous litigation strategy of the medical profession has focused on increased legislative involvement. To counteract the rise in suits, physicians feel compelled to seek relief from state legislatures, arguing that doctors are committed to high quality care, that litigation is often unfounded, and that it only causes defensive medicine.[52] In general, relief has been sought in one of three ways: (1) "raising the threshold" for getting into courts; (2) limiting the amount of damages one can gain; and (3) recasting liability rules.[53]

There are several ways for legislatures to make it more difficult to get into court. One is to modify the existing American contingency fee system, which allows lawyers to accept as payment a portion of the compensation of the plaintiff. Indeed, some states have taken to regulating fees directly with percentage caps on the amount of the award that can be taken as payment.[54] This lower payment creates incentives for plaintiffs' attorneys to shift from malpractice to other torts. Another way to keep plaintiffs out of courts is to decrease the statute of limitations, giving the injured party less time to discover and prove that the injury was a result of a tort. Yet another method is to force the plaintiff to be screened by a panel of experts before being able to go to trial. This delays the litigation process greatly.

Another effective method for discouraging litigation is to institute damage caps. Legislatures can put ceilings on both economic damages and compensation for pain and suffering, in the hopes that such caps will decrease the amount any one case is worth to a plaintiff's attorney.[55] Other simpler ways of reaching the same endpoint are changing the collateral source rule, which has traditionally provided that facts concerning the plaintiff's other sources of income are not to be put in as evidence, and instituting a periodic payment regime for damages.[56] All of these changes would tend to decrease the initial lump sum payment owed the attorney, who has no doubt spent many hours bringing the case to trial.

Finally, and perhaps most directly, legislatures can change the liability rules that common law courts have modified. Some legislatures, for instance, have attempted to reinstate the locality rule.[57] Others have tried to limit the use of res ipsa loquitur.[58] All of these statutory modifications can potentially decrease the amount of malpractice litigation.

Attorneys and others argue that tort reform is nothing other than a strategy of powerful medical and insurance lobbies.[59] Perhaps more important, many have challenged such statutory intervention on behalf of defendants as unconstitutional.[60] While some patient advocates have tried to enlist the aid of federal courts on this question, most have been loath to find state statutory modifications unconstitutional.[61] However, state courts have been willing to accept the due process "quid pro quo" argument that legislation is unconstitutional if it offers relief only to one side of an adversarial dispute.[62] As Paul Weiler notes, "The courts, moreover, have perceived that powerful physician organizations have pushed for reforms, knowing that they would cut back on the rights of injured patients without offering them anything like the quid pro quo of limited but guaranteed no-fault benefits which had been a part of almost all prior tort reform legislation."[63]

In essence, the courts have again shown themselves willing to reiterate that changes in common law were meant to reinstate the public morality of the liberal state, and that statutory modifications meant to block such reforms are an affront to the liberal constitution. Attorneys, challenging the constitutionality of statutory reforms that make it more difficult for plaintiffs to sue, argue that such reforms decreased the compensation and deterrent functions of malpractice common law, harming the individual patient and favoring the medical profession. Of course, they reinforce this argument with rhetoric concerning the number of injuries in hospitals and the relatively small number of suits.

But there is reason to believe this contention is more than rhetoric. To address the need for more empirical information on these issues a team of researchers at Harvard University has undertaken a study of medical injury and litigation. One of our primary goals was to develop up-to-date and reliable estimates of the incidence of adverse events and negligence among hospitalized patients. To accomplish this, we reviewed a random sample of 31,000 medical records from New York State using techniques we have previously described.[64]

Using weighted population figures, we estimated that of the 2,671,863 discharges in New York State in 1984, there were over 98,000 adverse events of which 27,177 were negligent. Using these figures, we estimated the statewide incidence rate of adverse events to be 3.7 percent and the negligent adverse rate to be 1.0 percent. Although most adverse events resulted in minimal (56.8 percent) or temporary-partial (13.6) disabilities, 2.6 percent caused permanent total disability, and 13.5 percent resulted in death. Moreover, the negligence rate was greatest among patients who suffered the more severe adverse events. We estimated that there were over 500 permanent total disabilities and almost 7,000 deaths due to negligent adverse events in New York State in 1984.

From our sample, we found that less than 5 percent of the cases we defined as negligent led to litigation. Thus it appears that only a small fraction of negligent cases were taken to courts. Of course, there were some suits arising out of hospitalizations in which we could find no evidence of negligence.

These results will likely fuel contentions that malpractice reform that provides only relief for physicians and hospitals from suits does not serve society's interest. In view of this and other data, state legislatures should begin to incorporate broader requirements concerning quality of care into malpractice reform packages. The authors and advocates of such bills could argue that these requirements provide the quid pro quo missing in earlier tort reform packages: physicians get relief from suits but in return must allow more supervision of the work they do. Some of these reforms have already taken place at the federal level and provide relief from antitrust scrutiny for staff physician oversight of other physicians, a subject we will return to in chapter 10.[65] Other such reforms are concerned with enhancing peer review by providing protection from defamation suits for physician reviewers in hospitals.[66]

By far the most important of the initiatives to improve the quality of care at the state level has been the effort to improve state disciplining mechanisms.[67] Increasingly over the last five years, state attention to discipline of physicians has accompanied reforms in malpractice law.[68] States have traditionally taken a leading role in licensing and evaluating physicians, although much of their function has been formal and involved little real oversight. The state boards have been inadequately funded, are limited in their authority, and are often dominated by physician members.

The malpractice crisis has spurred changes. At the federal level, the Health Care Quality Improvement Act of 1986 has required creation of a national data bank for reporting disciplinary and malpractice actions against all physicians; this resource should tighten up accrediting and licensing efforts.[69] States have gone several steps beyond this. In Massachusetts, for instance, the new Medical Malpractice Reform Act of 1986 requires physicians themselves, as well as hospitals, insurers, and medical societies, to report disciplinary actions and malpractice claims to the Board of Registration in Medicine.[70] Each health care facility must develop patient care assessment plans and file these with the board. The board also received new subpoena power under the act and its staff grew from six to twenty-eight in one year. Other states, including Florida, California, New York, and Texas, have instituted similar reforms.[71]

The upshot of all this legislation is greater oversight of physicians. Chances are, given physicians' posture toward medical malpractice suits and quality assurance, this supervision will continue to be necessary. A frivolous litigation strategy blinds physicians to any perception that society's concerns about malpractice may be concerns about quality of care. Physicians of course continue to resist the deterrent effect of malpractice litigation by attempting to minimize the amount of such litigation, but they demonstrate little evidence that they are committed to quality assurance programs that might make malpractice suits redundant. The result of the professions' strategy in the courts is that society will attempt to "police" physicians, an outcome that all must feel is unfortunate.

The Ethical Approach to Malpractice and Quality Assurance

As outlined in chapter 4, a medical ethics for the liberal state, just doctoring, must reject paternalism, further patient autonomy, and endorse the altruistic role of physicians in a relationship based on their concern and respect for their patients. It must also include an honest appraisal by physicians of the social circumstances of the practice of medicine, and a renewed deference to the public morality of the liberal state. These factors come together in a health care sphere that respects liberalism, while evincing a spirit of cooperation and egalitarianism.

The medical profession's attitude toward malpractice and quality assurance has failed to meet this model. Although the profession is committed to providing the best care possible, it has guaranteed the quality of that care through informal, often hidden sanctioning. The profession has made no effort to demonstrate the efficacy of its review programs, as should be expected in the open liberal state. Instead, patients have had to be satisfied with paternalistic reassurances of the quality of the care they received. This approach does not demonstrate respect for patient autonomy.

The medical profession has resisted every judicial effort to empower patients through changes in malpractice doctrine. In their attempt to defend their prerogatives, physicians have again failed to demonstrate any respect for the values of liberalism. Their response has engendered state efforts to oversee the quality of medical practice. This has created an atmosphere more akin to police regulation than to cooperative health care, which I have argued should be the goal of medical ethics as just doctoring.

What, then, is the place of medical ethics with regard to malpractice and quality assurance? The answer seems fairly simple, at least at first cut: physicians must develop methods of quality assurance measures that are both effective and open to public review. If we are to demonstrate that the "patient comes first," we must be able to show that we are giving great thought to, and helping to bring about, better care. Indeed, I would argue that this should be a major priority of medical ethics, although it is rarely discussed in such terms.

Ethical quality assurance must be public, for secretive or hidden efforts do not respect the public morality of the liberal state or the negative freedom of the patient. Moreover, the results of quality reviews must also be made public, just as they are in other industries. This allows the individual to make informed choices, another tenet of the liberal state. It also means that in addition to tissue committee and morbidity and mortality conferences, physicians must undertake other forms of quality assurance that will bring about better care.

There are many new quality assurance techniques taking shape which can be included in a just doctoring approach to the problem of substandard care. In the evolving literature on this subject, measures of quality are usually subdivided into process and outcome measures. Process measures evaluate care through reliance on criteria or elements of care that professionals agree are relevant and measurable.[72] Outcome measures are perhaps more straightforward in that they focus on the short-term and long-term results of care. Outcome measures are, however, more difficult to develop. For instance, those outcomes now used as measurements include mortality and readmission rates. Both of these measures are heavily influenced by the mixture and the severity of cases that go into the class of outcomes being measured. For example, the sickest patients might refer themselves to the best hospital. That hospital may have a rather high mortality rate overall, but that high mortality would presumably be related to the higher incidence of very sick patients, not to the quality of the care delivered. Another way to assess outcomes is simply to have patients rate the care they have received.[73] Again, however, there are problems with the validity of this kind of measurement.

Given these troubling aspects of outcome measures, there is a great deal of interest in process measures that can be shown to affect quality of care. For example, anesthesiologists at Harvard University have recently adopted standards for anesthesia for common surgical procedures. The standards specify simple monitoring techniques, or practice guidelines, that are based on clinical experience as well as claims experience.[74] The standards themselves can be specified on one-half of a page, and they appear to have significantly decreased the number of claims brought against Harvard anesthesiologists.[75] However, anesthesia may prove to be an atypically easy area in which to develop such criteria; similar criteria for obstetrics require dozens of pages, for example, and thus may be much less easy to adopt. Further research into practice guidelines must be a priority for the medical profession, just as it has become for the federal government.[76]

In addition to exploring methods for quality assurance, physicians must also ensure that an appropriate institutional context exists for review initiatives. For example, fears of litigation can disrupt efforts to monitor the quality of care. Physicians involved in quality review can become embroiled in litigation in two ways.[77] First, patient-plaintiffs seeking to establish that the care they received was substandard can petition the records of quality assurance offices concerning the care they were provided.[78] Those physicians carrying out the review might be asked by the court to testify about such cases. Second, quality assurance can lead to litigation when embittered physicians who have been cited by quality monitors sue the hospital and the physician reviewers for libel, defamation, or antitrust violations.[79] Most states provide some protection for physicians against such suits, but there are loopholes in state laws, and tort lawyers have continually sought to expand the scope of litigation in both areas.[80] Both types of suits make physicians uncomfortable about participating in review programs. If quality assurance is to become more rigorous, presumably physicians will have to be insulated to some degree from such suits.[81]

One form of quality assurance obviates the need to focus on particular physicians or patients. Some health care policy analysts have begun to advocate managerial methods of quality assurance.[82] Taking cues from modern management techniques that have been widely adopted in Japan, these analysts argue that physicians are only part of the whole process of medical care.[83] Mistakes, oversights, or inefficiencies at any step can lead to bad outcomes. The analysts suggest that the entire process of medical care must be examined if we are to bring about better quality care. The attractiveness of this approach is that it moves the focus from the physician to the health care team, and it thus overcomes the perception of quality assurance as an incrimination of physicians.

In summary, the response of physicians, motivated by a sense of medical ethics as just doctoring, to the malpractice crisis should be a renewed commitment to better quality care, as evinced by greater participation in quality assurance programs and scrupulously honest efforts to develop efficacious and open methods for improving medical care. Physicians must prove to society that they can regulate themselves and that society will benefit from this regulation. The liberal state will not at this point accept simple reassurances from physicians. We must prove that new approaches to quality assurance will work. If we do so, society may be willing to maintain protection for physicians who participate in such programs. In lieu of this demonstration by the profession of its commitment to quality, physicians will undoubtedly face stronger and stronger external regulation and oversight. This threat can only strengthen the appeal for ethical quality assurance efforts by all physicians.

The Ethics of Compensation for
Iatrogenic Injury

I have argued that medical ethics must be cognizant of policy issues and physicians should openly address these issues. Some might argue that given my orientation, it seems peculiar to argue that physicians should concentrate on quality assurance alone. My critics might ask, should not patient compensation be a part of the profession's concerns about malpractice? If tort law does not provide appropriate and equitable compensation, should not physicians work for a better system?

My answer is a qualified yes. It is apparent from the empirical studies discussed above that the current system of compensation through tort litigation has serious drawbacks. As I have argued at length, one element of medical ethics, including medical ethics as just doctoring, is the physician's altruistic commitment to the patient. This commitment must not only include respect for the public morality of the liberal state but also dutiful action on behalf of patients—action not expected in other relationships in the liberal state. The key to medical ethics in the liberal state is that the physician retains a "patient comes first" attitude of other-regardness, while respecting fundamental rights.

Given this basis for medical ethics, the reliance on tort law as the sole source for compensation for an injured patient seems peculiar, and perhaps counterproductive. The tort law has several functions. Of these, we have discussed deterrence and compensation. Another function, which has been advocated by several legal scholars over the past decade, is the corrective justice aspect of tort law.[84] The fact that tort law requires the injurer to pay the injured is not coincidence according to these scholars. Rather, they believe that tort law plays a special justice function in the liberal state, allowing the injured party to "even" himself with the injurer. This corrective justice is said to play an important symbolic role in the liberal state. It is not, however, a necessary part of modern liberalism as discussed in the first few chapters of this book.

Corrective justice has moderate appeal in some instances in the liberal state. Certainly the individualistic and egalitarian aspects of liberalism are reinforced when plaintiffs seek redress from impersonal corporations in product liability claims. Yet corrective justice makes little sense when considering a close relationship between doctor and patient that has now been complicated by medical injury. Thus medical ethics in the liberal state argues for alternatives.

Indeed, given the principles of just doctoring, administrative compensation for medical injury is preferable to tort law for several reasons.[85] First of all, a no-fault compensation system means that the injured party only needs to show that she was injured during treatment to gain compensation. This means that both negligent and nonnegligent injury are compensated. Our research suggests that about one-quarter of all adverse events are negligent. Since only negligently caused injuries are compensated in a tort regime, this means that 75 percent of all injuries in our country go uncompensated. Thus a no-fault approach provides broader coverage for patients, a goal of our "patient comes first" ethic.

Second, the no-fault system does away with the corrective justice aspects of the tort system. In Sweden and New Zealand, where no-fault compensation plans now exist, injuries are considered for compensation once they are reported to the authorities. Increasingly, injuries are reported by the physicians themselves. The physicians, as part of their ethical commitment to the patient, try to help procure compensation for the patient.

Physicians are so inclined for several reasons. Compensation is available for all injuries, not just those caused by negligence. Thus in helping the patient procure compensation, the physician is not admitting error. In addition, the physician in this system can accept that errors do occur. She knows, as do all of us, that mistakes are made by everyone in every line of work. She is not expected to be perfect. She knows that the authorities supervising physicians are keeping statistics on errors made by physicians, and she can thus be assured that an isolated mistake will not lead to discipline.

In the tort regime, the courts increasingly hold physicians liable for injuries suffered by patients so as to provide both broad compensation and deterrence signals for a profession that does not appear actively to police itself. This makes it well nigh impossible to admit error. The possibility of a physician's ethical commitment to patient compensation evaporates in the face of the corrective justice of the tort system. In the no-fault regimes of Sweden and New Zealand, the assumption is that accidents will occur, and both patient and physician have reason to cooperate in the effort to gain compensation for the patient. The "patient comes first" ethic can flourish.

This is not to say that the deterrence function is lost. On the contrary, there is the possibility of administrative systems for monitoring physician performance. Much of the information for these monitoring committees would come from episodes that lead to compensation. Physicians and other health care workers could participate in oversight committees and seek to uncover patterns of substandard care. If the patterns were the result of a single practitioner, steps could be taken to limit this person's practice. If the patterns were a result of a "systems" error, this information could be shared with all health authorities.

In this regime, physician altruism can flourish, and yet there is no infringement on the liberal rights of the patient. The physician can help the patient gain compensation for an injury. In addition, physicians can work selflessly to help improve medical care by pursuing quality assurance programs without fear of tort litigation.

Consider for example, the case I outlined at the beginning of this chapter. My patient died of salicylate poisoning. If he had a family or heirs, I and others associated with his care would have faced a series of very difficult questions regarding compensation for his family. While we did not believe we had provided substandard care, we all questioned whether we could have given better care. Yet we likely would not have recommended that the family sue us to gain compensation.

If we had been in a no-fault system, we could have recommended an application for compensation and forwarded the case to the appropriate authorities. They could have then considered whether compensation was due the patient's survivors. They could have also made a separate finding on the standard of care provided the patient. If it was substandard, we would have been on notice. If any one of us had continued to display questionable judgment, his practice would then be restricted. Perhaps new systems for alerting physicians to potential diagnoses could have come out of discussion engendered by the case. Thus the whole incident could have been handled in an honest manner that allowed ethical behavior on the part of the physicians and reiterated the profession's commitment to high quality care.

Of course, the fear of those who oppose no-fault compensation is that the deterrence function of tort law will not be replaced by sincere efforts to bring about better quality care by physicians. They believe that physicians will simply try to maintain authority over the practice of medicine and will not be amenable to disciplining themselves. They argue that the courts are necessary to interest the doctors in quality assurance, and that tort litigation is the sine qua non of better quality care.

Those who advocate tort litigation to deal with medical error and patient injury have history on their side. Physicians committed to ethical care of the patient may agree with me that a no-fault approach has much promise for the reinforcement of ethical behavior by physicians. However, the only way they can convince the skeptics is by renewed efforts to develop quality assurance programs and to discourage substandard practices and police substandard providers. Quality assurance efforts are critical to convincing society that the ethical commitment to the patient can provide the kind of motivation that heretofore has only been provided by threat of court sanctions. Thus the answer to medical ethics as just doctoring, for the present and future malpractice crises, must be better quality oversight by the medical profession. Once this commitment is clear, physicians' efforts to develop no-fault approaches will be recognized as an ethical commitment to the patient, not a self-serving ploy.

7

The Challenge of AIDS

We have discussed the notion of medical ethics in the liberal state by analyzing two sets of common law developments— informed consent and malpractice litigation. In these discussions we emphasized how developments in the common law represented attempts by courts to enforce the integrity of liberal law in order to align the behavior of physicians with the public morality of the liberal state. Thus medical paternalism has been curbed as the practice of medicine has been forced to respect the patient's negative freedom. The lack of respect shown by traditional medical ethics for patient's rights has been cured, at least partially, by judges enforcing the law. In this regard, the liberal society has told doctors that patients must be accorded the respect due every citizen in the state.

In this chapter, we will review aspects of medical ethics that are not defined by the law, but rather by the physician's "duty." While recognizing that medical ethics in the liberal state requires that physicians acknowledge the negative freedom of its citizens, we have not argued that medical ethics should be restricted to the set of duties or obligations owed by each and every citizen of the liberal state to his fellow citizen. To the contrary, a medical ethics for the liberal state involves notions of duty other than those typically owed by one citizen to another. Medical ethics involves altruism. This altruism enhances the sense of cooperation in the liberal state and helps bring to life the public morality of equal respect and concern for others that is central to liberalism. It helps transform the pluralism of liberalism into an "overlapping consensus," and helps create the sense of community without which the liberal state could not function. In short, medical ethics encompasses some duties that go beyond activities the law can enforce.

Today, one of the best ways to understand the role of altruism in medical ethics is to consider the physician's moral role in an epidemic. Again, allow me to refer to a recent personal experience. A friend was acting as "ward attending physician" for a month and had to go out of town. He asked if I could cover for him, meaning I would have to make rounds with the house physicians on his team. This involves reviewing the patients admitted to a team of interns and residents throughout the day and helping that team develop a treatment plan. In addition, I would have to deal with any problems in patient care that were troubling the team of physicians. This is usually quite enjoyable as the house staff at our hospital are very intelligent and caring and the discussions about patients are stimulating. This time, however, my experience was unexpectedly tense.

On rounds in the morning we did not see every patient. While we were talking about the new admissions, the resident physician in charge of the team told me that they were having trouble with Mrs. D. This middle-aged patient had a long history of intravenous drug use and had been admitted with a blood clot in the left arm. The thinking of the team was that the blood clot had been formed because the patient had injected some contaminated cocaine. They believed the clot was infected, and so they thought that several weeks of intravenous antibiotics would be needed. The patient had repeatedly taken out the intravenous lines in her arms over the course of the weekend, and had left the hospital once to "shoot up." The patient wanted a central intravenous catheter, that is a catheter placed into a large vein of the neck or shoulder. The house staff was hesitant, as these catheters, while in some ways easier to maintain than peripheral ones, can also readily be used to inject illicit drugs. Since chronic intravenous drug users such as this patient usually scar their veins injecting drugs, making it more and more difficult to find veins to shoot into, a central line is often a great opportunity to "get high." While angry about the team's hesitance to put in the central catheter, the patient clearly wanted to continue with therapy: she was not going to sign out "against medical advice," a very common disposition for intravenous drug users. This scenario was not in any way out of the ordinary. What was troublesome was the patient was threatening at times to spit on people, and she carried the human immunodeficiency virus (HIV).

While at a lunch meeting, and before I had met Mrs. D., I was paged and told that there was trouble, and that I should come to the patient's room. When I arrived on the floor, I was met by senior nursing administrators who told me the patient had to leave the hospital. They explained to me that the patient had spat at a nurse who was helping her and had threatened others. The house staff agreed that they could not do anything for the patient and that she should leave.

The patient, however, did not want to leave. I felt immediately embattled, and I still had not met Mrs. D. Everyone agreed that the patient was competent to make decisions, and that she wanted to stay in the hospital. No one seemed to think she had done anything criminal, and indeed, it was not clear whether she had spat at the nurse, or simply spat when the nurse was near. I related that I could not really do anything until I saw the patient. What I really wanted to do was to get away from the doctors and nurses, most of whom I knew as extremely cool and competent professionals, but who in this case were extraordinarily agitated.

Going to the patient's room, I had to pass an array of security personnel, all outfitted in gloves and safety glasses. Entering the room, I expected to find some large and threatening figure. Instead I found a thin and agitated woman, instructing someone on the telephone to hire an attorney. Clothes were scattered about, and it looked as though the other patient in the room had beat a hasty retreat. Mrs. D. finished her conversation and, fixing me with an intense stare, told me she would not leave the hospital. She explained that she had not spat at anyone, and that she knew she needed care. I agreed she needed antibiotics, but told her she would have to calm down. At the same time I realized privately and sadly that this was really an untenable situation for everyone involved.

I knew that the patient could only lose. It seemed clear from our initial conversation that while competent, she could not control her rage. She said, asserting with great anger, that if she did not get more methadone, she would go out and buy dope. However, she had already received so much methadone that she had fallen asleep in the bathroom, precipitating the violent encounter with the nurse. She knew she was sick and needed antibiotics, and was even willing to back off the central line request, but she only wanted to be cared for by certain nurses and wanted to leave the hospital whenever she wished.

Moreover, it seemed to me very likely that if confronted with authority, she would leave the hospital. Having spent at least ten years abusing intravenous drugs, and ten years needing immediate gratification from them at great risk to her health, did not produce patience and conscientious self-regard. If she was confronted, I was sure she would leave, even though we warned her that her health was endangered by the infected clot. This is a scenario I had seen played out countless times in the past. Indeed, the drug user's lack of self-regard can be used as a tool for turfing, or getting rid of the patient.

This patient had originally sought care at a community hospital. Even though they knew she was addicted to heroin and would suffer withdrawal without methadone, the health care workers she met in the emergency room of this hospital told her she would not receive any narcotics if admitted there. She left, quite understandably, after signing a form that instructed her she was leaving the hospital against their medical advice. I had little doubt that years of this kind of treatment had left this patient with an ironic understanding that it was always easier to leave than confront hospital authority. Thus while she doggedly stuck to her contention that she wanted to stay, I knew a confrontation would eventually drive her away.

A confrontation was inevitable because the health care workers felt threatened. I am generally impressed by the sense of duty that most hospital workers bring to their job. I am familiar mainly with the house and nursing staffs of large urban medical centers, and so this defines my perspective to a large extent. On the wards of these hospitals, human suffering is close at hand. There is usually a certain serious, often grim atmosphere, which is then lightened only by gallows humor. Nonetheless, there is a feeling of comaraderie, a belief that there is an important job to be done, that makes the work seem special. Moreover, one frequently sees compassion and gentleness in caring for vulnerable sick people. The nurses are of course in the forefront in this regard, as it is they who really take care of the patients. And they perform this task, in my mind, with a sense of tragedy, as their important job often goes unnoticed and their grave responsibilities are attended to with little real control over the situation.

Be this as it may, neither they nor the house staff, nor for that matter the staff physicians, want to feel threatened in their work. When they are threatened, it is usually by some patient who is behaving violently. Typically, security or the police can be called to subdue such an individual, and work goes on. However, health care workers now face another threat—more frightening because it is so ill-defined—from patients who carry the human immunodeficiency virus (HIV). They know that HIV infection often leads to death from complications of the acquired immunodeficiency syndrome (AIDS). They see young people dying of this infectious disease. They read that Hepatitis B is a much greater threat, as is death from an automobile accident. But most have never seen anyone die from Hepatitis B, and they also know that everyone has a relatively large risk of dying in an automobile, but only they, health care workers, have the risk of contracting HIV at the workplace. It is their own special threat, a risk which they will take seriously no matter what the risk calculations show.

This risk hung in the air on the wards as I left the patient's room to talk to the nursing administrators, now gathered in a nearby conference room. A couple of security officers had put on yellow gowns, along with glasses, hats, and gloves. A small crowd of people had gathered a respectful distance from the patient's room. The situation was charged; in the conference room, even more so. The nurses made it clear. This patient could not stay in the hospital. There had to be rules; nurses could not be threatened. When everyone else went home that night, only nurses would be left. She had spat, and she would probably do so again.

I did not see how we could send the patient away. She had no home, no arrangements to go to a shelter. More to the point, she was sick and wanted to stay. I thought if I could buy time, maybe the tensions would settle down and so would the patient, and then the staff. I demanded that we get a hospital attorney on the ward. This was a stalling action, as I knew the legal situation. The patient denied spitting at a nurse, and even the nurse who had been the target could not say that she had been spat at by the patient. Thus there was no way to make even a weak criminal case (if there had been, the patient would have been put into police custody and shipped to the city hospital). Moreover, the law regarding abandonment clearly requires one to continue to care for a patient who is seriously ill. Our legal duty was to keep her and treat her.

I felt that the same was true of our ethical duty, as might anyone else not involved in the situation. But I could not directly challenge the nurses, because I had seen the patient's rage and I knew the "threat" before them. The attorney gambit looked like it might work, however. The attorney took his time, and when he arrived, he reiterated the abandonment line. The nurses moderated, a bit. There was an opening.

Unfortunately, it closed quickly. I went back to talk to the patient. It was going well. We would forget about intravenous lines and treat her with intramuscular injections. She would get a single room. She would try to moderate her behavior. But then I used the wrong choice of words to explain something to her. Again she flew into a rage. She threw trays around the room and screamed. Security bristled. The patient said, all right, she was leaving, that was it. She began to pack. The staff seemed relieved. I could not entreat her to stay, perhaps because I knew she would not. The confrontation was too much for her. She left, with an infected arm, and likely a number of other medical problems.

None of this was too unusual, except for the "threat" of her infection. The risk of contracting HIV had lent an extraordinarily urgent mood to the encounter. The relief when the patient left was palpable; it would not have been so if the patient had been some other troublemaker. There was also a certain embarrassment because many of the people present had wanted a sick person to leave the hospital. I felt, and I think others did, a peculiar uneasiness. I am normally rather unaffected emotionally by my work in the hospital, but I felt drained as I went to the elevator to leave. I walked over to the public health school to a meeting, for which I was an hour late. It was a meeting on the staffing needs caused by the HIV epidemic. I blurted out an account of the incident. People were vaguely sympathetic, but one colleague noted dryly that while these problems are new in Boston, in New York they happen every day over and over again. This put my thoughts about the legal and ethical duties to treat HIV infected patients in a new light.

Indeed, the HIV epidemic goes to the heart of medical ethics in the liberal state. Up to this point we have been concerned about the manner in which physicians must learn to respect the negative freedom of patients. Here we must debate the extent to which physicians must willingly give up some of their own negative freedom in order to demonstrate their concern and respect for all patients, including those with AIDS. We will also discuss the manner in which AIDS highlights the nature of just doctoring, which requires that physicians address important issues of public health. In general, the challenge of AIDS allows us to understand new dimensions of just doctoring.

The (Rather Minimal) Legal Duty to Treat

In previous chapters, we discussed the manner in which legal innovations reminded physicians that they needed to seek informed consent and to provide good quality care, as well as evidence that the care was good. Some might think, having read the case study I just outlined, that the law should also require doctors and nurses to care for all the sick, including those with HIV. This argument may, however, misconstrue the nature of the law as integrity. The law, especially the common law, protects negative freedom, and thus it provides formally equal concern for all individuals. It also ensures that minorities do not suffer at the hands of majorities, by providing for certain substantive civil liberties. Moreover, the liberal legislature decides democratically the manner in which inequalities can be overcome—the overall balance between negative freedom and inequality. Ideally all citizens receive equal concern and respect, but that is only a goal. In any real liberal state, there will be inequalities, even inequalities that conflict with the ideal of equal concern and respect. Thus some people, because of the nature of their disease, might receive less than equal treatment. The liberal state might be unwilling to constrain the negative freedom of others, for instance, health care workers, so that equal treatment is provided. This appears to be the case with the common law and AIDS: the doctor's freedom to choose is respected, even to the detriment of sick people.

The traditional paradigm for establishment of the doctor-patient relationship is the contract.[1] Under common law, physicians have been allowed to refuse to care for patients in nonemergency settings. Physicians are also allowed to limit the care they provide to certain kinds of problems or to certain subspecialities.[2] However, once a physician begins to treat a patient, a relationship is assumed and care must be continued until the patient no longer needs treatment for this specific problem.[3]

This does not mean that a physician must continue to treat a patient until the patient decides to go elsewhere for therapy; if the patient is not acutely ill, the physician may end the relationship after giving enough notice for the patient to find a new physician.[4] If a physician ends the doctor-patient relationship while the patient is in need of care, the physician may be found to be in breach of the implied contract, and a patient may sue under the doctrine of "abandonment."[5] Abandonment doctrine thus prohibits a physician from unilaterally refusing to care for a patient once a relationship has been initiated, unless that patient's health is stable and sufficient notice is given of the physician's intention to withdraw from the relationship.

Abandonment doctrine will have a relatively small role to play in assuring access to health care for patients with AIDS. If a physician is treating a patient who has AIDS, he can withdraw, but he will have to give ample warning and recommend another physician for the patient. Moreover, the physician cannot withdraw if the AIDS patient is acutely ill. AIDS patients are frequently ill, and many times the illness is critical. Does this mean that once a physician enters a relationship with an AIDS patient, he is committed to treatment of that patient for life? Some commentators have answered this question in the affirmative, but I think this demonstrates an incomplete understanding of the clinical course of AIDS as well as the law of abandonment.[6] The disease tends to smolder, then it flares up with opportunistic infections. In the majority of AIDS cases there are times in which patients are quite stable and a new therapeutic relationship could be forged without detriment to the patient. Moreover, the care of patients with AIDS is becoming more sophisticated, and primary care practitioners, for instance, may cite lack of specialist knowledge as the reason for terminating a relationship with a patient with AIDS. Thus the doctrine of abandonment does not prohibit a physician's withdrawal from a relationship with an AIDS patient.

The same is true for a patient who is HIV seropositive. People who carry the HIV may be completely asymptomatic and may not require any intense therapy. While such patients may potentially become quite sick, they are usually not acutely ill, and proper notice can be given with no problem. Nor will the doctrine of abandonment prevent doctors from requesting antibody screening before they initiate care for individuals. Since there may in the future be new drugs available to treat seropositive patients, a primary care physician can argue that the care of seropositive patients also requires specialist knowledge. Thus the refusal to care can be couched in terms of concern for the patient.[7]

In the case of Mrs. D. cited above, the patient would have had grounds, had we forced her to leave, for an abandonment suit. We were already providing care for her, and she was acutely ill. Thus the common law would have found us in violation of her negative freedom and the expectation of being treated fairly.

However, hers is not the typical case, although it is the most frightening for many health care workers. Physicians studying this paradigm might well decide that they will limit their care to people who do not have AIDS. They can justify this refusal to care on the grounds that they do not understand all the problems that can develop in people with AIDS, and that AIDS for them is like cancer; it is best handled by specialists. Underlying this seemingly prudent decision, however, will be the realization that they simply do not want to have to face the incredible social problems presented by many patients with HIV infection, or the fear of contracting the virus from the patient. (The situation is even more difficult for nurses, who have more contact with patients in general, and who might decide that some career other than hospital nursing seems more attractive.)

Fears of contracting the virus may lead to real shortages of practitioners available to care for people with HIV infection. Especially as the epidemic deepens and moves into urban communities which have long been underserved, it may be difficult to find enough physicians willing to undertake the small risk associated with caring for patients with AIDS. In this area, the common law of abandonment tends to emphasize the negative freedom of the physician, and it thus does little to correct the inequalities that might develop around care for those infected with HIV.

Of course, the common law is not the only means the liberal state employs to develop legal duties. The law as integrity is not restricted to traditions of judicial law. In addition to the common law sanction of abandonment suits, there are statutory controls over physicians' practice that could serve as sanctions against physicians who refuse to care for seropositive patients. Physicians are licensed by the state, and the state retains some control over the manner in which physicians practice. This power could be used to prohibit physicians from discriminating against patients who are seropositive.

In New Jersey, for example, the state's licensing authority has stated that physicians cannot discriminate against patients with AIDS or AIDS related complex (ARC).[8] The state does not, however, require treatment if the physician states that she does not have the skill or experience to treat the disease. Thus, while state licensing authorities may be able to mandate that if a surgeon is qualified to do an open lung biopsy, he cannot refuse to do one on an HIV seropositive patient, the state will not be able to mandate that all primary care practitioners must care for HIV seropositive patients. This means that even laws emphasizing the civil rights of individuals may prove ineffective in guaranteeing the equal concern and respect that is the ideal of liberalism.

Hospitals and other health care institutions are governed by a set of doctrines different from those covering individual practitioners. (Of course, many physicians are employed directly by hospitals, and the doctrines that apply to institutions will apply to the physicians employed there.)[9] Hospitals that have emergency rooms must treat all patients who arrive in unstable condition.[10] Unfortunately, this right to emergency care at a hospital that offers emergency services does little to guarantee that people with AIDS will have unfettered access to health care. If an AIDS patient is suffering from a medical emergency, it is clear that he or she has a legal right to care in a hospital with an emergency service; but the law provides little more than emergency care. Once the acute medical problem stabilizes, the hospital and its employees are able to sever the therapeutic relationship.[11] However, the federal government, prompted by the phenomenon of "dumping" indigent patients in county hospitals, has instituted sharp penalties for hospitals that send unstable patients to other facilities.[12] While these penalties will help ensure safe transfer, they do not guarantee access to health care at any particular institution. Indeed, it is likely that private hospitals will increasingly send indigent AIDS patients to county or public hospitals.

These provisions will accommodate at least some individuals with AIDS, but they will not assure the kind of continuing primary care that may be the cornerstone of treatment for HIV in the future, especially as more drugs emerge for the treatment of the asymptomatic carrier.[13] Indeed, patients like Mrs. D. may continue to find that legal guarantees of emergency treatment are essentially empty promises. Every emergency room physician realizes that a confrontation with an intravenous drug user over the availability of narcotics will drive the patient away. Thus the law can do relatively little, in real terms, to secure treatment for individuals with HIV infection.

The Ethical Duty to Treat

I have argued that in certain spheres of activity, voluntary moral behavior, involving altruistic actions, contributes to the liberal state's sense of community and helps balance the demands of negative freedom with the ideal of equal concern and respect. The cooperativeness of the liberal state, the sense of the state as a community, is brought about not only by the law as integrity but also by concern for others, both at the individual level and within certain spheres of concerted activities.

The principles of just doctoring define medicine as one of these spheres and constitute the practice of medicine as a moral activity that contributes to the sense of cooperation within the liberal state. Thus it is clear that medical ethics must naturally address the potential inequalities that would occur if we relied solely on the law to bring about care for those infected with HIV. Just doctoring must include a duty to treat. Before defining that duty, however, we should review the nature of the threat posed by HIV to those who care for patients infected with it.

The magnitude of the problem posed by HIV in this country alone is well known. Since 1981, there have been nearly a hundred thousand reported cases of AIDS. It is estimated that approximately one million individuals carry HIV, and that many of these individuals will eventually develop AIDS.[14] Although there are increased rates of infection in African American and Hispanic communities,[15] there is no way to know whether or not a person is an asymptomatic carrier without a blood test.[16] Thus many patients may be unrecognized HIV carriers.[17]

Fears about occupational transmission have developed relatively recently. At the beginning of the epidemic, there was little discussion of this issue, probably because the risk of transmission was thought to be nearly nonexistent.[18] However, in the summer of 1987, the Centers for Disease Control (CDC) reported three cases of HIV infection in health care workers who were splashed with HIV seropositive blood, a manner of exposure that was previously thought not to be a hazard.[19] Soon thereafter other researchers demonstrated that the HIV infection rate was much higher than expected in patients admitted to emergency rooms.[20] These reports demonstrated that occupational transmission of HIV would not be limited to needle injuries involving AIDS patients. At about the same time, the first suit was filed by a physician against a hospital in which he claimed that he was exposed to HIV and developed AIDS after a blood tube accident.[21] More suits by health care workers have followed.[22]

These suits have heightened health care workers' awareness of the dangers of HIV as an occupational disease, and there are signs of changes in professional attitudes. Surprisingly large numbers of surgeons support mandatory testing and refusal of surgery for HIV seropositive individuals.[23] Very few dentists accept new patients with AIDS.[24] Thus, although the risk of occupational infection is still thought to be very low,[25] physicians and other health care workers, as well as the hospitals in which they work, may soon begin to limit care.[26] Indeed, new data suggest that the risk of contracting HIV for a medical house officer is greater than the risks for police officers of being shot, or for asbestos workers of dying from asbestos-related disease.[27] A recent debate at San Francisco General Hospital provides a disturbing picture of our current situation. Researchers there have demonstrated that the occupational risk of contracting HIV is quite low; nevertheless, the chief of orthopedic surgery at the hospital has advocated a policy of physician discretion regarding elective operations on HIV seropositive patients.[28] Thus a sense of disquiet is spreading, retarded only by rational arguments concerning the minuscule risk of exposure if one adheres to the standards of the CDC and Occupational Safety and Health Administration (OSHA) on safety procedures and precautions.[29] The risk is real, if small, and the law can do little to force physicians to care for those infected with HIV.

Even if the risk were more substantial, just doctoring would require that physicians not discriminate on the basis of type of illness; indeed, it demands an assurance of equal care for those infected with HIV. But what are the limits of this ethical duty to treat?

This can be answered in part by addressing the ethical approaches to the duty to treat. Some create open-ended duties. Ezekiel Emmanuel has noted, for example, that "the objective of the medical profession is devotion to a moral ideal—in particular healing the sick."[30] In other words, the ethical obligation to heal entails treating all sick people. Abigail Zuger and Steven H. Miles have framed the relationship of principle to obligation in a slightly different manner. They argue that the practice of medicine itself requires the physician to act virtuously, to exemplify honesty, compassion, fidelity, and courage.[31] Since refusing to care for HIV seropositive patients is without virtue, physicians have an obligation to treat everyone. John D. Arras elaborates on this principle of virtue, noting that "in refusing to treat, physicians violate their own professional commitment to the end of healing."[32]

Yet, a theory of medical ethics based on classic liberal principles finds few special ethical obligations attending the occupation.[33] Agreeing with Robert Sade that the relationship between doctor and patient is contractual in nature, and that the doctor's rights in such a relationship are symmetric with those of the patient,[34] a physician can state, "I practice medicine and I find nothing in the enterprise that creates a special obligation to treat HIV-related illness." More to the point, a physician can say to a colleague, "You recognize an ethical obligation to treat, I do not. I argue that the practice of medicine itself does not create such an obligation. Just as patients are free to choose doctors, I am free to decide whom to treat."

This is certainly the position taken by many physicians and some medical societies who assert that the practice of medicine does not entail treating all HIV seropositive patients.[35] When coupled with a willingness to refer HIV seropositive patients to HIV clinics, this kind of behavior is not on face unvirtuous or unethical. These arguments, then, emphasize the negative freedom of the physician, to the detriment of the patient who is HIV seropositive and cannot find care.

Those ethicists and physicians who base their ethical duty to treat in a beneficence model seem to be unable to counter the negative freedom argument made by other physicians. Instead of pointing out its deficiencies, these ethicists appear only to recognize and lament the problems posed by the changing structure of the practice of medicine and the pluralism this creates. They rue the growth of the metaphor of medicine as business and the influences of pluralism on the liberal state. Indeed, it often sounds as though they would like to be rid of liberalism and instead base the state, as well as professional ethics, on heroic notions of virtue.

Medical ethics as just doctoring does not need to turn its back on the (real) liberal state. To the contrary, just doctoring arises out of and is compatible with modern liberalism, and this compatibility is revealed in its arguments about physicians' duties to treat patients infected with HIV.[36]

Since the just doctoring model of medical ethics takes as its first principle equal concern and respect for the sick, the "patient comes first" model, and since this principle is universalizable as to the class of all patients, it is unfathomable that physicians would refuse to care for patients simply because the patients are HIV seropositive. The history of medical ethics, and every notion of the physician's commitment to the patient, requires studied ambivalence toward the disease when one is called to care. Since the patient must come first, discrimination on the basis of illness is not a possibility.

Moreover, medicine constitutes a sphere within the liberal state, a sphere defined by physicians' altruism. Liberalism is dependent on this and other spheres to help bring about the sense of cooperation that unifies the state. Liberalism itself is based first and foremost on the notion of equal concern and respect. Therefore, even if physicians did not partake at all in the notion of altruism, the liberal state would probably require that their negative freedom be limited so that all would receive care. The duty to care defined by medical ethics obviates the need for the liberal state to take coercive steps to guarantee equal concern and respect for all patients regardless of their disease. It involves self-imposed limits on the physician's negative freedom for the good of patients.

The notion of health care as a sphere of moral activity that creates duties beyond those usually expected in the liberal state provides further grounds for the duty to treat. Since all physicians share the same set of duties to patients, moral imperatives are arguably as universalizable to the class of physicians as they are to the class of patients. Thus physicians owe duties not only to patients, but also to other physicians. In this regard, it would be grossly wrong for some physicians to refuse to undertake the risks associated with caring for HIV seropositive patients, forcing others to assume more risks. Physicians share equally in the requirements of the duty to demonstrate equal concern and respect for patients. This means they must all be willing to act altruistically, and to share in the risks presented by the care of those who are infected. Just doctoring prohibits free-riding by some physicians because health care is a particular good with moral principles that apply equally to all health care providers. In short, the social morality of medicine expressed as just doctoring extends beyond the public morality of the liberal state.

The requirements of just doctoring are not, however, as open-ended as the duties specified by a beneficence model. In a beneficence theory, it is unclear what sort of risk might be too great to expect that physicians would serve unselfishly. More important, the beneficence approach to a duty to treat does not leave any room for self-regarding or prudent action by physicians. It does not allow physicians to argue that they should be compensated if they contract the virus in the line of duty or to consider mechanisms for dealing with HIV infection as an occupational disease.

Medical ethics as just doctoring remains within the confines of the liberal state. That is, while the social morality of medicine extends beyond the public morality of liberalism, it does not undermine it. Therefore physicians do retain some negative freedom. They voluntarily give up some portion of that freedom when they become health care providers and enter the moral structure of the health care sphere. The negative freedom of physicians is thus not extinguished, but it is diminished somewhat by the need to show the greatest possible respect and concern for all individuals, to certify the equality at the heart of liberalism. However, doctors are still liberal citizens and they are not expected to be saints, to use George Annas's expression. Indeed, just doctoring allows physicians to consider, in a realistic fashion, those incentives that will enable them and their colleagues to undertake their ethical duty with as much support as possible.

What does this amount to? Just doctoring, while reiterating the duty to treat, allows physicians to advocate measures that will support caregivers who do contract the virus. They can submit reforms to the representative democracy for its consideration. These reforms will probably center on means for compensation for HIV-related illness for health care workers. Thus just doctoring requires us to consider the available means for compensation through the law, again emphasizing the close relationship between medical ethics and the law.

It also allows health care workers to consider the various levels of risk that accompany different jobs. Since they face significantly higher risks, surgeons may expect greater protection from infection than other specialists, and may expect better assurance about compensation.

If a health worker contracts the HIV at his workplace, he will likely be seropositive for life, probably will develop AIDS, and could be disabled for a long period of time before dying.[37] There will be tremendous costs associated with these accidents, both in economic and emotional terms.[38] These are the costs that society must be prepared to shift from the injured party to other pockets.

The costs of accidents have traditionally been shifted from the injured to other "deep pockets" by insurance and the tort law.[39] But for a variety of reasons, tort law will not provide much compensation to health workers infected with HIV at the workplace.[40]

The relative inapplicability of tort doctrine to HIV transmission accidents does not foreclose the possibility of compensation for the injured worker. In fact, workplace injuries are typically compensated by an administrative approach called "workers' compensation" in most jurisdictions.[41] Workers' compensation also has drawbacks as a means of shifting the cost of occupational HIV infection. One big drawback of workers' compensation is that the benefits are inadequate, especially in occupational disease cases.[42] A further problem with death benefits, and indeed with all workers' compensation benefits, is that they are tied to the amount the person is earning at the time of injury. This will affect student nurses and physician members of the house staff, who could expect higher incomes after completion of training. State legislatures can, however, increase compensation levels and create presumptions to overcome some of these problems.

Since workers' compensation is often inadequate, HIV infection also creates a need for health, disability, and life insurance. While more than 75 percent of Americans have some form of health insurance, and many have life insurance, far fewer have disability insurance.[43] Most health care workers would not necessarily be covered for all the economic repercussions of an HIV infection. Hospitals could, however, broaden the coverage they offer as terms of employment, and provide health, disability, and life insurance for employees as a benefit. This would seem a prudent step for hospitals to take in the near future.

In return for providing low-cost insurance for health workers, insurers might require some form of testing for HIV antibody. They would fear, as might hospitals, that HIV seropositive individuals would seek health care employment as a result of attractive insurance policies available to workers. Thus, to qualify for an insurance plan, health care workers might first have to submit to testing. Current employees who tested positive would be removed from work that could infect patients but would suffer no loss of salary or benefits. The employees who tested negative would qualify for insurance, as would any new employees who tested negative. Prospective employees who tested positive would not be given jobs that have a demonstrated risk of infecting others. Those who refuse to test would not be subject to job discrimination, but would not qualify for special insurance benefits.

This kind of testing will probably be required to develop a workable insurance scheme for defraying the costs of occupational HIV infection. A plan along these lines seems appropriate if we are to shift effectively the costs of HIV occupational accident. Moreover, it is essential to a system that respects the negative freedom of physicians without diluting the duty to treat, and without diminishing the equal concern and respect owed every patient. It acknowledges the limits of physician altruism, as we must in the liberal state.

Of course, consideration of means of compensating physicians who contract HIV at the workplace must be part of efforts to reduce the risk of such transmission of the virus. Just doctoring requires that every effort be made to develop new means for avoiding transmission, and for ensuring that existing guidelines are careful followed.[44] Prevention is a much better path than compensation for obvious reasons.

However, there will be accidents that cannot be avoided by universal precautions, and thus compensation policies cannot be ignored.[45]

Now some health care workers might argue that in addition to universal precautions, hospitals and health care workers should be allowed to test patients for HIV antibody, whether or not the patient requests testing.[46] They argue that they would be able to protect themselves better if they knew the HIV status of every patient. While just doctoring allows physicians to consider means for maintaining their own negative freedom, it does so only if those means do not diminish the goal and principle of equal respect and concern for each patient. Thus any consideration of mandatory testing requires that physicians look broadly at the potential impact of such testing on patients. Once again, just doctoring requires analysis of concepts and issues at some distance from the doctor-patient relationship.

Screening for HIV Infection

One of the great advances in the fight against HIV has been the development of low-cost and accurate tests for the presence of antibodies that the body makes once it is infected with HIV. These tests can tell us whether asymptomatic individuals are infected with the virus.[47]

Although quite accurate, the test is not problem free. Diagnostic tests are evaluated according to their specificity and sensitivity. Sensitivity is usually not a large concern with HIV tests; however, specificity is very important. Specificity refers to the probability that the test will be negative, given that the disease state is absent. A test lacking in specificity has a high false positive rate. Although the point is somewhat complicated, it is important also to discuss the positive predictive value. This is the probability that a disease is present, given that the test is positive. Positive predictive value incorporates issues of specificity, as well as prevalence of a disease state. A specific test can have poor positive predictive value in a population in which the disease is not prevalent.[48]

The tests for HIV have increasingly good specificity. However, the positive predictive value for the test is quite low in low-risk populations because the prevalence of the disease is so low.[49] This means that any mass screening will be troubled by numerous false positive test results: many people who are not infected with the virus will test positive. Given that most of us are now familiar with the biological and social repercussions of infection with HIV, it is easy to see that significant numbers of false positive results are an intolerable prospect. For this reason alone, mass testing of those admitted to hospitals is a bad idea.

But what if the tests for HIV continue to improve and the false positive rate continues to drop? And what if prevalence continues to increase, especially in certain emergency rooms,[50] and at specific hospitals,[51] as it has. And what if the estimates of the risk posed by occupational transmission of HIV continue to increase, as they have over the last four years? Is it then reasonable to argue that health care workers and institutions should be able to test all patients, regardless of whether they would freely consent to testing? Can the negative freedom of physicians (the right to take precautions when a patient is possibly infected) provide a foundation for mandatory testing? This is an issue that medical ethics as just doctoring must address.[52]

Certainly there are many health care workers who believe that mandatory testing is reasonable and appropriate. In Great Britain, for example, many feel that requiring consent for HIV testing is not a desirable social imperative.[53] In this country there also appears to be a great deal of testing, at least in some states, of individuals without their consent.[54] Many doctors, it seems, would argue that we often perform a battery of tests on individual patients without seeking their specific consent to the testing. Why is HIV any different, they ask, than a simple CBC (complete blood count)?[55]

The simple answer has been that the risks of a false positive result outweigh the benefits to the person who is tested. In the past we had very few good interventions for treating HIV infection or AIDS. A false positive result would lead to great and unnecessary personal suffering for a patient. Therefore, a risk-benefit calculus led to the conclusion that mandatory testing could not be justified. In light of this, the World Health Organization, the Centers for Disease Control, the American Medical Association, the American Hospital Association, and the Presidential Commission on the HIV Epidemic have all argued against mandatory testing for patients.[56]

But the assumptions underlying the risk-benefit analysis are changing. Consider that there are now more and more pharmacological agents that look as though they may prove to be useful in the therapy for HIV infection.[57] For instance, the drug AZT is recommended as therapy for those who are HIV seropositive but who do not yet have AIDS given certain other conditions, such as low T4 lymphocyte cell subsets. More experimental drugs are coming down the line. Thus it may be beneficial to treat HIV infection, and thus beneficial to test and treat people early.

In addition, assume that concerns continue to grow about the safety of those who must, as part of their work, come into close contact with individuals who are infected with HIV. These concerns could lead to mandatory testing. Indeed, they have begun to do so. In Missouri, for instance, a new AIDS statute requires HIV testing for all individuals who enter a correctional institution, presumably at least in part to protect correction officers.[58] One should expect that similar statutes will be passed in other states, and the slippery slope leads from prisons to hospitals.

In view of these developments, should health care workers encourage mandatory testing of hospitalized patients? From my viewpoint of medical ethics, it seems the analysis must still center on the encumbrance on the patient represented by such testing. Physicians have negative freedom as well, but just doctoring requires that it must be weighed relatively less than the negative freedom of patients. The altruism that makes health care a sphere of ethical activity requires that the patient come first. This does not mean the physician must totally disregard her own welfare, but it does mean that her autonomy is of less concern in the calculus. Thus while we would grant that knowing the HIV status of a patient might afford marginally greater protection for the health care worker, we must weigh and assess the burden of the test results on the patient.

These burdens can be insurmountable. Consider the following case related by Dr. Renslow Sherer:

In 1985, I was the primary physician for a young man whose life was ruined by the inappropriate disclosure of a positive human immunodeficiency virus (HIV)—antibody test. A physician ordered the test without consent and notified the local health department of the positive result. The health department notified the individual's employer and he was promptly fired. These events became common knowledge at his workplace and in his rural Midwestern town and he was shunned. His landlord asked him to move. Ten days after testing, the life he had known for the past ten years was permanently ruined and he left town. With the loss of his job came the loss of health insurance and insurability; he has been unable to obtain health or life insurance since then.

In this case, no purpose was served by obtaining the HIV-antibody test. The patient had been diagnosed with acquired immunodeficiency syndrome (AIDS)-related complex which has a 95 percent correlation with HIV infection six months earlier at Cook County Hospital. He was aware of his diagnosis and its implications. He had been following safe sex guidelines for the preceding 18 months and had never donated blood or semen.[59]

This passage makes clear the potential devastation of an HIV test. Let us look at the effects in some more detail. First, it is obvious that to be known as an HIV carrier is often to be stigmatized. Since many people are inordinately fearful of infection with HIV, their knowledge of one's status can lead to unreasonable reactions. The patient easily may become isolated from friends and face social exclusion. This can and does lead to depression and increased rates of suicide among individuals who are HIV seropositive.[60]

Second, the dissemination of the information can cause the loss of essential insurance policies. Most insurance companies want to reduce their expenses from AIDS-related claims. Therefore, they are unwilling to write health policies for individuals who are HIV seropositive. In addition, there are constraints on the availability of life insurance for people who are HIV seropositive.[61] Thus an individual who tests positive through mandatory screening at a hospital may find that he loses both life and health insurance, as did the patient described by Sherzer. Those who are HIV seropositive may also face discrimination in their workplace. There have been many examples of people who have been harassed by coworkers, or even fired by employers, because their status as HIV carriers became common knowledge.[62] Carriers may also face housing discrimination.

These problems tend to pale, however, compared to the threat of quarantine. There appears to be both public and academic support for coercive public health intervention for those who are HIV seropositive. Some have now recommended quarantine as a solution for "recalcitrant" individuals who carry HIV.[63] While these proposals concern only those people who repeatedly endanger others through sexual contact or through sharing needles for intravenous drug abuse, there are no bright line definitions for the term "recalcitrant." Thus proposals regarding limited quarantine would soon lead to broader use.

Of course, quarantine, discrimination in housing and at the workplace, and even, to a certain extent, loss of availability of insurance are unacceptable burdens on the liberty interest of individuals who are HIV seropositive. In the liberal state, which values the concept of pluralism and the ability of each citizen to set his or her own agenda within the sphere of negative freedom, such encumbrances are intolerable. Indeed, in our country, we have a series of constitutional protections designed to prohibit such encumbrances.[64] The Fourth Amendment of the United States Constitution explicitly protects citizens from unreasonable searches and seizures. This seems to include searches and seizures of one's body and thus, presumably, laboratory testing.[65] In other words, our liberal Constitution prohibits mandatory testing against an individual's will. Given that just doctoring must conform with the public morality of the liberal state, it must be unethical for physicians to recommend mandatory testing. Even more important, since just doctoring involves an altruistic commitment to the patient's best interest, and since the individual's best interests may very well not be served by mandatory testing, there seems to be no basis within medical ethics for anything but opposition to mandatory testing of patients.

One may counter that the best interests of the patient might be met by early treatment of HIV infection, and that this early treatment can occur only if we know the patient's HIV status. Of course, the rational approach to accomplishing this goal is not mandatory testing. It is, rather, careful education of the patient about the options available for therapy. Once the physician explains the benefit of early treatment (and thus the benefit of testing) to the patient, and the patient refuses, then the liberal state is served only by respecting the patient's decision. In our discussion of informed consent, we concluded that the informed patient should be able to make decisions regarding medical therapy. An individual who wants therapy for an HIV infection and who is well educated about the benefits of this therapy can undergo voluntary HIV testing. Those who do not wish to know their HIV status because they are unconvinced of the efficacy of therapy, or because they fear the potential constraints on their freedom should others acquire knowledge of their HIV status, should be able to refuse testing. Medical ethics as just doctoring supports this notion and must therefore be opposed to mandatory testing.

One further argument in favor of mandatory testing is that many of the problems associated with testing can be obviated if test results are kept strictly confidential. Thus no one loses insurance or faces discrimination if their test results are positive. The problem with this is that no one can be assured that results will be kept strictly confidential. Moreover, physicians must be concerned that even though they promise patients that the test results will be kept confidential, the state might decide otherwise. Indeed, it is conceivable that a majority might some day support the publication of such results in a liberal state. We must, as just doctors, be concerned for the welfare of the minority, especially when this minority consists of all individuals who are HIV seropositive. Therefore, we must be aware that even though confidentiality appears to be assured, there are no airtight guarantees. Confidentiality of results alone does not provide grounds for mandatory testing.

Many of these same arguments apply to converse testing proposals, that is, proposals that all physicians should be screened for HIV. While the chances of an HIV infected health care worker transmitting the virus appears to be low,[66] one such case has been reported by the CDC.[67] Given patients' informed consent rights discussed in the previous chapter, one could make an argument that the liberal state could require testing, especially of physicians involved in serious invasive procedures.[68]

Medical ethics as just doctoring does not create an ethical duty to mandate screening. For many of the same reasons cited above regarding testing of patients, mass screening of health care workers appears inappropriate. Physicians retain their liberty rights, and without clear and rather substantive benefit to the patient, these should not be forfeited. Individual physicians may choose to be tested, especially if they are at high risk, and are often involved in potential percutaneous transfer of blood products with patients. They may also choose to disclose the results to patients. But, until there is evidence that there is some measurable risk to patients, any form of screening of physicians and nurses is inappropriate. Of course, this does not mean there is symmetry in the justifications for patient versus health care worker screening. Indeed, the altruistic commitment of physicians to patients may mean that a certain level of risk would justify screening for physicians, but not for patients.

These are issues all health care workers must begin to debate, and for which they must help develop policies. Just doctoring requires public policy development by health care workers and the public. Medical ethics in the liberal state must consider and elaborate propositions on various issues that were previously considered matters for courts or for governments. Health policy issues are an important part of medical ethics. Thus it is appropriate for physicians to consider the effects of discrimination on their patients. They should understand that their concern for patient welfare must extend beyond the disease process and into social implications of disease. Moreover, medical care, especially under the conditions of an epidemic, butts up against public health issues. Here again medical ethics moves beyond the individual relationship between doctor and patient and addresses social and political issues. For instance, consider the question of whether the physician has a duty to warn individuals who may be put at risk by contact with the physician's HIV seropositive patient.

Duty to Warn and the Public's Health

Public health is an enterprise based on equality. It considers the individual's negative freedom far less than it does the broader concern of how to procure the best possible public hygiene. It addresses the health needs of citizens as a group. For example, public health officials curb the negative freedom of individuals to dispose of wastes as they see fit in order to ensure that the danger posed by those wastes does not fall selectively on one group of people, that is, those living near the chosen dump. The public health requires use of the police power of the state to protect innocent parties. Public health officials also attempt to minimize public health problems overall through the police power of the state. For instance, they attempt to decrease use of fluorocarbons in order to halt the destruction of the ozone layer, a public health problem that affects all the members of a society.

One can imagine several ways in which public health officials might employ the power of the state to ensure that the burden of the HIV epidemic does not fall selectively or unfairly on some individuals, or to curb the overall spread of the epidemic. Consider, for instance, ways to slow the transmission of the HIV. One approach, long used by public officials, would be to undertake contact tracing.

Contact tracing is the practice of identifying individuals exposed to communicable diseases.[69] It can mean assistance for voluntary efforts to trace one's contacts; it can also mean aggressive tracing of infections through health department interviews.[70] The public health officials identify the contacts and warn them that they may have been exposed to the virus. These individuals can then choose whether or not to be tested to ensure that they are not also silently spreading the disease.

While contact tracing has always relied on voluntary disclosure and respect for confidentiality, some argue that AIDS hysteria might create pressures to change the traditional public health approach. They fear that infected patients who refuse to disclose contacts might be subject to penalties and their identity as HIV carriers disclosed. Moreover, they fear that since contact tracing involves public health authorities, it might open the door to further use of the police power of the state and ultimately to quarantine. Thus civil rights organizations and the gay community are profoundly opposed to systematic, aggressive contact tracing by public health authorities.[71]

Civil libertarians also argue that the efficacy of contact tracing is unknown. While contact tracing appears to have worked well and cost-effectively in a small trial in South Carolina, there are reasons to believe this will not be the case elsewhere.[72] Given the long latency between infection with HIV and the onset of symptoms, the difficulties in identifying contacts in urban populations, and the previous failures of contact tracing to curtail sexually transmitted diseases, such as Hepatitis B, which are not readily treated with antibiotics, it appears that the benefits of contact tracing are questionable.[73] Given the potential costs to society of a policy that may move us toward quarantine, it seems that medical ethics as just doctoring would take a stance against this kind of public health measure.

Yet the goal of contact tracing is undeniably good, that being to curtail the spread of the virus. In the pursuit of contacts of HIV infected patients, public health authorities demonstrate their concern and respect for those who have been put at risk—a concern the carrier may not have shown. Just doctoring shows regard for seropositive patients by pointing out that they may be subject to discrimination through contact tracing policies. These tensions come about frequently in the liberal state and must be managed through accommodation and compromise.

Physicians, following principles of just doctoring, should be willing to help bring about the values embodied in policies like contact tracing, yet also provide highest regard for the patient's negative freedom. One way to do this would be to have private physicians warn third-party contacts of HIV seropositive patients rather than employing the state to do so. If physicians were to take on this task, there would be less danger that state power could be used against individual patients who are HIV seropositive, which would help protect the patient's right to privacy. Since the "patient comes first," it makes sense that physicians who are "just doctors" would be willing to warn third parties as an alternative to contact tracing by the state. However, this proposition requires that just doctoring be accommodated with existing laws about doctor-patient confidentiality.

The law regarding confidentiality is quite complicated. The common law did not recognize that doctor-patient communications were privileged.[74] Rather, the confidentiality of these communications was created by state legislatures.[75] By 1983, all but two states had enacted statutes providing some kind of protection for medical records and communications; this protection was referred to as the doctor-patient privilege. These statutes are usually written with a number of exceptions to the privilege for issues such as reportable venereal diseases, battered children, and workers' compensation claims.[76] In some states, courts have argued that these "public policy" limitations create an exception that allows warnings for innocent third parties,[77] although physicians can be held liable for groundless breaches of confidentiality.[78]

With regard to contagious diseases, courts have tended to find a general duty to warn on the part of health care professionals.[79] This common law duty to warn in contagious disease cases is buttressed in some states by statutory public health laws that require warnings for contacts of contagious individuals. It would appear, then, that common law and statutory law generally support confidentiality and certainly frown on groundless breaches of confidentiality, but they do require warnings for innocent third parties who may be endangered by the contagious disease of a patient.

The legal duty of physicians to warn those endangered by their patients has expanded generally as a result of cases concerning psychiatric patients, the most important of which is *Tarasoff* v. *Board of Regents of the University of California*, in which the California Supreme Court found that a psychotherapist had a duty to warn a third person whom his patient had threatened to kill.[80] *Tarasoff* has had a tremendous impact on the practice of psychiatry as well as the law governing it. The California court premised the duty to warn on a finding that violent behavior toward a particular individual was foreseeable. The emphasis on foreseeability has diminished as courts have found a general duty to warn, even when the victim is a stranger to the patient.

The importance of *Tarasoff* and its progeny cases in determining whether a health care worker has a duty to warn contacts of HIV seropositive patients cannot be understated. Using an analysis similar to that used in several post-*Tarasoff* cases, a court could rule that health care workers are liable for failure to warn not only known contacts of seropositive patients, but any possible contacts. Thus *Tarasoff* and the common law it has engendered create a potentially very broad duty to warn in HIV cases.

At the present, however, the common law principles that emphasize warning are constrained by statutory law regarding the confidentiality of HIV antibody status. The states in which the prevalence of HIV seropositivity is greatest have also been the states that have recognized the importance of confidentiality.[81] In the mid-1980s, these states tended to buttress the privacy of HIV antibody testing results with statutory requirements concerning confidentiality. In California, any disclosure of a patient's HIV antibody test results to a third party has been punishable by imprisonment for up to a year or a fine up to $10,000.[82] In Massachusetts, the state law is clear that no health care worker can disclose the results of the antibody test without the written consent of the person tested.[83] Statutory requirements for confidentiality of HIV test results in most states with large numbers of AIDS cases would thus appear to insulate health care workers from a duty to warn.

Nevertheless, many of these states' legislatures are now considering amending their blanket confidentiality provisions to allow individual physicians to warn. The Association of State and Territorial Health Officials is considering the same kind of exception to its endorsement of confidentiality of HIV test results.[84] California has already amended its strict confidentiality provisions to allow a physician to inform the spouse of an HIV-infected individual. The New York State legislature has passed a bill that allows physicians to warn third-party contacts and also allows doctors to gain the assistance of trained public health counselors.

It would seem that medical ethics as just doctoring would endorse third-party warnings by physicians as an alternative to contact tracing. The duty to warn allows the physician to consider the exigencies of the situation with the particular patient. Moreover, the physician can weigh the potential restrictions on the patient created by breaking confidentiality against the risk to the innocent third party. Perhaps more important, a physician warning a third party forestalls the need for involvement of the state, and the potential for abuse of civil liberties that state involvement may entail. In short, just doctoring requires that physicians play a public health role if that role serves the goals of the liberal state better than does any alternative. In this way, physicians can accomplish the good of protecting innocent third parties without threatening patients' civil rights.

In summary, if medical ethics is to define appropriate public health responses to combat the spread of HIV, physicians must think broadly about their duties to patients and the relations of those duties to other legal and policy matters. Of course, once we begin to consider the relation of the public's health to the principles of just doctoring, we must discuss the issue of public support of initiatives that will bring about better health.

Public Expenditure on AIDS Treatment

As we discussed in the first chapter, the liberal state tends to be based on a market distribution of goods, as the market allows each individual to decide how to use his or her resources. This freedom of choice will in theory bring about the greatest possible equality of concern and respect for the individual members of society. However, the liberal allows modification of the market in order to overcome the inequalities that develop in any real market economy. If necessary, the liberal will accept a broad welfare state if the market proves to be too inequitable. Public health expenditures are examples of this kind of equality-promoting modification.

Again we return to AIDS, and to the patient I discussed at the beginning of this chapter. The patient was impoverished, having spent most of her money on illicit drugs. She was also HIV seropositive. She was thus a candidate for several types of intervention. First, we would want to begin to measure certain subsets of her T lymphocytes in the blood. We could also measure levels of $beta_2$-microglobulin and p24 antigens in order to predict the course of the disease. These tests would also tell us when to initiate therapy.

Therapy for HIV infection is in the early stages of development, but there do appear to be some important interventions. One is AZT, a drug that has been shown to stabilize immunological status in those infected with HIV. The data on zidovudine is so encouraging that the federal government now recommends treatment with this medication for all individuals infected with HIV who meet certain clinical criteria. Other drugs, for example, imuthiol, are now undergoing trials. We are also trying to treat some of the opportunistic infections associated with AIDS, such as pneumocystis carinii pneumonia (PCP), with early intervention and prophylaxis. All of these therapies might be indicated for my patient.

Yet she has no money to purchase them, and they are expensive. Therapy to treat the HIV state (antiretroviral therapy) might cost up to eight thousand dollars per year. Physician visits and serological tests could amount to over five hundred dollars. Prophylaxis against PCP would be another two thousand dollars per year. Thus the costs of early intervention across the board might range between two and eight billion dollars per year for the United States alone.[85] My patient clearly could not have afforded these potentially valuable interventions.

Since health care is a sphere of ethical activity within the liberal state, and since it provides support for the liberal state's commitment to equal concern and respect, I suggest that just doctoring requires public expenditures for the treatment of patients who are penurious. While recognizing that this will decrease the negative freedom of those who will have to pay more taxes, physicians arguably should support these expenditures in light of their commitment to altruistic caring. Denial of treatment because of inability to pay offends any sense of justice or morality that issues from the notion of medical ethics I have described.

Of course, the liberal state is often unwilling to circumscribe further the negative freedom of its citizens in order to fund more public programs. Some would argue that "just doctors" must realize that there are other goods in society that need funding besides medical care. They would assert that it is naive of doctors to expect society to bankroll physicians' sense of justice. There must be some limits on care, in other words, and just doctoring should address these limits. Thus it is appropriate for us now to leave AIDS and to turn to the issue of limits on care and just doctoring.

It is also appropriate at this point to reemphasize the fact that much of my discussion in these chapters is not descriptive but prescriptive. I do not believe that many, let alone all, physicians conceive of medical ethics as just doctoring, at least in the way I define it. My description of just doctoring is meant as an argument to physicians and other interested parties. It is my conception of the best structure for medical ethics.

8

Limits on Care

In the last chapter, we began to address the question of the physician's ethical duties with regard to limits on patient care. This issue is well within the ambit of medical ethics, because just doctoring considers not only the particular patient's care but also the institutional structure in which that care is given. In so doing, just doctoring does not dilute the relation between doctor and patient; rather it requires physicians to engage in ethical analysis of political and economic issues that affect the care of the individual patient. Just doctoring does not decrease the ethical commitment to the patient, but it does increase the scope of considerations for medical ethics. This aspect of just doctoring distinguishes it from traditional medical ethics, as we discussed in chapter 4. In just doctoring, the blinders on institutional arrangements are removed.[1]

Consider again the case of an HIV carrier who also abuses drugs. I had a patient recently who was HIV infected and who had been actively "shooting up" at the time of his hospitalization. He became genuinely concerned about his situation, and while we treated his infection, he voluntarily tapered himself off the methadone therapy we had initiated. He wanted to be rid of drugs, to "straighten himself out."

He was worried, however, that he would not be able to stay away from cocaine and heroin if he went back to his home after discharge. Therefore, he asked if we could not arrange some alternative housing as well as support through addiction services. He had no money, and so we considered publicly available programs. The social worker assigned to our team put together a list of options. Unfortunately, the upshot was that he would have a long wait before he could get into a group home, and before he could receive adequate counseling and addiction treatment. When he was discharged, his only option was to return home to the poisonous milieu from which he had fled. He was soon abusing drugs again.

Just doctoring requires that physicians consider the institutional context in which they provide care. The ethics of medicine does not begin and end at the doors of the hospital. The commitment to the patient, based on the liberal value of equality, requires that we do everything possible for this patient's health in terms of antibiotics and wound care. It also requires that we make every effort to place him in a group home where he can get support and counseling that would help him "stay straight."

As a just doctor, I might also be required to address the fact that there are no outpatient treatment options available for my patient. Do they not exist? Are there so few because the city has little money? Is the problem simply that my hospital's social workers are not aware of options for outpatient care? Just doctoring cannot require me to invite this gentleman to come and stay with my family while he waits for a treatment bed. But it does require that I try to understand the political context of the problem and make some effort to address it.

Consider another example. I have had patients in the past who were intravenous drug users who injected filthy materials into their veins. These materials tend to lodge on the heart valves and cause infections, destroying the valves. For one patient, we replaced his own valve with an artificial one. Later the same month, the patient was readmitted with the same problem, having infected the artificial valve. Leaving aside the tort and antidiscrimination issues contained in such a policy, suppose that my hospital had instituted a policy that would not allow second operations for drug abusers who infected an artificial heart valve by using drugs. What does medical ethics demand of me in such a case?

As a physician committed to a patient's welfare, I would do everything medically possible for the patient during his hospitalization. I would even develop a set of reasons why the "no surgery" policy should not apply to this particular patient. No matter what happened in the end, however, I would, as a just doctor, also try to address the issues that gave rise to the policy. Separate from my care for the individual patient, I would have a duty to understand the origins of such a policy, and its rationale. If I found them unacceptable, I would try to have the policy changed. This would not supersede my advocacy for my patient. Rather, it is a natural extension of my duty to that patient.

Moreover, I am not surprised by limits on care, since I practice medicine in a liberal state. I realize that there must be limits on the resources that we as a society put into health care. This is another aspect of just doctoring that distinguishes it from traditional medical ethics. Traditional medical ethics required simply that the doctor do everything possible for the patient, whatever the cost. We can no longer afford such an attitude. We must ration scarce medical resources.

The issue of rationing has remained generally submerged in discussions of medical care in this country. We have not wanted to face it, perhaps because it is antithetical to the constant growth in health care resources upon which the industry has relied, perhaps because Americans have been unwilling to accept the notion that access to health care must be limited. In any case, just doctoring demands explicit discussion of rationing.

These are the issues to which I now turn. Perhaps the best way to address them is to review the reasons why limits on care are much more apparent in this country now than they were twenty years ago. We will also contrast our American experience with those of other liberal states, especially Canada and Great Britain. We will then outline different types of limits on care and discuss the ethical approach to each of them in the liberal state.

The Reasons for Limits: Cost Control

In chapters 3 and 4 we reviewed in some detail the historical development of health care institutions. We discussed the peculiar relationships between doctors, hospitals, and third-party insurers, and how those relationships removed physician and patient decision making from the market. I asserted that these arrangements, and the insulation of medical care from the liberal market, were doomed. In part, this change gave rise to my theory of just doctoring. In the following two chapters, as we begin to explore the ethics of just doctoring vis-à-vis the institutions of medical care, we will at times highlight the arguments with more technical discussions of economic

arrangements, thereby supplementing some of the points of chapters 3
and 4. In particular, to understand rationing of medical care, it is
necessary to understand the social costs of such care.

The past three decades have witnessed huge increases in our national health expenditures.[2] These increases in health care costs have in
turn led to huge increases in federal outlays for Medicare and Medicaid. For example, in 1967 the total federal expenditures for Medicare
were $4.5 billion.[3] In 1975, the figure was $15.6 billion, and by 1982
it had increased to $50.9 billion. In fiscal year 1987, Medicare pro-
vided health insurance coverage for 31 million Americans at a cost of
$80 billion, while Medicaid covered 28 million poor Americans and
the total cost to the federal government was $27.4 billion. Overall, by
1987, health care consumed 11.5 percent of the Gross National Product in the United States, compared with 8.6 percent in Canada and
even less in Britain.[4]

Many have attributed the increases in health care costs, which have
outstripped general inflation consistently over the past two decades, to
the economic arrangements that exist in American medical care. They
argue that the physician controls both supply and demand of health
care goods. As we discussed in chapter 4, this leads to a peculiar set
of economic and ethical relationships, in which the physician consistently faces moral hazards.[5] The organization of hospitals compounds
the risk. Indeed, M. Pauly and T. Redisch have characterized the nonprofit hospital as a physicians' cooperative that assures physician economic prerogatives.[6] Since the patient is not a fully informed consumer of health care goods, she can do little to constrain health care
costs. Relying until recently on federal insurance programs and private
commercial insurers that reimburse at the "usual and customary fee"
level, hospitals have very little incentive to control physician behavior.
Thus only the deep pockets, the commercial insurers, and the state and
federal governments have any incentive to constrain health care costs.
Using empirical methods, Joseph Newhouse suggests that the insurance arrangements underlying medical care in this country account for
a significant proportion of the increase in health costs.[7]

Others have identified a number of additional contributors to the
rise in hospital costs. One corollary to the moral hazard theory concerns the number of hospital beds. Roemer's law, as it is known, holds
that physicians will fill all available beds in a given geographic area.[8]
They can do so because they control supply and demand.

The introduction of new technology is perhaps an even more important reason for the increase in health care costs. Through acquisition of new technology, and by using the new technology to supplement rather than replace old technology, physicians are able to create demand (and to fill hospital beds).[9] While the portion of the increase in health care costs that can be attributed to new technology is debatable, there can be little doubt that it is substantial.[10] New techniques and procedures continue to be integrated into medical practice with little oversight, at least until recently.[11]

All these contributors to the increase in health care costs are interrelated. Consider the example of a friend's father who was recently admitted to our hospital. He had had some vague chest pressure, and his doctor thought it might be angina pain. A resting electrocardiogram was not helpful in making the diagnosis, and so an exercise tolerance test, involving electrocardiography while the patient exercises, was employed. The test was equivocal, so the doctor chose another similar exercise test, only this time the patient was injected with thallium, to enable the doctors to see any defects in the blood flow of the heart.

The exercise test with thallium was positive for ischemia, or decreased blood flow to the heart, and so the patient was referred for cardiac catheterization. Catheterization would provide us with information about specific blockages in the coronary arteries that were causing the ischemia. The patient's catheterization revealed some disease in two vessels of the heart. His doctors recommended angioplasty, or balloon dilation of the blocked vessels. He assented. The procedure went well, but on the first day after the procedure, he developed chest pain, with electrocardiographic changes. The patient's doctors told him he would have to undergo coronary artery bypass grafting surgery. He assented, did well in the operation, and is now free of pain.

This patient was a very well educated man. In addition, his son, also very intelligent, was involved. Moreover, his son is a rising star in the litigation department of a local law firm, a position which not only garners some attention (if not respect) around the hospital, but which also trained him to ask the right questions of experts. Thus the patient and his family were as capable of being as informed as any patient can be. Nonetheless, they were almost completely dependent on the recommendations of their physicians, as most of us would be.

The physicians were not a greedy and calculating lot. Each decision they made was reasonable, each step correct. However, in the end the patient's insurer ended up with a lot of medical bills, based largely on numerous tests that in hindsight may have been unnecessary. The point is not that hindsight is always 20/20, but that physicians will use all available technology in their decision-making process, and it is not typically a process in which the decision makers concern themselves with costs. In this manner, the American health care system's total costs have grown enormously.

Of course, others might argue that lawyers and judges are at fault for at least some of the costs of health care because fears of litigation induce physicians to do needless tests. So-called defensive medicine does not increase the quality of care, but it does decrease the possibility of suit. The influence of defensive medicine is, however, difficult to assess (see chapter 6); it may be quite great or quite small. While it is a powerful emotional argument for most physicians, they also recognize that it is very difficult to identify specific acts of defensive medicine, except, perhaps, emergency room X-rays.[12] Moreover, recent investigations suggest that the threat of malpractice litigation is a bona fide deterrent of bad medical practice, and this presumably induces higher quality care. Therefore, we might be willing to accept some defensive medicine in return for better quality care.

No matter what the cause, in the mid- to late-1970s, both state and federal governments began to address the problem of rising health care costs and unnecessary care. One should expect little else from the liberal state. Both traditional and modern liberals recognize that the liberal state has limits. Modern liberalism, as interpreted by Rawls, guarantees certain fundamental or primary goods. These could include, for instance, housing, health care, and education. However, guarantees of primary goods do not mean that everyone receives equal amounts of those goods: the government does not guarantee that everyone will receive an education at Princeton, or a four bedroom house with a yard.

The same is true for health. While there is general agreement in the liberal state that access to basic health care should not depend on one's ability to pay, this does not mean that limitless resources can be designated for the health care industry or that every individual can expect to receive equal quantities of care. The liberal guarantee of equal concern and respect for all requires that some level of health care be available to all. It does not, however, preclude rationing health care. Nor does it preclude efforts to control costs that bring about some rationing.

This is not, of course, to say that all liberal states will pursue the same course. Some, for instance Canada and Great Britain, envision health care as primary to individual welfare, and thus make greater efforts than the United States to provide a decent minimum of health care for all.[13] Nor does this mean that these countries spend more; rather, they commit resources to less costly, perhaps more effective, care options. These approaches must be of interest to a just doctor in any liberal state, but for now let us review the American experience.

Initial American state legislative efforts to control costs emphasized rate regulation and certificate of need rules.[14] The latter policy initiative was meant to decrease the total number of hospital beds, and also to reduce and control use of technology such as CT scanners. The former, rate regulation, was intended to force hospitals to develop cost-saving measures by capping their reimbursement levels.

Since these initiatives were only partially successful, after 1980, the Reagan administration developed a two-prong cost control strategy: increasing competition in the health care market and prospective payment for Medicare. Because the Reagan administration was philosophically committed to market solutions for problems of scarce resources, the competitive strategy was especially congenial.[15] While the paradigm of nonprofit hospitals had long dominated medical care, in the late 1970s and early 1980s for-profit institutions were steadily increasing their share of the market.[16] The federal government encouraged the profit motive, and also encouraged innovations in health care insurance, especially health maintenance organizations (HMOs) and preferred provider organizations (PPOs).[17] Advocates argued that these new organizational forms would provide administrators with incentives to control providers' clinical decision making. They would also provide the informed consumer with more choice in health insurance.[18] The federal courts provided help as well.[19] The new strategy appears to have developed a competitive outlook among health care administrators and certainly has accelerated the changes in the health care industry that we noted in chapter 4.[20]

One new policy initiative should be discussed in more detail, as it helps reveal the nature of rationing in our health care system. In 1983 the administration endorsed a prospective payment plan for Medicare hospital costs. In the past, Medicare had reimbursed hospitals on a usual and customary fee basis. This "open-pocket approach" had fueled the great increase in Medicare outlays in the late 1970s and early 1980s.

Very quietly, Congress enacted a prospective payment system in

Title 6 of the Social Security Amendments of 1983.[21] Since under the new system, hospitals would receive only a predetermined amount of payment for the care of a patient with a particular kind of problem, the amendments created new incentives for hospitals to limit the amount of care provided each hospital day, and to limit the number of hospital days. Prospective payment thus represented a revolutionary change in hospital services reimbursement under Medicare.[22] It appears that the prospective payment system has indeed led to a moderation in the rise in Medicare costs.[23]

Many have questioned the justice of prospective payment systems.[24] They argue that prospective payment is unjust because it can lead to rationing of care, the burden of which falls disproportionately on a few. For example, prospective payment creates incentives for hospitals to move patients out as quickly as possible. This means that patients will be transferred to nursing homes with more expediency, and that patients in nursing homes will be sicker than patients in nursing homes in the past. Those who are sick, but not sick enough to warrant further hospitalization, may receive poorer quality care than they would have received had they stayed in the hospital.[25]

In other words, prospective payment represents rationing.[26] In particular, its cost-cutting measures decrease access to health care for elderly patients. We as a society are unwilling to provide the open-ended care for the elderly that was offered in the "usual and customary fee" financing relationships. This fact must be clearly understood by all who are involved in promulgating similar regulations. While the liberal state is not in theory opposed to rationing access to care, it is opposed to rationing of health care when that rationing fails to provide equal concern and respect for all individuals. Prospective payment means that elderly individuals will have fewer resources committed to their care than will other individuals. This is acceptable to the liberal state so long as the burden falls rather evenly among the elderly. Justice is served so long as there is some equity in rationing measures.

It is of great importance, however, that rationing in programs like prospective payment is not hidden from public view lest the equality and fairness issues also remain concealed. Thus physicians should recognize that cost cutting involves rationing and that concern for patients requires that the cost cutting not fall disproportionately on certain minorities. A primary concern of just doctoring must be that rationing is openly recognized and that any unfairness or inequality it creates must be addressed. For example, prospective payment should be scrutinized closely, to discern whether it unfairly limits care. Since it lacks a "severity of illness" correction factor, it may be that the more severely ill will receive less care than do others—that is, there will be unintended inequality in care. Therefore, medical ethics as just doctoring encourages efforts to bring about a more just system of prospective payment, for example one that takes into account severity of illness.[27]

This viewpoint differs considerably from traditional medical ethics. The ethics of beneficence inherently opposes any cost control in which physicians play a role. Those who support a theory of beneficence argue that patients, not costs, must come first.[28] In other words, since the patient comes first, the physicians cannot involve themselves in efforts to reduce the total cost of health care, especially efforts that affect clinical decision making. This attitude, which we discussed in detail in chapter 4, goes hand-in-hand with the isolation of the physician from considerations of justice and of political and economic issues. It is the attitude, I have argued, that led physicians to promote a system of health care that depended, unrealistically, on unlimited resources.

I believe physicians must put the beneficence model behind them. Medical ethics as just doctoring requires that physicians consider the political context in which care occurs. This includes consideration by physicians of the need to moderate health care costs. Thus physicians must accept prospective payment and other similar regulations. Their ethical duty is not to resist the effort to control costs. Rather, one's duty as a just doctor is to help make those cost controls work in the best possible manner, and also to ensure that cost control is as good and just as possible.[29] One must openly recognize it as rationing, and must help to ensure that the rationing is fair.

Rationing is in essence a social decision to limit resources available to some so that others can benefit. Prospective payment means that the government spends less on medical care for Medicare beneficiaries. Presumably, other social programs will benefit. Nonetheless, we cannot deny that rationing does limit the negative freedom of specific groups of people. As discussed in chapters 5 and 6, one goal of just doctoring has been to constrain the ways in which doctors limit patients' negative freedom. Thus recognition of the relationship of just doctoring to cost control raises some new questions. What role should physicians play in more explicit forms of rationing, apart from cost control measures?

Perhaps even more to the point, should physicians advocate new models of health care delivery that provide a more equal level of care for all citizens? Does a Canadian model featuring fee controls and central financing make better medical ethical sense in a liberal state? For now, we will leave aside this more fundamental question and explore the physician's role in rationing in our own American health care system.

Limits on Care at the End of Life

Until recently in this country, we have not been concerned about the issue of physician-imposed limits on patient care. Discussion has focused instead on the right of the patient to refuse care. Over the past few decades, we have witnessed a steady evolution of society's attitude toward the care of the terminally ill, an evolution that has supported patients' negative freedom. The limits of patient autonomy, the role of the family's substituted judgment, and the prerogatives of physicians have been openly debated. Courts have endorsed the notion that patients' decisions to limit care should be respected. These cases have largely been based on respect for the patient's autonomy, and are consistent with decisions on informed consent.

The details of this evolution are revealing. In the decision *In re Quinlan*, the New Jersey Supreme Court became the first court to allow withdrawal of life support from an incompetent person.[30] Since Karen Quinlan's own views on continued life support were somewhat unclear, the court recognized that a substituted judgment could be made on her behalf by a family member, in this case her father.[31] Many other courts have followed the *Quinlan* precedent with regard to withdrawal of a variety of medical therapies.[32] Most recently this right of refusal has been applied to such "ordinary" supports as feeding tubes.[33] Other courts have reiterated that competent patients should be able to refuse therapy, and that an incompetent patient's previously stated wishes involving life support should be honored.[34]

These court decisions have tended to reassure physicians that the law countenances withdrawal of care, especially after the Massachusetts

Supreme Judicial Court, and several legal academics, clarified the intention of that court's ruling in *Saikewicz*.[35] Again, it is quite clear that the courts in most of these cases were basing their decisions on the patient's autonomy, not on the prerogatives of the medical profession. In other words, concerns about the negative freedom of the patient not reiterations of the positive freedom of the physicians, led the law as integrity to endorse patient desires for limits on care. Thus the liberal state permits self-assumed limits on care for individual citizens. Physicians were able to accept these rulings because, in theory, they were committed above all to the patient.

There are, however, strains within this apparent consensus. Although the judges' opinions in court cases clearly indicated that it was the patient's liberty, not the physician's paternalism, which drove the decisions, it appears that physicians may have misinterpreted the message. The clear intention of the courts notwithstanding, physicians have begun discussing guidelines for terminating such care as ventilators[36] and renal dialysis without emphasizing the importance of the patient's wishes.[37] There are now articles that suggest that physicians need not consult patients about treatment for "no code" status if the physician deems such therapy to lack medical benefit.[38] Some physicians argue that doctors should consider not "offering" patients cardiopulmonary resuscitation and, by implication, other life support measures when such therapy seems to them inappropriate for the patient.[39]

Physicians have also begun to report on their clinical experience with decisions to overrule patients', or their families', wishes for continued "full care." One group of doctors acknowledge that they have issued unofficial orders not to revive dying patients that violate the patients' and families' express wishes.[40] I, myself, have reviewed cases in which a hospital ethics committee limited patients care against their, or their families, stated preference.[41]

The reasoning that underlies decisions by doctors to overrule patients or their families is explicitly ethical and emphasizes the principle of beneficence.[42] Physicians believe, quite reasonably, that patients have no right to demand medical care that is without benefit.[43] They also argue that care should be limited when it is futile.[44] Thus they argue that it is in the patient's best interest to limit care at times, no matter what the patient, or the incompetent patient's family, says. As in informed consent, this line of reasoning demonstrates how beneficence theories of medical ethics can lead to great disrespect for patient autonomy. The "physician knows best" attitude leads to replacement of patient negative freedom with doctor positive freedom.

Courts have now begun to reiterate that decisions about limitations on care are a matter of patient autonomy. As such, they are nontransferable. Thus a New York court has recently required previously made explicit statements reflecting a firm commitment of the patient him- or herself before allowing termination of life support for an incompetent individual.[45] More importantly, the Supreme Court has recently ruled that the federal constitutional privacy rights cannot be used to justify withdrawal of support for a patient in a persistent vegetative state unless the patient's wishes were clearly stated.[46]

These decisions should provide some warning to physicians that limits on care for individual patients are a matter of individual autonomy. Rationing based on an individual physician's judgment that further care has little likelihood of increasing the patient's potential for survival, or of increasing the number of "quality" days the patient will live, is not explicitly linked to a concern for scarce medical resources, and should not be allowed. The law will step forward to restrict physician's prerogative through decisions like *Cruzan*. It is hoped that such decisions will also prompt more health professionals to discuss with patients their desires for "heroic measures" and crystallize these desires in "living wills."[47]

Nonetheless, the concept of limits on care for the elderly should be a part of society's concern about scarce resources.[48] Over the past decade, several studies have shown that persons who are dying tend to consume a disproportionate amount of scarce medical resources.[49] For instance, one study showed that 5.9 percent of Medicare beneficiaries who died in 1978 required nearly 28 percent of all Medicare reimbursement for that year. Moreover, many individuals who receive intensive care in hospitals, that is very expensive care, die soon after their discharge from the hospital.[50] Recent research suggests that increased hospital use does not, in aggregate, lead to greater life expectancy.[51] Thus the provision of hospital care for the elderly is a likely target for those who would try to decrease the overall costs of medical care by rationing resources.

As we discussed, this sort of reallocation is strictly within the bounds of the liberal state. Limiting care for the elderly will create more funds, presumably, for health care for others. Moreover, we might be able to provide better preventive and primary care to a larger group of individuals by limiting intensive care for elderly patients.

Thus limits on care demonstrate equal concern and respect for all individuals in that the resources now used disproportionately by some, the elderly, are redistributed to others.

But, this kind of reallocation raises a serious question: should the individual physician be able to make this kind of decision? Do we as a society want physicians making controversial decisions about terminating care? Should we continue to allow the erosion of the once widely accepted notion that a competent patient or the family of an incompetent patient determines the nature of limits on care?[52]

I believe that the answer must be no, for at least two reasons. First, we must recognize that the doctor-patient relationship does not occur in a world ruled only by ideals of justice and ethics. Rather, it operates in a much more emotionally charged environment. The intellectual and physical weaknesses of human beings, both doctor and patient, are constant companions of medical care.[53]

Second, as we discussed in chapter 5, doctors have not in general demonstrated their willingness to communicate openly with patients. This is especially true in the cases of patients who are critically ill. Several studies have demonstrated how little discussion there is with patients about "life and death" issues.[54] Perhaps some of the most striking findings of my review of an ethics committee's experience were those situations in which the treating physicians had assumed that their patients were incompetent, while the ethics committee found the patients rational and reasonable in their requests for "full care."

All of this indicates that the isolated doctor-patient relationship lacks a basis for decisions about limiting care without patient or family consent. Physicians can too easily fail to understand the irrational impulses that contribute to their actions; they assume they are certain even when they cannot be. Therefore it seems a very bad idea to grant physicians greater authority in decisions to limit care by leaving allocation decisions totally within the doctor-patient relationship.

If not the physician alone, then who else should decide when scarce resources demand cutbacks in care? Rationing of care for the elderly involves issues that all concerned about medical ethics, indeed all citizens of the liberal state, must now address. It seems to me that physician decisions must be made within guidelines developed by a broad social consensus.

Given the gravity of the decisions to limit care, and the importance of this issue to all members of society, it follows that there should be general social participation in the development of a rationing program.

The effort to limit care for the elderly will generate controversies of great importance to the liberal state, because that effort strikes at the heart of liberalism—the trade-offs between negative freedom and equal concern and respect for each citizen. Limits on care will mean that some individuals will be denied care, even care they can afford (and might have saved for) so that others can receive more care in the future. Developing guidelines acceptable to the democratic majority will require broad input, especially from patients and their advocates. The wider the participation, the more readily acceptable will be the results. Therefore, efforts will have to be made to submit such issues to the public at large, or at least to their representatives in legislatures. This process will be critical to the just resolution of rationing.

The development of just guidelines is not an easy task. While an across-the-board prohibition on intensive care for those over the age of eighty, such as that proposed by Daniel Callahan, makes great sense in terms of being simple and just, this alternative may not be efficient.[55] For example, some eighty year olds are still very vigorous, and some people under the age of sixty-five may be quite debilitated. This means that intensive care for debilitated individuals under the age of sixty-five will save fewer days of enjoyable life than would intensive care for abler patients over the age of seventy-five (that is, assuming we can define what is enjoyable about one's life). Thus the physically vigorous elderly person may be someone we want to support with life-extending treatment whereas we would not do so for many younger but debilitated people. All these issues must be studied and debated.[56]

In a book concerned primarily with medical ethics, we must ask again, what should the role of physicians be in the debate on the rationing of care? On the one hand, I have argued that it is foolish to think that physicians will not play a role in cost cutting. Specifically, I have asserted that prospective payment mechanisms will influence physicians' decision making and that it is important for them to be aware of such influences. On the other hand, I have said it is not a good idea to allow physicians to make ad hoc decisions about limits on care for elderly patients, for this gives them far too much authority. These seemingly contradictory arguments are really two sides of the same coin. In issues of rationing—whether we are talking about prospective payment plans or the limitation of care for the elderly—there should be guidelines for the physician to follow.

For the practice of medicine in a prospective payment program, those guidelines are fairly clear-cut. The physician must provide good quality care, despite incentives for discharging patients earlier than might be done under other reimbursement arrangements. To fail to meet the standard of care would be to violate ethical imperatives as well as to open the physician to charges of malpractice.

In the case of the physician's decision to limit care, however, the guidelines are far from clear. A physician using her clinical judgment is on familiar ground when faced with decisions on standard of care for illnesses. She is much less prepared when trying to decide about futility of care, even less so when trying to integrate considerations of quality of life and costs of therapy. Therefore, physicians' prerogatives to ration care (in the form of decisions to limit care for the elderly against their wishes) should be restricted. Just doctors need the support of social consensus before becoming involved in this form of rationing.

While we want to curtail physician decision making in this area, physicians should still be involved in the policy debate. Indeed, physician viewpoints will be particularly valuable in the process of developing a consensus. More to the point, physicians have an ethical duty, as just doctors, to help society develop fair guidelines. Physicians are committed to protecting patients and to maintaining the status of health care as a cooperative sphere within the liberal state. In addition, however, physicians as just doctors realize that there are social limits on the expenditure of funds for health care. Allocation decisions will have an impact on both individual patients and the health care industry. Physicians must therefore address such decisions and help society reach the most just allocation. As L. Churchill suggests, then, physicians should play an active role in the "macro" allocation decisions, and then honestly apply the guidelines developed to particular decisions on rationing.[57] They should also invite the oversight of nonphysicians, perhaps using ethics committees to review a sample of the bedside allocation decisions. Openness and honesty are critical. Just physicians must be willing to separate their role in the larger debate on rationing from the decisions they make for each patient.

What form will the larger debate take? This is very difficult to say with regard to rationing based on age. Discussions in this area have only begun, and there are clearly many problems to be resolved.[58] Rather than try to specify the nature of allocation decisions based on age, it is perhaps easier to move to an area in which we have had more explicit and detailed discussions of rationing. That area is organ transplantation. A brief review of the history of organ transplantation in this country can help define the role of just doctoring in the development of rationing guidelines.

Rationing Organs

The procurement of human organs for transplantation provides perhaps the clearest example of rationing of health care goods in our society. Nowhere else is it as clear that a liberal state must trade off the negative freedom of individuals for the virtue of equal concern and respect. Scarce organs must be allocated according to explicit criteria. Economics and ethics interact very directly.

The transplantation of organs involves very expensive technology. There are indeed serious questions surrounding the cost-effectiveness of transplantation. Although it is an example of truly impressive technology and is potentially quite useful, one must continually ask whether widespread transplantation of organs is something that is good for society. Hence, transplantation is an obvious target for social rationing.

The history of organ transplantation in this country reveals that the government has played a central role in rationing decisions.[59] Most important, the government has financed the transplantation of organs, beginning with kidneys in 1972.[60] The End Stage Renal Disease Program stipulates that kidney transplants are to be paid for by the federal government under Medicare. This financing has led to the underwriting of nearly eight thousand kidney transplantations per year in the United States.[61] In the mid-1980s, when it became clear that the immunosuppressant drug cyclosporine would increase the survival rate of organ transplant patients, the federal government developed further legislation on the financing of organ transplantations. The National Organ Transplantation Act of 1984 formed a task force to deal with policy issues underlying organ procurement and distribution. In addition, it created the Organ Procurement and Transplantation Network.[62] The Act also banned the purchase and sales of human organs. In 1986, Congress again addressed issues of organ transplantation. This legislation established new rules for the procurement of organs. More important, it required that all transplantation programs must meet a certain set of detailed requirements, including rules regarding staffing patterns and qualifications of surgeons, as well as appropriate survival rates for the patients.

These efforts by the federal government to finance and regulate transplantation address the allocation of scarce resources. For kidney transplantation, the federal government has decided to deal with scarcity by underwriting. However, this program costs more than $300 million per year. Since the costs of kidney transplantations have been so great, the government has been reticent about underwriting in a similar fashion the transplantation of hearts, livers, or bone marrow. Instead, the government has opted for a patchwork of volunteer efforts, matched by spotty funding for certain centers and governed by the statutes noted above.[63] In particular, the federal government has been reluctant to underwrite transplantation on a broad basis until it is clear that the therapy is no longer experimental.

This has been particularly true in regard to heart and liver transplantation. Although heart transplantation sparked a great deal of interest in the late 1960s, survival rates were miserable and many centers abandoned the procedure.[64] Several researchers did, however, continue to explore heart transplantation and immunosuppression. In particular, Dr. Norman Shumway at Stanford University Medical Center carefully worked out the technical and medical aspects of the transplantation process. Given his increasing success, and the declaration by certain Blue Cross programs that the transplantation process was no longer experimental, the Department of Health and Human Services decided to undertake a complete study of the efficacy of heart transplantation.[65] Following on this study, the Health Care Financing Administration (HCFA) began to fund a limited number of heart transplantations in certain centers that could demonstrate good patient outcome. In particular, the HCFA would only pay for heart transplantations of disabled individuals, and would only pay for them at cardiac transplantation programs that had documented evidence of twelve or more surviving patients in the previous two years.[66] The same sort of story has evolved for liver transplantation, although its annals have often included more melodramatic episodes.[67]

In summary, decisions involving organ transplantation in this country reveal a certain admirable rationality. The End Stage Renal Disease program was thought, at the time it was instituted, to be a relatively efficient and not very expensive alternative. The government would simply underwrite the cost of transplantation. With hindsight, it is now clear that the renal disease program is inordinately expensive; indeed, it is probably not a program that the federal government would underwrite today. While the government is unwilling to pull the rug out from under those who now expect transplantation (and dialysis), the lesson has been learned. Heart transplantation and liver transplantation will only be underwritten insofar as their efficacy can be demonstrated. The government has very carefully selected criteria for underwriting transplantation. Since the procedure is so expensive and since private financing is unavailable in the majority of cases, the government's tightening of its purse strings limits its availability. The government has thus made an explicit decision to ration heart and liver transplantations until it is clear that these procedures are cost effective. In other words, the liberal state has declared that it will not decrease the negative freedom of individuals through higher taxes so that procedures which may not be cost effective can be completed.

None of this, however, sheds much light on the role of physicians in the allocation of scarce resources like organs. It is notable that in other societies, physicians play a particularly central role in the rationing of renal dialysis and kidney transplantation. For instance, in Great Britain, rationing is undertaken at the level of the general, or primary care, practitioner. British practitioners employ few explicit criteria when making these decisions. William Schwartz and Henry Aaron relate that an English consultant, when queried why he had not recommended renal dialysis for a particular patient, replied, "Everyone over 55 is a bit crumbly." In other words, such patients are not really suitable candidates for therapy.[68] General practitioners in Great Britain receive signals from nephrologists at major regional centers on the guidelines for transplantation, and they translate these into rationalizations for individual patients.[69]

While this is the approach in one liberal state, it does not seem to be the best approach for all liberal states, and is not necessarily a model for just doctoring. The theory of just doctoring involves equal concern and respect for all individuals, as well as consideration of each individual's negative freedom. The use of rationalizations for individual patients, while acceptable in some liberal states, would not be acceptable in ours and would not be acceptable for just doctoring. Open communication as well as altruistic commitment to individual patients is what converts health care into a sphere of moral activity within the liberal state. Thus, just doctors must be honest with their patients about criteria for organ transplantation.

As we concluded in the previous section, the best role for physicians is twofold. First, they should help society develop guidelines for rationing; second, they should honestly apply these guidelines to clinical practice. Physicians have long been involved in the development of such criteria. For instance, in the early 1960s when renal dialysis was just beginning, the artificial kidney center at Swedish Hospital in Seattle, Washington, developed an admission and policy committee. This committee was given charge of decisions about which patients would be granted access to the small number of available dialysis machines. The committee, including several physicians, developed a set of criteria that included marital status, number of dependents, occupation, future potential, and past performances.[70] Applying these explicit criteria was quite difficult. Moreover, some of the criteria seemed to be biased in favor of patients who were similar to those individuals who served on the committee. Nonetheless, this approach suggests a role for physicians, at least with regard to biological criteria.

As noted above, we have largely abandoned rationing of kidneys or dialysis. The federal government underwrites the effort. Most individuals who have many medical indications for and no medical contraindication to transplantation can be referred for procedures. The same is not true for heart or liver transplantation. In these cases, all disabled individuals who fit the Medicare criteria must queue up at designated centers and wait for available hearts or livers. Acceptance at these centers must be and is based on severity of the patient's disease, a biological criterion that doctors are best equipped to assess. Thus the just doctor's role should be to monitor the queue and ensure that the line is formed according to severity of the illness, and not according to other factors such as ability to pay, or ability to donate funds to a nonprofit institution.[71] This is one aspect of the role of just doctoring in rationing of organs.

The example of bone marrow transplantation reveals another aspect of the role of just doctoring with regard to transplant rationing. Bone marrow transplantation involves providing new bone marrow for those suffering from certain types of cancer. These individuals undergo chemotherapy, which eradicates their cancer burden, but also kills all off the fast-growing cells in the bone marrow. Therefore, they require transplantation of bone marrow after the chemotherapy has eradicated the cancer. This therapy is used most frequently in tumors of the blood-forming system, such as leukemia and multiple myeloma.

One of the biological issues that distinguishes bone marrow transplantation from other forms of transplantation is the abundance of bone marrow. Unlike transplantation of the liver or heart, and in some ways unlike kidney transplantation, bone marrow transplantation does not involve the use of scarce organs (although finding an appropriate match can sometimes be difficult). Moreover, donating bone marrow does not significantly impair the donor. Therefore, there is no scarcity of potential donors as there is for heart or liver transplantation.

As a result, the rationing of bone marrow transplantation has tended to revolve around the health care expenditures required for this technology. Unlike heart and liver transplants, debates on bone marrow transplantation emphasize the total cost of the procedure, rather than the ethical issues surrounding the harvesting of organs or the solicitation of organ donations. It reflects primarily allocation decisions, not the rationing aspects of scarce organs. Like other forms of transplantation, bone marrow transplantation is very expensive. Costs for treatment of lymphoma or leukemia using bone marrow transplantation methods range from $100,000 to $250,000. Many insurers are unwilling to pay for such expensive therapy. Moreover, medical centers that provide bone marrow transplantation are often unwilling to undertake the process unless the patient can provide a large down payment. Yet bone marrow transplantation is now accepted therapy for various types of leukemia and lymphoma. Moreover, long-term survival rates are quite good, especially in treatment. Perhaps most important, bone marrow transplantation is used in certain types of refractory pediatric leukemias.[72]

The federal government has not assumed a specific role in bone marrow transplantation and does not underwrite its costs as the government has done for renal transplantation through the End Stage Renal Disease Program. Nor does the federal government regulate the centers that perform bone marrow transplantations in the same manner in which it regulates those that perform heart and liver transplantations. Thus bone marrow transplantation has been left to the control of administrators, scientists, and physicians at the various teaching centers that have pursued this technology.

Like other forms of organ transplantation, the costs associated with bone marrow transplantation have led to emotionally charged individual cases. Consider, for instance, a case from late 1987 in Oregon. A seven-year-old boy with leukemia required a bone marrow transplantation. However, the Oregon legislature had curtailed Medicaid funding for heart, liver, pancreas, and bone marrow transplant patients, owing to a fiscal shortfall. As a result, the seven-year-old was denied transplantation. Private fund-raising efforts fell short of the $100,000 necessary to guarantee the transplantation. The child died. There is little doubt that his death was related to rationing of health care resources.

The Oregon legislature was well prepared for the public outcry surrounding this case. Since the early 1980s, grass roots organizations in Oregon had attempted to increase public understanding of allocation decisions of health care. In 1982, a conference involving these groups posed two important questions: "How does society value expensive curative medical care relative to preventive services being progressively curtailed in government budget?" and "Can the present implicit rationing of health care be made explicit and concur with community values?"[73] After this conference, committees organized a series of town meetings. During several hundred meetings, thousands of citizens exchanged opinions and educated themselves.[74] There can be little doubt that the impact of these grass roots agencies played a role in the framing of the problem by the Oregon legislature, and led to the decision to curtail funding for transplants.

Recently, the Oregon legislature has passed a law that would require the governor to appoint a commission to develop a prioritized list of medical services funded by state Medicaid programs. This commission would be guided by citizen input. In return for restrictions on services, the law loosens somewhat stringent eligibility standards for Medicaid, and increases by 77,000 the number of people who are covered by Medicaid. Part of the plan depends on developing scientific data on treatment outcomes and the effectiveness of certain therapies. Only with these data will the commission be able to develop an appropriately prioritized list.

As we discussed in previous chapters, however, the appropriateness of procedures can be very difficult to gauge. There has been very little research into variation in care between geographic regions, but the evidence we do have indicates that appropriateness is an ill-defined concept in medical care.[75] For instance, there is very little information on the cost effectiveness or appropriateness of bone marrow transplantation.[76] Moreover, it is unclear how many days of our lives are saved per dollar in bone marrow transplantation, as opposed to more preventive services. These vexing problems lie ahead for the Oregon commission now attempting to rank various procedures according to cost effectiveness.[77]

Nonetheless, the consideration of bone marrow transplantation by grass roots organizations, such as those which have developed in Oregon and other states, provides us with a rational approach to the rationing of health care within the liberal state. Perhaps more important for our purposes, these models suggest explicit roles for medical ethics as just doctoring. As I have argued, just doctoring involves altruistic concerns for the individual patient, as well as respect for that patient's rights and negative freedom. Moreover, the just doctor must show equal concern and respect for the entire class of patients. Finally, just doctoring moves medical ethics beyond the simple doctor-patient relationship, without abandoning the patient for greater societal goods.

Now consider the just doctor who is caring for a seven-year-old child with leukemia. It appears that bone marrow transplantation may prolong the child's life, perhaps even bring about a cure. However, the child's family is poor and the child qualifies only for Medicaid. Moreover, Medicaid in the state where the child lives will not fund bone marrow transplantation. What should a just doctor do? One answer might be that this just doctor should organize fund-raising efforts and try to raise the $100,000 necessary to purchase this child's bone marrow transplantation. Another answer might be that the physician should lobby the medical center to obtain free care for his patient. However, this might trespass the physician's commitment to equal concern and respect for all patients. Why should this one patient receive special treatment at the medical center that is unavailable to other poor children? Indeed, there may be little that the individual physician can do for a child facing death from leukemia.

Just doctoring, however, requires that physicians address the larger social issues. Since we live in a liberal state and since the liberal democracy determines how funds are to be allocated, the just doctor must realize that there will no doubt be limits on the availability of health care. But, the just doctor should assure that whenever those limits do occur, they are distributed in a way that reflects the values central to liberalism, values that solidify the sense of medical care as ethical and altruistic. Joining in grass roots organizations, helping to engage the public's attention, and helping to form lists of priorities are ways in which physicians can discharge their duties as just doctors. Physicians should be encouraged to join these popular movements and to urge their own patients to become involved in these efforts. Encouraging the public's interest and developing priorities in the allocation of scarce resources is an acknowledgment by members of the liberal state that they themselves must decide how society allocates those resources. Moreover, this kind of participatory democracy emphasizes that health care is a collective good and that priorities in health care must be established by all members of society, not just doctors or politicians. So I would argue that just doctoring goes hand in hand with grass roots efforts to help citizens understand and discuss rationing decisions.

Just doctoring makes an additional ethical demand in this area. This is not a duty that all physicians can discharge, but all should be committed to it. That is, physicians must begin to develop information about the appropriateness and efficacy of individual procedures. For too long the development of health care technology has been driven by the personal interests of researchers and the imperatives of the market. We now have huge numbers of therapies and diagnostic tools in our technological armamentaria. It is time we begin to evaluate these seriously and to provide the kind of baseline data that individual citizens and grass roots organizations will need to prioritize allocations of health resources. Thus, as we mentioned in chapter 5, physicians must be willing to participate in trials that define efficacy and appropriateness.

Rationing, Health Insurance, and the Poor

Clearly, rationing of health care resources does not fall evenly within society. The child who died of leukemia in Oregon died because his family was unable to afford transplantation. Had he lived in a wealthy family, the $100,000 necessary to obtain his therapy would have been available. Access to health care in this country is a matter, in many circumstances, of financial status. The poor will likely bear the brunt of rationing. The ethical physician must be aware that there are limits on health care resources and that these limits lead to rationing. In addition, she must be concerned that rationing of resources primarily affects the poor. It follows that rationing based on ability to pay should be a major concern of medical ethics as just doctoring. Before we address this problem, it is necessary to review again the manner in which we finance health care in this country.

In chapter 3, we noted that health insurance is a relatively recent development in this country. By the beginning of the 1950s, however, 40 million people were enrolled in private hospital insurance plans, and by the mid 1960s, Blue Cross had an enrollment of 67.2 million people, or 37 percent of the civilian population under age sixty-five, while commercial insurance companies provided for 100 million people, or 57 percent of the civilian population under sixty-five.[78] Commercial health insurers benefitted from tax laws that treated health insurance contributions from employers as a tax-exempt fringe benefit.[79] By the early 1960s, the combination of health insurance, not-for-profit hospitals, and physicians as private contractors dominated the organization of medical care, as we discussed in chapters 3 and 4.

Following the Democratic landslide in the 1964 elections, it was clear that the public favored a Medicare initiative that would provide comprehensive health insurance for the elderly. As related by David Blumenthal, Congressman Wilbur Mills, working closely with the administration's Wilbur Cohen, put together a compromise program that covered both hospital and physician's services, but made physician's coverage voluntary rather than compulsory.

At present, Medicare provides health insurance for all who are eligible for Social Security, old age, and disability insurance programs.[80] Eligibility is also extended to nearly all elderly individuals not covered under the Social Security program and certain others with end-stage renal disease.[81] There is no cost to enroll in Part A of Medicare, but to enroll in Part B, one must pay monthly premiums.[82] Medicare has consistently paid for reasonable and necessary services for the sick, including new technologies to treat illness.[83] Its reimbursement structure is enormously dependent on the individuals and organizations that act as intermediaries and contractors for payment of services.[84]

At the same time Congress enacted the Medicare legislation, it also created the Medicaid program.[85] Essentially, Medicaid provides matching funds from general federal revenues for states that choose to provide health care assistance to low-income families, especially welfare recipients. Two of the primary eligibility criteria for Medicaid are incorporated from standards of two other cash assistance programs, Aid to Families with Dependent Children (AFDC) and Supplemental Security Income (SSI).[86] In addition, states can make Medicaid available to the "medically needy."

All states have AFDC programs that provide cash assistance to single-parent families. Federal law requires that the states provide Medicaid funds to all AFDC recipients. Moreover, states have the option of extending benefits to "those eligible for assistance but institutionalized; those who would be eligible if child care costs were paid from earnings rather than through social service plans; and those eligible for but not receiving AFDC."[87] Individuals covered through this set of eligibility criteria account for slightly less than 25 percent of Medicaid expenditures.

Disabled persons of any age and low-income elderly persons qualify for Supplemental Security Income (SSI). People eligible for SSI are also generally eligible for Medicaid, although states can impose stricter eligibility criteria for Medicaid.[88] The same set of extensions that apply to AFDC also apply to SSI.[89] Fifty percent of Medicaid expenditures go to those eligible through SSI criteria.

Finally, twenty-nine states provide coverage to the "medically needy." To qualify as medically needy, the medical expenses incurred by a family must be large enough to reduce their income to a specified level.[90] Federal law prohibits setting the "spend down" level below 133 percent of the maximum AFDC payment in the state. Many states set the spend down level considerably higher. Recently, Congress has expanded and mandated Medicaid coverage for pregnant women.[91]

As might be expected, the Medicaid program creates a federal patchwork of health coverage for the poor. Because the eligibility criteria for Medicaid are tied to AFDC and SSI, eligibility reflects the extent of state commitment to these two other cash assistance programs. For instance, the maximum monthly AFDC benefit for a family of four in Mississippi is $120.00; in New York it is $676.00. In Texas, only 25 percent of poor children were covered by Medicaid in 1980, whereas in Massachusetts, 72 percent of poor children were so covered.[92] In those states without medically needy programs, the coverage through Medicaid is especially spotty.[93] In addition, federal welfare and Medicaid changes enacted by the Reagan administration in 1981 led to cutbacks in Medicaid eligibility.[94] Thus Medicaid provides coverage for only about 40 percent of those living below the poverty line.

In summary, while explosive growth of commercial health insurance provided the funds necessary to pay for increasing hospital and provider costs, there were still concerns about access to care in the early 1960s. The Medicare program provided fairly comprehensive federal assistance for the elderly ill. On the other hand, the federal Medicaid grants to states created rather patchy coverage for the indigent who are sick. This means that lack of insurance continues to be a troubling problem for our country and that many—especially the uninsured—have little access to health care.

Another way to look at Medicare and Medicaid is from the point of view of liberal justice. In the early 1960s, the United States was concerned about the inequality that existed in access to health care, especially for the poor and the elderly. As a result, new taxes developed revenues that were used for the development of programs to assist the poor and the elderly in their purchase of health care. Our government decided to encumber the negative freedom of individuals with more taxes on income in order that greater equality in access to health care could be developed.

While the patchwork approach of Medicaid seemed appropriate in the mid-1960s, we are now again concerned with problems of inequality in access to health care. The health care sphere or vocation does not contribute to cooperation within the liberal state when it is weakened by serious inequities. Rationing based on ability to pay affronts the altruistic notions of medical care. The growing concern about access to health care must be all that much greater for just doctors, who are committed to the altruism of the health care.

The concern about the problem of the uninsured has led to numerous estimates of the extent of insurance coverage.[95] The estimates of the sources of insurance are generally consistent.[96] Nearly 65 percent of the population receive their insurance through their employment. Medicaid provides coverage for 8.1 percent of the population. CHAMPUS, the federal health care system for members of the military and their dependents, provides another 4.2 percent of coverage.

While the number of uninsured people is generally recognized as having increased throughout the past decade, it is not clear exactly how many Americans are without health insurance.[97] In the summer of 1989, the preliminary March 1988 Current Population Survey (CPS) results were published.[98] The CPS, which has been conducted each month by the Bureau of Census continuously since 1942, now estimates that there were a total of 31.1 million Americans lacking health insurance during 1987.[99]

Concerns about access to care has spawned debate in this country about the benefits of government sponsored comprehensive health insurance. As noted above, unions and certain groups within the Democratic party have long advocated national health insurance.[100] Many advocates, however, became pessimistic about the cause in the aftermath of the Carter administration's failure to enact even preliminary legislation. In the last few years, coincident with revelations of the scope of the uninsured problem, there has been renewed interest.

Although there are a number of different approaches to universal health coverage, few have proposed a British-style National Health Service for the United States.[101] More attention has focused on legislation that requires all employers to provide health insurance to employees.[102] Others recommend the Canadian approach, which leaves many current institutional structures in place but features comprehensive public insurance and global budgeting for physicians and hospitals.[103] But proposals are viewed by many in the business community as extraordinarily expensive and unrealistic.[104] Indeed, the debate about the problems of the uninsured continues to be driven largely by concerns over cost containment in medical care and the role of government in constraining these costs.[105]

Of course, the new emphases on profit and prospective payment mean that the health care industry is generally less able to subsidize nonpaying patients with revenues earned from paying patients.[106] More often, it appears that for-profit hospitals prefer to shift care for those without insurance to public and large municipal hospitals.[107] Without the cross-subsidies they had traditionally relied upon, even these large municipal hospitals feel the bind of the increasingly cost-conscious environment. This means that there are strong incentives to avoid hospitalizing those without insurance, and to discharge those without insurance as quickly as possible. The same set of constraints also applies to health care providers outside of hospitals. Thus concerns about health care costs have led to strategies which, in theory at least, ration the availability of health care for those without insurance.

This means that rationing of care will not be limited to large-ticket therapies like bone marrow transplantation. While it is true that states may decide to trade-off funding for transplants in order to increase access to preventive and prenatal care; even without such highly visible "swaps," rationing will occur. The lack of public funding for those unable to buy insurance could lead to more limited access to a large number of services. This is not a small problem.

What position should just doctoring take on rationing of care based on the ability to pay? We have said that physicians should not be involved in private decisions about rationing. Rather, they should apply fairly distinct guidelines that have been developed by broad social consensus. Moreover, I have argued that physicians should take part in the development of this consensus, and should urge their patients to become involved in setting priorities.

This should also be the position just doctoring takes on the quiet rationing of care based on availability of insurance. It follows as well that physicians should not tolerate private rationing by hospitals or health care providers that is based on ability to pay. The inequalities in access to health care based on ability to pay should be considered publicly and with the input of physicians' altruistic concerns about patients. It may be that after public consideration of these issues, some inequalities may still remain. Even the commitment to equal concern and respect will not eradicate all substantive inequalities. The just doctor realizes this. In addition, however, she realizes it is ethically wrong and unjust to allow the burden of health care costs to fall on the poor through the likely unintentional operation of our medical system. Rather than fuming about their patients' inability to buy appropriate medicine, as I have done in the past, just doctors have an ethical commitment to review the health care industry and question publicly those aspects that lead to inequality of access.

Indeed, physicians and all health care workers in a liberal state have an ethical duty, under just doctoring, to realize that limits on care are part of overall allocation decisions, and that these decisions are framed by methods of financing and delivering care.[108] Moreover, we in the United States must realize that other liberal states have taken other approaches. Health care cost increases, as we have seen, are at least in part attributable to the manner in which health care is financed. Perhaps changes in financing would bring about more equal access and less need for rationing policies without requiring commitment of new resources.[109]

9

The Economic and Political
Structure of Medical Practice

We have seen the consequences of a beneficence-based medical ethics that fails to look beyond the individual doctor-patient relationship. Traditional medical ethics in which the "patient comes first" inculcates paternalistic attitudes toward patient care, belittling the patient's negative freedom. In addition, the "patient comes first attitude" blinds physicians to the institutional context of care. Specifically, the beneficence model exacerbates the moral hazard created by the physician's relationship to the insurers of medical care, and it has thus fueled the increase in health care costs.

As I have argued, medical ethics is not simply a private matter between doctor and patient. Physicians must realize that at least some of the ethical nature of their practice depends on the recognition that, while the altruistic features of traditional ethics must be preserved, they practice medicine in the liberal state. This understanding has motivated my effort to describe medical ethics as just doctoring. Just doctoring explicitly recognizes the norms and underlying moral structure of the modern liberal state and describes a medical ethics consistent with liberalism, but it also retains the altruism of traditional medical ethics. In particular, just doctoring envisions health care as a sphere of cooperative activity within the modern liberal state, an enterprise that helps to establish a sense of community. Such spheres of activity within the liberal state remind us that the polity is more than liberal law and a free market; it is also a community in which concern for others means more than economic freedom.

Of course, the modern liberal state is grounded in the concept of negative freedom. In a perfect world, negative freedom, operating in a market economy, ensures equal concern and respect for each individual. Each person may pursue what he values without interference. But the modern liberal also recognizes that we do not live in a perfect world. Individuals have unequal talents and start their lives with different advantages and disadvantages. In order to show equal concern and respect for each person, the market must be modified, and the negative freedom of some must be limited so that all can have opportunity to thrive under liberalism. For example, we have progressive taxation, which funds programs that help provide appropriate nutrition and housing to the poor. Moreover, we fund public education. In the health care area, we underwrite care for the poor and elderly. The modern liberal countenances these necessary restrictions on the market, even to the point of allowing government control of some areas.

Much of the democratic activity of the modern liberal state concerns the ways in which we limit individual freedoms so as to benefit the welfare of all. The liberal state explicitly recognizes that there should be restrictions on the market in order to promote equality. Nonetheless, the liberal also acknowledges that there are limits on resources. Taxation spent on housing means that less is available for health care, unless new taxes are instituted. Thus there is a dynamic relationship between individuals' negative freedom, the market, and the commitment to equal concern and respect.

Since spheres of cooperative activity within the liberal state are there to promote a sense of community, it follows that attention to equality is especially focused within those spheres. This is true in medical care, as we have seen. The notion of just doctoring is offended by inequality of care. The patient must be attended to, whatever his affliction or socioeconomic background. This much is clear from our analysis of the AIDS epidemic and of rationing of care. This is not to say that just doctoring ignores negative freedom. To the contrary, in its commitment to informed consent and to limits on care, just doctoring reiterates the importance of the patient's right to choose.

Since the compromise between negative freedom and equality is so central to liberalism, and since that compromise is expressed in the economic and political structure of institutions in the modern liberal state, it follows that just doctoring, as opposed to traditional medical ethics, must be intensely concerned about the economic and political structure of medical practice. Of course, this is the issue that has motivated much of the discussion in this book, but to this point we have not discussed the specifics of the institutions of medical care.

Several parameters must guide the discussion. First, the negative freedom of the patient must be considered. The public morality of the liberal state must be respected. Second, the compromise between equal concern and respect, on one hand, and negative freedom and the market, on the other, plays a role. Third, the status of health care as a sphere of cooperative activity weighs heavily. From the foregoing arguments, it might be concluded that the market should be highly regulated in health care so that equal concern and respect can be shown to all patients.

This is not, however, entirely the case, as I suggested in chapter 4. Increasingly, many advocate the wider use of market concepts in medical care. To understand why efficiency concerns have become so prominent, and to assess how just doctoring fits into the structure of health care institutions, we must review the forces that have led to calls for broader use of the market in medical care.

Markets in Medical Care

Health care in the United States has been defined for the last fifty years by the interrelationships of doctors, hospitals, and health insurers. The patient usually provides payment for medical care through an insurance relationship. He, or his employer, purchases insurance that covers all, or most, of medical care expenses. The insurer pays the provider directly or reimburses the patient for the expenses incurred by hospitalization as well as for the physician's fee. Even those patients whose medical care is provided by the federal government fit into this overall framework.

The independence of the physician from third-party payers as well as hospitals has been critical to the structure of medical care in this country. The physician has typically billed the patient or the insurer separately from the charge for hospital services. Thus the physician works as an isolated economic entity, even as a member of a group practice. This ensures the economic independence of the doctor-patient relationship, an imperative of traditional medical ethics.

Another important facet of the structure of medical care in this

country has been the passivity of the health insurer. In the three decades after the Second World War, health insurers rarely, if ever, in-
terfered with the doctor-patient relationship. Indeed, the first and still
most influential of insurers, Blue Cross and Blue Shield, were formed
by a coalition of hospital organizations and physicians. Their support
of traditional physician-hospital relationships remained solid until the
1980s.

Another important element of the traditional structure of medical
practice has been the not-for-profit status of the majority of hospitals
in the United States. As discussed in some detail in chapter 3, hospitals
arose out of alms houses and other charitable organizations in the late
eighteenth and early nineteenth century.[1] Most were incorporated as
nonprofit institutions under both state and federal law, and have maintained their original standing under the Internal Revenue Service
Code.[2] At the beginning of the 1980s, 70 percent of all hospitals were
nonprofit or voluntary, while another 22 percent were governmental
or other special hospitals.[3] Only about 8 percent of hospitals were
for-profit institutions.

Hospitals have retained their nonprofit structure for a number of
reasons. Historically, hospitals evolved out of charitable organizations
and most likely have found it easiest to retain that corporate structure.
The not-for-profit status also provides access to ready sources of capital through philanthropy.[4] But perhaps a more cogent reason behind
the nonprofit structure has to do with the nature of patients as consumers of health care.

Henry Hansmann has argued that not-for-profit institutions are a
sensible choice when a client is a poor consumer and must trust the
good will of another.[5] When consumers are particularly uneducated
about a product, they are at risk in the market. They may have no way
to evaluate the product being offered and thus will find it difficult to
take advantage of the efficiency and fairness of the market. In this
situation, consumers may opt for not-for-profit institutions, which
presumably have little interest in maximizing their profit at the expense
of the consumer. Therefore, the consumer can trust the producer's
assertions about a particular product. In this manner, a not-for-profit
institution makes more sense than a for-profit institution, even in an
economic universe otherwise dominated by markets and profits.

This seems to be a reasonable way of understanding nonprofit
health care institutions. The patient is usually a poor consumer of
health care and takes whatever is offered, because it is very difficult to

assess the quality and appropriateness of the product (it is even very difficult for the producer to assess the quality and appropriateness of the product). Rather than having to act as a consumer, the patient may therefore wish to trust the physician and the hospital to provide good quality care. Specifically, the consumer relies on a fiduciary relationship with the hospital and the physician. This of course goes hand-in-hand with traditional medical ethics, which asserted that patients should trust physicians and that physicians in turn will do what is best for the patient.

There is another way in which the "patient comes first" ethic has been served by not-for-profit hospitals. Since most hospitals retain this form, there have traditionally been few strong administrators. Moreover, managers of nonprofit hospitals have no shareholders to whom they must answer (although until the mid-20th century, there was typically a very active lay board of governors).[6] Instead, hospital administrations have typically shared power with physician medical staffs. This means that physicians have largely been able to dictate policy and direction for not-for-profit hospitals. In essence, then, the not-for-profit hospital can be interpreted as having acted as a physicians' cooperative,[7] which has assured, in turn, that the hospital does not interfere with the isolated doctor-patient relationship. Physicians have admitted patients to hospitals, and hospitals have provided the unregulated setting for patient care. Traditional medical ethics, steeped in physician paternalism, has thus been protected by nonprofit hospitals.

Economists have noted that there are also obvious financial motives for structuring hospitals in this manner.[8] In a "physicians cooperative," doctors can maximize profit while evading oversight by outside institutions. Robert Clark has argued that the clearest reason for maintaining the not-for-profit status of hospitals is income maximization for physicians.[9] Moreover, he makes the case that such a status allows physicians to hide this motive from patient. He believes that the nonprofit structure creates no incentives for improving the quality of care or for critical evaluation of appropriateness of procedures. The antidote, from his point of view, is increased utilization of market methods in health care, and in particular, increased emphasis on profit taking by health care institutions. His hope is that an emphasis on profit will lead to better education of consumers and a curbing of physician prerogatives.

As we have seen, insurers have until recently done little to interfere

with the physician's clinical judgment. Since many insurance companies have been closely associated with or controlled by providers, they
have usually chosen to pay bills rather than scrutinize them. This being
the case, physicians have had every incentive to provide as much care
as reasonably possible. In other words, physicians have faced great
financial temptations, to which they have sometimes succumbed. Even
the most moral physicians have found little need for evaluation of cost
effectiveness or appropriateness of procedures or diagnostic modalities. It is in this light that we must view the lack of information on
even the simplest of procedures. Of course this has led to higher and
higher hospital and health care costs, with the national health expenditure going from $12.7 billion in 1950 to $604.1 billion in 1989.
Even more disturbing has been the increase in per capita costs, from
$82 in 1952 to $2,354 in 1989.[10]

Although concerns about costs have been well expressed for over
thirty years,[11] by the late 1970s government began to develop ways to
restrict capital outlays by hospitals, as we discovered in chapter 8.
States considered[12] and enacted certificate of need laws.[13] Others un-
dertook prospective budgeting.[14] But these measures have been
viewed as only partially successful.

Many analysts have advocated that there should be more for-profit
enterprise in medicine, both to curtail hospital costs and, no less important, to constrain the behavior of physicians. Those who take such
a position are largely persuaded by the contention that physicians have
been able to take advantage of the existing framework of medical practice to maintain control over medical care and to maximize profit. This
perception, at least in part, underlies the general effort to institute a
competitive marketplace ethic into medical care. More broadly, competition is meant to help mitigate the increases in health care costs,
whether through changes in the structure of health care or through
curbs on physicians' prerogatives. In any case, the two goals must be
seen as interrelated.

This understanding of the role of competition in medical care reiterates a theme that runs throughout this book. That is, many of the
recent legal and political efforts to change medical practice have shared
the implicit goal of limiting physicians' power and promoting patients'
negative freedom. In the health care marketplace, patients are to be
consumers: in other words, they should have choice in their medical
care. In a competitive marketplace, providers present to the patient
their approach to health care, and the patient chooses an approach that
is, theoretically, the least costly and most efficient. Openness and hon-

esty in medical care, the theory goes, will result from use of market concepts. The ambitions of the marketplace are well expressed by E. P. Melia and colleagues:

Using management consultants from the insurance companies and panels from the medical staff hospitals, in this optimistic view, will cause cost control mechanisms to contain costs within contract limits. To ensure quality while controlling costs, physician groups will develop diagnostic protocols and standard treatment plans where they are appropriate. Sanctions will be imposed on nonconforming group members that will include required attendance at noon conferences and grand rounds as well as required use of protocols jointly agreed on by physicians, hospitals and insurance companies; required courses in medical education focused on individual weaknesses or needed skills and strengths. . . . Both hospitals and physician groups will find that the quality of care does not suffer but that in fact it is improved by the reduction of unnecessary tests, procedures, treatments, hospital days and surgery. . . . Some hospitals and groups will prove to be more efficient than others or will provide a higher quality of care and this difference will be reflected in future contract negotiations, thus encouraging hospitals and physician groups to compete with regard to care and quality of care. . . . Cost effective preventive care, health education and self-help will be more readily accepted by consumers and practitioners, further reducing costs and improving the public health.[15]

Thus great hopes are held out for marketplace approaches that constrain physicians and other providers' prerogatives and allow the consumer-patient to make reasonable decisions about health care. Most promarket analysts believe that any change in the direction of an efficient market is to the good because it transfers the locus of decision making, to use Clark Havinghurst's term, from physicians and hospitals to patients as consumers.[16] Moving from the regulation of health care by physicians to an open market that increases consumer choice is thought to be critical. Indeed, many market advocates would argue that rate setting and certificate of need regulations by states are inappropriate interventions because the institution of market concepts will replace any need for state regulation. Again, the most important aspect of the market approach appears to be the reinforcement of the negative freedom of the patient as consumer and the curbs on the physician's ability to control the shape of medical practice.

Not all observers are so sanguine about a shift toward the competitive marketplace. Eli Ginzburg, for instance, argues that a once rather flexible system of care has been completely destabilized by the introduction of marketplace concepts.[17] He is concerned specifically about the demise of the small community hospital, an institution that he feels has great symbolic as well as medical value. He also argues that a competitive market will be incompatible with notions of cost containment. In fact, he argues that health care costs may increase as a result of the implementation of marketplace concepts.

These fears are echoed by Arnold Relman, who has consistently stated that moral hazards faced by physicians in an insurance relationship pale in comparison to the potentially difficult ethical problems that arise when physicians are placed in profit-seeking institutions.[18] Relman argues that profit taking is an unacceptable practice for physicians. He relies on altruistic notions of medicine which suggest that physicians ought not profit at the expense of patients. Indeed, even a leading health care economist, Mark Pauly, suggests that medical care may be a different sort of good than other goods that are distributed through the marketplace.[19] This is a view many people may share. (I am always surprised to find in the classes I teach at the law school that students frequently relate that they believe individuals are poor consumers of health care and that the notion of patient as consumer is inappropriate.)

Certainly, many doctors believe that their patients are often mystified by issues of medical practice. Of course, just doctoring requires that physicians make every effort to inform and educate the patient. Even when this goal is pursued vigorously, however, it may be that patients are not perfect consumers, and that great mischief awaits a system of medical care totally integrated into the market.

This is clearly an issue of great importance for just doctoring. To explore it further, let us look in some detail at the way in which American medical care might operate in a competitive marketplace and try to trace out the problems faced by physicians who attempt to act ethically within that marketplace. This will help indicate potential problems as well as the appropriate posture for medical ethics as just doctoring in the competitive marketplace.

The Market in Medical Care: The Profits in Managed Care

Most who recommend competition in health care realize that patients may be poorly equipped to take advantage of the marketplace. Nonetheless, they believe that appropriately designed competition can help bring down health care costs even if the consumer remains somewhat poorly informed about clinical issues. In particular, they argue that insurance options can be marketed to individual consumers as well as to third-party payers. Thus competition among various insurance arrangements can lead to greater choice for consumers and potentially lower costs. Critical to the goal of lower costs is management of care by the insurer.

As mentioned in chapter 8, there are a variety of insurance arrangements in the health care industry. In traditional indemnity plans, the insurer directly reimburses the patient for medical expenses, and there is no financial relationship between the provider and the insurance company. Service benefit plans, such as those championed by Blue Cross and Blue Shield, involve a direct contract between provider and third-party payer. A patient insured by Blue Cross/Blue Shield is not indemnified; instead the insurance company pays the provider directly. Neither of these traditional programs envision much management by the insurance company of the provider's practice.

New approaches to health care insurance do entail such management. In essence, the third-party payer is large enough and sophisticated enough to accumulate the expertise necessary to manage and modify clinical decision making by health care practitioners. An insurance company, for instance, can hire physicians to set up protocols for various diagnostic or therapeutic modalities. These protocols may be just as effective as more costly alternatives. Thus managed care helps create competition by exerting influence over physicians to provide cost-efficient care and by passing those savings along to the patient-consumer. The patient-consumer therefore must be informed about the various benefits associated with the insurance plan, which is probably easier than keeping him informed about the appropriateness or inappropriateness, and the efficiency or inefficiency, of medical practice. Thus, in this regard, advocates of the competitive marketplace seem to have reasonable expectations of patient care.

There are a variety of different forms of managed care.[20] Preferred provider insurance requires that the enrollee choose their medical care from selected providers, all of whom have contracted with the insurer. The contract between the insurer and the preferred provider entails a set charge for visits or procedures, as well as other requirements, for example, mandatory second opinions for surgery. Another form of managed care is the individual practice health maintenance organization. The individual practice association (IPA) health maintenance organization (HMO) is similar to the preferred provider insurance plan except that the providers tend to share in the financial risks of the insurance organization, and patients enrolled in the IPA HMO usually do not receive any reimbursement if they go to a nonparticipating provider. An even greater degree of management is found in the pre-paid group practice HMO. In this arrangement, a medical group is employed by the HMO and services are highly rationalized and or-ganized. The prepaid group practice HMO exerts great control over the number of physicians employed and their clinical judgment.

The prepaid model is what is generically referred to as an HMO. HMOs have a long history in this country.[21] The first HMOs were organized in the Pacific Northwest, in Tacoma, Washington. Mill owners and lumberyards contracted with physicians on a prepaid basis for medical services.[22] Early HMOs engendered much opposition, es-pecially from organized medicine, which led to antitrust litigation (in which the HMOs were generally vindicated), but by the late 1940s, the first large scale HMO was developed by Dr. Sidney Garfield, in collaboration with Henry Kaiser.[23]

In the 1950s and 1960s, other HMOs developed in sporadic fash-ion. By 1970 there were between 30 and 40 prepaid group practices in operation in the United States. In the early 1970s HMOs received a great political boost. The Nixon administration advocated the HMO concept as a potential method for constraining health care costs. The administration was convinced by arguments made by Dr. Paul Ell-wood, who had long championed HMO concepts. Indeed, it was Ell-wood who coined the term "health maintenance organizations." The administration agreed to support over 100 HMO projects. In the five years after 1970, the number of HMOs increased from 33 to 166, and they have continued to grow ever since.

Because prepaid group practice HMOs offer the greatest potential for management by the insurer of physician decision making, much of the attention of those interested in evaluating the competitive mar-ketplace has been focused on these organizations. Many have asked whether health maintenance organizations actually increase competi-tion and bring down costs.[24] While some preliminary evidence does suggest significant decreases in the rate of hospital admissions for those who participate in an HMO, other evidence fails to reveal re-ductions in hospital use for the HMO enrollee.[25] Moreover, there is a great concern that HMOs may produce cost savings at the expense of other sorts of insurance plans as a result of patient self-selection.

As we develop alternative insurance schemes, patient self-selection becomes an increasing problem. If sicker or older patients consistently select a certain insurance arrangement, that program will be at greater financial risk than its competitors. If HMOs are selectively marketed to healthier individuals, they will skim the healthier patients from the total patient population and leave other insurers with the sicker and more expensive patients. Thus some observers have suggested that any cost saving demonstrated by HMOs may simply be due to redistribution of sicker patients.[26] Indeed, the problem of self-selection and the financial risks it creates raises questions concerning the potential for multiple insurance options as a means of constraining health care costs.[27] It also raises questions concerning access to health care, as we will see.

Whatever questions remain about the potential for prepaid group practice HMOs and other managed care alternatives to help reduce health care costs, there is little doubt that these institutions are going to be an important part of the structure of medical care in this country. We now see that HMO concepts have begun to work synergistically with traditional insurance, as insurers offer more and different managed care options.[28] For example, in Minneapolis, long a friendly market for HMOs, traditional Blue Cross and Blue Shield programs have begun to offer preferred provider options. Included within these options are programs that provide full coverage for preventive medical services and routine physical examinations. These kinds of developments blur the difference between fee-for-service entities and health maintenance organizations. As alternatives grow and prosper in other metropolitan areas, these combinations will undoubtedly occur widely.

Traditional medical ethics and traditional notions about medical practices do not fit easily within the managed care framework, especially the prepaid group practice concept. Physicians who work in a prepaid group practice HMO are generally employees of the HMO. They are expected to follow certain care protocols and to adjust their clinical practice to accommodate the efficiency and cost-consciousness of the HMO.[29] No longer in a situation in which she is unconstrained by concerns about resources and can thus presumably "do everything for the patient," the physician practicing in an HMO is quite aware of the economic costs of diagnostic and treatment modalities. Indeed, there may be a number of financial incentives for primary care physicians within HMOs. For example, a physician may get extra pay if she is more productive, that is, if she sees more patients per hour; or she may face financial penalties if she orders too many outpatient tests; or she and her colleagues may receive a bonus if extra money remains in a referral fund at the end of the year. All of these incentives aim to decrease referral by primary care physicians to subspecialists and to decrease testing of patients. The bottom line is that such incentives tend to save HMOs money and this money remunerates to the individual physician.[30]

This departure from traditional fee-for-service arrangements plays havoc with the beneficence model of medical practice. No longer is physician decision making insulated from concerns about resources. The relationship between physician practice and remuneration is quite clear. Physicians are paid more if they "do not do everything" for the patient. One might well ask whether or not "the patient comes first." Many have suggested that this conflict of interest is too great and physicians ought not be subjected to such financial temptations.[31] Of course, these observers seem to overlook the fact that physicians also profited greatly from traditional medical relationships. Indeed, those who advocate a competitive marketplace believe that the absence of any economic incentives allows physicians to provide unnecessary care and elaborate unnecessary charges, thus maximizing their own income.

The truth no doubt lies somewhere in between these two poles. It is doubtful that the majority of physicians have taken gross advantage of their power in the traditional structure of medical practice. Most were generally motivated by concerns for their patients and thought they were providing correct and cost-effective care. The overwhelming increase in health care costs reveals fundamental problems, but it still seems inappropriate to refer to not-for-profit hospitals as an exploitation of patients by physicians. Yet, it is unreasonable to argue that traditional medical arrangements were the best possible. Traditional medical practice emphasized complete physician authority and therefore dismissed concerns about effectiveness and quality of health care. As we have discussed, physicians as members of the liberal state must realize that it is important to respect patients' ability to make decisions. Therefore, efforts to curb the prerogatives of physicians through marketplace concepts must be applauded from the viewpoint of medical ethics as just doctoring. Nevertheless, we must recognize that society does not want an unfettered marketplace in health care. This much is clear from recent developments in the government's role in health care regulation.

The Regulated Health Care Market in the Liberal State

The most committed marketplace advocates, as we noted, believe that the market can completely replace regulation within health care. They would, for instance, allow managed care options to evolve appropriately, with minimal governmental input. This makes sense only so long as we consider the consumer to be the large third-party payers who are trying to decide which option seems to be most cost effective. But there is also the individual patient to consider. The patient in a managed care option is, to a certain extent, at the mercy of the organization. It is the patient who will suffer if the physician, affected by economic concerns, decides not to order certain important tests or not to refer a complicated problem to a subspecialist. More bluntly, it is the individual patient who will suffer the consequences when efforts to cut costs lead to a lower standard of care.

The American government, reflecting liberal values, will not accept such trade-offs. The Reagan administration was once a strong advocate of managed care for Medicare beneficiaries, so as to reduce the cost of providing care to these patients. However, over the last few years, problems arising in government-contracted HMOs have led many to question whether or not it is a good idea to enroll elderly individuals in these HMOs.[32]

More important, Congress has become aware of the potential inattention paid by HMOs to quality of care, owing to their concerns about cutting costs. In particular, Congress has prohibited the splitting of fees based on physician referrals. While states have traditionally prohibited fee splitting in the practice of medicine, they have typically focused on fee splitting following the referral of a patient from one physician to another.[33] The managed care industry has, inadvertently, revived the prohibition on fee splitting of a different sort.

There are two sorts of fee splitting. One creates incentives for a physician to treat a patient (referral fees); the other creates incentives not to treat (antireferral fees).[34] The latter is more likely to be found in managed care situations as an incentive to decrease referrals. The Medicare fraud and abuse statutes specifically prohibit referral fees. Those found guilty of this felony face up to five years of imprisonment and $25,000 in fines.[35] A more recent federal statute prohibits antireferral fees and allows the Department of Health and Human Services to impose fines of up to $2,000 upon those who reduce services in return for financial reward.[36] Thus antireferral fees directly address the problems associated with economic incentives that seek to limit the care of enrollees in managed care programs.

This new prohibition on antireferral fees, as well as the concern about enrollment of Medicare beneficiaries in HMOs, suggests that while the administration and members of Congress may well support managed care options and general competition within the health care market, they will not forego all regulations. Most important, the government will continue to be concerned about the potential vulnerability of patients within competitive marketplaces. This means that regulations of physician practice will continue even as, or if, we move to broader use of marketplace principles in medical care.

Of course, it should not only be up to the government to provide protection for individual patients. Although just doctoring is not hostile to market values in medical care per se, medical ethics is also defined by its concern for others. "The patient comes first" attitude is the acceptance of the standards of liberalism. Indeed, just doctoring recognizes that communitarian and cooperative values must be part of the health sphere. These values are not always a part of the market, and in this regard, one would expect that just doctoring would elaborate restrictions on marketplace notions.

This certainly should be the case for incentives to make or avoid referrals. As we have seen, managed care options depend heavily on antireferral incentives in order to provide more efficient care. This is appropriate insofar as we recognize that there are a number of ways to approach any clinical problem, and that there should be incentives to choose the most cost-efficient way. However, physicians have an ethical duty to react strongly against managers who suggest substandard methods for assessing medical problems because of their cost. One of the major tenets of just doctoring, in fact, one of the major tenets of any notion of professional ethics, is that one must provide the best care possible. Physicians cannot tolerate economic incentives based on notions of efficiency that compromise care for individual patients. In this regard, Relman and others who support traditional medical ethics are correct in saying that the patient must come first. Just doctoring requires that financial incentives that could lead to substandard care should be, to the extent it is possible, curtailed. Just doctoring can operate within the marketplace, but only a marketplace that is regulated by concerns for individual patients and by skepticism of financial incentives for physicians. Physicians have an ethical duty to oppose antireferral incentives that compromise care.

Antireferral incentives are not the only target of just doctoring, nor of existing government regulation of the health care market. Indeed, the role of just doctoring in the competitive medical marketplace, and its integration with and support of government regulation of the market, becomes clearer as we look at other potential abuses of patients in the marketplace. As we mentioned, Medicare fraud and abuse statutes prohibit referral fees.[37] Fraud and abuse litigation have increased greatly with the introduction of marketplace notions into medical care.

The reasons for this increase are fairly straightforward. It is now more generally acceptable for physicians to invest in for-profit institutions, such as free-standing laboratory facilities.[38] The potential for profit probably increases physicians' incentives to invest in such laboratories; even more so, it increases their incentives to refer patients to such testing facilities. The inspector general of the Department of Health and Human Services has found that referral of patients increases greatly when physicians own the laboratories to which the patient is referred.[39] These self-referrals are at least partially constrained by Medicare fraud and abuse statutes.[40] Some politicians and physicians have called for complete prohibitions on such self-referrals.

Medical ethics as just doctoring would support close regulation. While accepting that the marketplace may bring about more cost-efficient care, just doctoring will not stand for physician profit making at the expense of the patient. Even if we acknowledge that it is beneficial for physicians to determine whether laboratories provide good quality care, it does not follow that it is necessary for physicians to take an absolute investment interest in such firms. Moreover, it seems there is little to be gained from physicians' capital investment in such facilities; presumably an efficient laboratory would be able to attract capital elsewhere. Even in situations where we might accept that a physician-owned laboratory is appropriate, for instance, when the alternatives are substandard, close scrutiny and oversight are critical.

The presumption must be that there is little to be gained from such arrangements, and much to lose. Referral to labs owned by the referring physician, or to labs from which the physician receives a kickback, creates the impression that the physician is seeking to profit from the diagnostic endeavor beyond the usual fee. There is, moreover, a possibility that these arrangements will induce unneeded care. They undermine the altruistic doctor-patient relationship and belittle the health care industry's status as a sphere of cooperative activity within the liberal state. Medical ethics is, to at least some extent, a matter of symbols. The abuses of physician-owned labs create great negative symbolism. They mock, rather than support, altruism.

Just doctoring requires physicians and the organized medical profession to review marketplace concepts, like self-referrals, and rigorously question whether they might exploit the patient. Medical ethics as just doctoring realizes that there are important symbolic values within the health care sphere; physician altruism must be emphasized. Insofar as the patient comes first, just doctoring must prohibit physician profit taking in the health care market, at least profits from referral to facilities in which the physician retains an interest.

Consider yet another issue arising from the institution of marketplace concepts in medical care. Since health care insurers are now at risk when hospital stays grow longer, many insurance companies, under the pressure of the competitive marketplace, have undertaken utilization review. Utilization review involves insurance company oversight of indications for admission to hospital, as well as oversight of the care provided during the hospital stay.[41]

These programs definitely reduce health care costs, probably by decreasing inappropriate care. However, the physician cannot hide behind the utilization review program when he has provided poor quality care. Just doctoring demands that if the physician believes that a patient's condition requires more hospital days than a utilization review committee might allow, the physician is ethically required to maintain the patient's hospitalization. Physicians cannot be paralyzed by cost-containment programs if they think that patient care might be compromised.[42] The concern for others central to medical ethics as just doctoring and its inherent commitment to good quality care must provide a firm foundation for physician judgment of cost containment and the medical marketplace.

Another example of the regulatory role of just doctoring in the medical marketplace concerns the care of emergency room patients. Under the common law, any hospital which has an emergency room must be willing to provide care for those patients who arrive with an acute medical problem.[43] Impoverished patients who come to emergency rooms may lack any form of health care insurance. These individuals will present problems for hospitals' financial budgets. With the move toward a competitive marketplace, there are fewer subsidies available to help fund the care of poor patients. Hospitals thus have new incentives for getting rid of patients who lack health insurance. Hospitals may, for example, treat the patient only enough so that he may be transferred to another hospital. The phenomenon of patient dumping is in part, a by-product of the competitive health care market.

The federal government has sought to prohibit such dumping.[44] The antidumping statute provides treble damages to a patient who is injured because of unfair transferrals, and hospitals that dump patients can lose all their Medicare funding. Although it is laudable that Congress has taken these steps, it is equally important that medical ethics assume a posture of strong opposition to dumping. The commitment to the patient that is part of just doctoring cannot justify activities that endanger patients, especially when the only reason for transporting the patient is that his care might be uncompensated by third-party payers.

In summary, while just doctoring accepts the marketplace in medical care, that marketplace must be modified to prevent serious disregard for a patient's well-being. The emphasis on quality that is part of medical ethics tolerates a very low threshold for profit taking. Any profit taking in medical care must be neutral with regard to patient care and should not accrue directly to the physician. Thus just doctoring generally supports only a regulated market in health care.

Of course, the appeal of the market in medical care, from the viewpoint of just doctoring, is that it restricts physicians' monopolistic control of medical practice. However, with the market must come some inequalities. Given the degree of the ethical opposition to gross limitations on access to care, a full blown market in medical care may not be appropriate. Perhaps even greater regulation than discussed above may be necessary.

Just Doctoring, Rights, and Access to Health Care

As outlined above, and in more detail in chapter 8, the institution of market-competitive concepts in medical care has had detrimental effects on access. In a competitive marketplace, health care providers, especially hospitals, must compete for patients. Moreover, third-party payers, especially insurers and the federal government, have restricted considerably the reimbursement structure for physicians and hospitals. While this may not have cut health care costs a great deal, it has created a sense within health care administration that less and less funding will be available for financing health care. This has led to an unwillingness to subsidize care for the poor. With less available in the reimbursement provided by insurers, there are smaller surpluses with which to subsidize the care of the indigent. Accordingly, since Medicaid provides only partial coverage for indigent health care, Congress has become more and more concerned about availability of health care for poor people.[45]

The just doctor understands that the implementation of marketplace concepts in medical care is in many ways an effort to place the patient on an equal footing, as a consumer, with the physician, who becomes a supplier. She welcomes this aspect of the marketplace. Nonetheless, she finds the inequalities produced by the market especially inappropriate in medical care as a sphere of cooperative activity within the liberal state. Gross inequalities display a lack of equal concern and respect, affronting both the values of liberalism and the ethics of just doctoring. Lack of access is a challenge for just doctoring, for every physician must help to decide the best ways to modify the market in health care without decreasing the negative freedom of patients. The just doctor must therefore support patient rights while maintaining a concern for access to care. The just doctor recognizes the manner in which a market in medicine can decrease physician prerogatives and increase the patient's ability to choose, yet she must still be concerned about access.

Some would argue that there is no real conflict between patient rights on one hand and concerns about access on the other. They would argue that patients have a right to health care, and that this should define equal access for all. In other words, they argue that concern for patient rights demands the elimination of the market where it creates inequality. Thus a commitment to the right to health care would lead one to replace the market with a national health service.

The notion of a right to health care has a relatively long history in this country. Of course, it is not a matter that concerns only physicians per se, but rather all members of the liberal state. In essence, those who call for a right to health care believe that this particular right is an inherent feature of any political structure. The argument is that any citizen in a civilized state should have a right to health care, some would even say a right to health. But is the modern liberal state such a civilized state? To answer this question, it is necessary to retrace issues we addressed in chapters 1 and 2 in regard to the foundations of modern liberalism.

Ill health presents a peculiar set of conceptual problems for liberalism. In the liberal state, choice is highly valued; it is one's freedom to choose that defines individuality. One actualizes oneself by budgeting one's own resources and selecting projects to be pursued. Health care is usually not conceived of as such a project. A decision to seek care is usually not a matter of free choice. Norman Daniels states, "For at least *some* health service needs, people cannot *just choose* to modify them when budgeting their fair share of social good."[46] A critical illness or debilitating injury strikes suddenly in many cases. One has no choice whether to seek help or not; health care must be sought.

Thus the liberal ideal of the rational man calculating a list of social goods cannot apply. The victim of an appendicitis attack or a car accident rarely sits back and decides whether health care is more important than that new convertible or big evening out on the town. Gene Outka correctly states that "health crises are often of overriding importance when they occur. They appear therefore not satisfactorily accommodated to the context of a free market place where consumers may freely choose among alternative goods and services."[47]

Another consideration follows closely on this. The pure procedural justice of the market, and its utility in bringing about equal concern and respect, rests on a partly hidden premise, which is that all people have essentially the same needs and that the choices one makes are not a societal concern. Personal choice, guided by personal responsibility for one's well-being, prevails. If you enjoy caviar and champagne, you have no one to blame if you cannot purchase heating oil later. Since each person has similar needs, each decides how to fulfill the basic ones and cultivate others that are not so basic.

This description of needs and personal responsibility does not, however, obtain in health care. The need for health care is grossly unequal among people, and it often has little to do with how responsible one has been regarding one's own health. The pure procedural justice of the market place fails, to some extent, to operate in the area of health care. Thus Daniels assesses the situation accurately when he writes that "perhaps because health care needs behave in this especially unruly way, [many liberals] deliberately [leave] consideration of them out of [their] theory."[48]

In a modern liberal state, one could argue that health care would be on the list of primary social goods, those things to which a citizen can say she has a right. That list, as Rawls sets it forth, is made up of the following: (1) a set of basic liberties; (2) freedom of movement between various opportunities; (3) income and wealth; (4) social bases of self-respect; and (5) powers and prerogatives of office. These goods appear to be the prerequisites of personal choice. They protect and circumscribe the negative freedom of individuals.

Continuing this argument, nothing so limits freedom of choice as does the handicap of illness. Thus P. Greene states that "access to health care is not only a social primary good, in Rawls's sense of the term, but possibly one of the most important such goods. . . . Even more apparently than governmental interference, disease and ill health interfere with our happiness and undermine our self-confidence and self-respect. . . . There seems to be little question that in the priorities of rational agents health care stands near to the basic liberties themselves."[49] The prevalence of health problems in a society and their great propensity to interfere with the chosen projects of the individual are strong arguments for the inclusion of health care as a primary good to be guaranteed by the society in the promotion of justice.

There are, however, serious objections to this stance. At least two major arguments have been made against health as a primary good. The first concerns the claim that health care is not a general enough good to be a primary good. As Daniels says, in defense of Rawls's wish to keep desires theoretical in the "original position," guaranteeing health care would be tantamount to opening Pandora's box:

Greene's construction proliferates too many other quality provisos. Surely, contractors might reason, adequate food is a primary social good of fundamental importance; so are clothing and shelter. Contractors would not risk having inadequate supplies of any of these goods. Therefore, they would choose principles that guarantee equal access at least to some basic level of each good. What is happening here is that the theory of primary goods is being turned into an elaborate list of fairly specific needs. But Rawls never intended the index to function as a "need satisfaction" indicator, and converting it into one does violence to Rawls' whole view of these goods. The primary goods are intended to be general, all purpose goods, which it is rational for the moral agent to want even if he does not know his *specific* ends or needs.[50]

This leads into the next argument against the inclusion of health care as a primary good: its cost would be tremendous. To accept a certain minimum of health within a society would call for a certain amount of money. But the funds required to guarantee a level of health such that it would be possible to say that no one in the society is prevented, because of health problems, from pursuing his or her own happiness would have to be unlimited. Even Greene must admit that "the provision of the 'best possible' health care is an unreachable goal whose pursuit can absorb all the resources of even the richest society. A right to health care as a positive right, then, cannot be affirmed like negative rights or liberties. It must eventually be defined in terms of its permissible claim on other resources, particularly those handled by the economic system. Very bluntly, the question is how much should a society spend on health?"[51] As Kenneth Arrow has argued,[52] the needs of some people for health could reduce the rest to poverty if all health needs were to be fulfilled.

Clearly, however, this overstates the case. Arrow is correct only insofar as a right to health care means doing everything possible to restore everyone to good health. But this is not the realistic goal of any health care system. Many liberal states, Britain and Canada to name two, provide universal health care to all citizens, yet spend less of their Gross National Product (GNP) on health than does the United States. Thus, at least to the extent that a right to health care means equal access to some level of health care, it can be part of the modern liberal state. As Outka concludes, "In light of all the foregoing then—and especially the contrasts drawn between need and desert—a case can indeed be made for the goal of equal access."[53]

As such, the right to health care merely requires modification of the market and general taxation to support indigent care. These kinds of measures are accepted by the modern liberal as important for the goal of equal concern and respect. If health care is to be a cooperative sphere of activity, there is all the more reason to bring about equal access to a basic level of care. But the liberal does not, in so doing, create equality of access to health care. Those who can buy more than what is guaranteed will do so:

Those who claim a right to health care often gloss over another important distinction. They may intend only a system relative claim to health care: Whatever health care services are available to any within the given health care system should be equally accessible to all. Such a claim may be met by removing services accessible to only a privileged few from the system. This equality of access demand is not a demand for an independently determined level of health care, only for equality relative to whatever level of services the relevant system provides. Contrast this right claim with one that requires some specifiable range of health care services to be made available to all. . . . Such a substantive demand might require specific expansion or contraction of the existing health care system, not just in terms of who is treated, but in terms of what services are offered. The two rights claims may have vastly different implications for reform.[54]

In a liberal state, one cannot expect that we will deny the individual who has scrimped and saved for the bone marrow transplantation she desires simply because public expenditures do not fund such transplantation. While there is much that is admirable in a state that attempts to create radical equality, it is not a liberal state. This underscores the requirement that the approach of just doctoring to health care rights must be in step with the public morality of liberalism.[55]

Nonetheless, it appears that there is some basis for an individual right to health care in the modern liberal state. Yet, as James Blumstein suggests,[56] rights language itself does not take us very far in defining appropriate access to health care. The claim of a right to health care simply does not elicit a definitive response by the liberal state. Indeed, this was the conclusion of the President's Commission for the Study of Ethical Problems in Medicine and Biomedical and Behavioral Research.[57] (One could argue that rights are the best way to protect an indigent person who is urgently ill, and cannot gain access to emergency medical care.[58])

This is not to say that the liberal state, and especially those committed to just doctoring, can afford to overlook inequity of access to health care. The liberal state is still committed to equal concern and respect for all individuals. This equal concern and respect should lead to substantive efforts by government to overcome inequality, even to the extent of modifying or eliminating the market in certain areas of the economy. Certainly, the modern liberal cannot tolerate a state in which access to medical care is strictly propositioned on the ability to pay.

Thus the law as integrity puts the onus on the liberal legislature to address concerns about equal respect for all individuals. This requires the government in the liberal state to examine those inequalities that exist in access to medical care and decide which inequalities must be eliminated so that the promise of the liberal state can be fulfilled. More importantly, medical ethics as just doctoring requires physicians to help the state determine the best arrangements for making medical access universal.

An Ethical Set of Health Care Institutions

Since health care is a sphere of cooperative activity that is especially important in demonstrating the liberal state's commitment to equal concern and respect for all its members, access to health care is of great importance. It follows that physicians should consider it part of their ethical duty to help work out the appropriate mix of market and nonmarket concepts in designing a framework for health care that provides equitable access. Physicians must consider, however, not only the concerns of patients and their access to health care, but also the availability of resources in society and the limits on care that must be tolerated. In this country, for instance, we have just witnessed the gutting of a catastrophic health program that was to provide long-term care for elderly patients as well as protection from the crushing financial consequences of their illness. The rationale for the cutbacks is concern for cost and the sense that government can no longer avoid fiscal responsibility. Therefore, it is unlikely that there will be huge new resources available for health care.

Those physicians who accept medical ethics as just doctoring must participate in an effort to define what constitutes adequate access to health care in light of limited resources. Physicians must help society decide what sorts of medical problems should be addressed for all patients. For instance, what kind of elective operations should be made available to all individuals? Certainly, resections of breast cancers are procedures which should be available to all. However, the same is probably not true of cosmetic reduction mammoplasty. Between these poles are a great number of other procedures and diagnostic modalities. The state should fund some of these in order to grant all citizens in the liberal state access to a level of adequate health.

The critical role for physicians is to define this spectrum and decide where the threshold for public financing lies. Thus physicians have a very important role to play in the problem of access to health care. Their clinical knowledge and sense of concern for the patient must be integrated into the development of lists of procedures to which the liberal state guarantees access.

Of course, American physicians and state governments have been determining adequate levels of care for some time. Consider, for instance, the case of *Weaver* v. *Reagen*.[59] Weaver and his coplaintiffs suffered from diseases caused by the human immunodeficiency virus. They sued the Missouri Medicaid program because the Missouri government had decided not to list the drug (AZT) under the program. In essence, this meant that the state had refused to consider AZT as a medication to which individuals should have equal access; the state was unwilling to pay for AZT for Medicaid recipients.

The plaintiffs argued that the Medicaid law requires that drugs such as AZT, which have been proven effective for a disease, should be on the Medicaid drug list. The state countered that perhaps AZT was not indicated for individuals who, while infected with HIV, did not meet the criteria of AIDS. In response, the plaintiffs had numerous expert physicians testify that indeed AZT was indicated for all individuals infected with HIV whether or not they had AIDS. These physicians, then, were testifying that a particular medication was indicated for a particular condition and in addition, that the medication should be available to all patients under the Medicaid law. The court found in favor of the plaintiffs, granting summary judgment and allowing all who qualify for Medicaid access to this medication. Thus, in an ad hoc fashion in the courts, physicians have helped determine what constitutes adequate levels of care. What is needed, however, is a more systematic approach by the medical profession.

But, to a certain extent, efforts such as those pursued in *Weaver* are simple tinkering. Just doctoring's commitment to adequate access requires that physicians address the financing and delivery of health care. In addition to helping to determine the definition of adequate levels of health care, physicians should participate in the development of the institutions that will guarantee that access. Physicians cannot sit on the sidelines and allow economists and politicians alone to determine these issues. The central and most special part of being a physician is to care for those who are sick. This sense of care involves commitment that goes beyond relationships typically expected within a liberal state. It gives physicians a special ethical, and thus a special political, perspective. As a result, physicians must act as advocates for the patient in designing institutions that guarantee access to an adequate level of health care.

Just doctoring must value universal and adequate access to health care. However, as we saw in previous chapters, it opposes dominating physician control over the financing and delivery of health care. The commitment to access argues for a positive right to health care. The opposition to physician dominance lends to a regulated, but competitive, medical marketplace. Can these, on first glance, conflicting options be accommodated by health care in a liberal state? I think the answer is yes, as a review of some other liberal states' experience can suggest.

In Great Britain, a national health service was created after the Second World War. The National Health Service removed a great deal of the inequalities to access and probably also tended to hold down health care costs. This is one model for the liberal state. The modern liberal can accept government control over certain functions of the economy, if it is necessary to bring about equal concern and respect. Of course, getting rid of the market does entail certain costs, and in Great Britain these costs are now being reexamined. The Conservative government wishes, for efficiency's sake, to reintroduce some market concepts in medical care and is committed to modifying the National Health Service.[60] It is instructive for our argument that many British physicians are opposed to these changes in the National Health Service, as they feel they may lead to greater inequalities in the provision of health care.[61]

The Canadian model may be more pertinent to the United States, as more and more physicians are realizing.[62] Since the 1950s, Canadians have moved to universal access by turning over the *financing* of health care to the government. Universal access has been in place since 1976.[63] In essence, the provincial governments, supported in part by federal government grants, engage in global budgeting with private, not-for-profit hospitals, on a prospective basis. There is no reimbursement to individual patients. Private physician-owned laboratories, and radiology centers do exist, but provinces control them by restricting their ability to bill the provincial plan. Specific schedules for physician fees are hammered out annually by representatives of the provincial governments and physician professional associations.

This approach has led to admirable savings, keeping the percentage of the Canadian GNP devoted to health care down to 8.6 percent. America, meanwhile, spends $604 billion a year on health care or more than 11 percent of its GNP.[64] If we could pare our health spending down to Canadian levels, the savings would amount to greater than $100 billion.

How does Canada obtain universal access at lower cost? There are several explanations. First, administrative/bureaucratic expenditures are greatly reduced by naming a single payer, the provincial government.[65] Second, given the global budgeting, including capital costs, provincial governments are able to effect control over hospital costs and technology use. Finally, the negotiation with physicians over fees keeps professional costs in check. The result is that Canadians use less intense resources for hospitalized patients, with no discernible decrease in the quality of outcomes.[66]

What is the physician's role in this system? They still make all treatment decisions and retain many professional prerogatives. Indeed, most are quite satisfied, even though there has been some labor/industrial strife.[67] Nonetheless, the government represents a counter weight to unlimited physician control over supply and demand.

From the viewpoint of just doctoring, there is much to admire in the Canadian model. It brings about lower costs and universal access. Moreover, it helps limit the moral hazards faced by physicians. This is not to say all American physicians will support it. Indeed, as acute an observer as Alain Enthoven has argued that the main obstacle to a Canadian model in the United States is the opposition of physicians.[68] Canadian physicians' incomes, especially for procedure-oriented specialists, are lower than those of their American counterparts. Of course, just doctoring, and its sense of commitment to patients, requires physicians to go beyond their narrow self-interest, and ask what the most ethical approach is to health care institutions. The Canadian model of universal access and governmental oversight fulfills many of the criteria set by just doctoring for health care institutions.

The Canadian model focuses on health care financing. The delivery still occurs through nonprofit private institutions and independent physicians. Perhaps other forms of delivery might make better sense for the American liberal state. For example, Alain Enthoven and Richard Kronick have advocated a consumer's choice health plan that includes universal health insurance. Two elements are critical to this plan.[69] First, the authors retain the competition among different sorts of managed care plans, so as to bring about cost efficiency and good quality care. Second, they recommend using an 8 percent payroll tax on the wages of all workers without health care insurance to fund broader coverage under Medicare and Medicaid. Certain cost-saving devices such as copayments and cost sharing would be included in this plan, thus keeping in place many of the attributes of our present system of health care, while both encouraging competition and increasing funds available to ensure that all individuals have access to some level of health care.

Perhaps the competitive elements of the Enthovan-Kronick plan could be married to the Canadian financing model, which would bring about the competition of a marketplace with assurance of universal access, both quite attractive from a just doctoring viewpoint.[70] Physicians would play a public, ethical role in this health care system, helping to determine levels of adequate access, and policing competitive forces to ensure that some patients do not suffer from market efficiency.[71]

I cannot sketch this health plan in detail in this book; that is for another day. My point is that physician's concern for others does not only apply to the individual doctor-patient relationship. A just doctor cannot be satisfied if only her particular patients have access to health care. Her sense of what is moral or ethical must be affronted if there are patients, even patients of other physicians, who lack access to a decent minimum of health care. Concerns for individual patients should translate into concerns for the class of all patients. Therefore, physicians should not assume the general posture of other citizens in the liberal state when analyzing the policy options in regard to health care. They must respond with the same commitment they display in their relations with their own patients. In this manner, the communitarian value of medical care will be appropriately affirmed, helping to develop the most appropriate means for bringing about access to adequate health care.

10

Concluding Thoughts: Trust and Antitrust

In an effort to specify in some detail the nature of medical ethics as just doctoring, as well as the ethical duties of individual physicians, I have reached a number of conclusions. Some of these have been quite general. I have insisted that physicians continue to maintain a sense of altruism in medical practice, a notion that the patient comes first. Medical ethics as just doctoring expects that physicians will accept duties that are different, often more rigorous, than those undertaken by other individuals in the liberal state. Physicians must be committed to patients and must be willing to act on their behalf, even when this requires sacrifices we do not generally expect of citizens. Given that sick patients are often vulnerable, such altruism must be a norm in the medical profession.

In addition, I have reiterated that physicians must respect the negative freedom, the individual rights, of patients. For too long, physicians assumed that they had a broad prerogative to define the nature of the patient's medical care. Thus patients were denied informed consent. Physicians must realize that medical practice occurs in the liberal state and that this requires respect for the negative freedom of all individuals, including patients. Therefore, physicians should be committed to informed consent for individual patients. In addition, physicians should not assume that they have the power to decide when and if care should be limited.

Just doctoring also requires that physicians work together. Collaborative effort defines a profession. In addition, ethical imperatives must be universalizable from the individual doctor-patient interaction to the broader class of both physicians and patients. Therefore, physicians' duties extend beyond duties to their own patients to the whole class of those who care and those they care for.

To say that just doctoring involves ethical commitments outside the individual doctor-patient relationship is not to limit the physician's altruistic commitment to her patient. Rather, medical ethics as just doctoring requires that physicians take extra steps, recognize extra duties. In short, physicians must study the institutions of medical care and develop information and alternatives that will benefit all patients.

In particular, I have argued that physicians should work together to develop information about the appropriateness and efficacy of procedures. To ignore the importance of this issue is to ignore the welfare of all patients. Furthermore, physicians should develop information about the quality of care. This requires that physicians, in addition to their altruistic commitment to their patients, should be willing to step forward and help assess whether or not the best quality care possible is provided at their particular institutions. Medical ethics as just doctoring requires physicians to pay attention to the institutional context of medical care and to take steps to improve the quality of care for all patients, not just their own patients.

The HIV epidemic demonstrates other principles that arise out of medical ethics as just doctoring. Physicians must band together to assure that access to medical care is available to all, and that individuals suffering from certain diseases, such as HIV infection, do not face irrational constraints on medical care. While the philosophical and moral basis for this proposition is the vulnerability of sick patients and the commitment of individual physicians to their patients, it results in a mandate for the medical profession to eliminate restraints on access that are based on patients' HIV seropositivity. Although physicians need not be saints, medical ethics as just doctoring demands that they address the fears that may lead to denial of care for people who suffer from HIV diseases. Thus imperatives that arise out of just doctoring include the need to maintain access and, if necessary, the need to address particular insurance relationships and benefit programs so that physicians who do care for patients infected with HIV are protected from the disasters of AIDS as an occupational illness.

Physicians must also be willing to address issues of access generally. When it appears that care must be limited, physicians should help society develop guidelines for comprehensive rationing. They should not, of course, make individual rationing decisions themselves but should apply guidelines developed out of the social consensus. Moreover, physicians have a duty to uncover the rationing that is often not apparent in our present system of health care and to expose episodes in which individuals have been denied medical care because of indigency.

Physicians should also help society decide exactly what equitable access to health care involves, and what constitutes adequate health care. Indeed, physicians should be committed as a group to the provision of adequate levels of health care for all individuals. Given the notion that medical ethics converts medical care into a sphere of cooperative activity in the liberal state, one ethical proposition must be that health care at an adequate level is available to all. This is an imperative, an ethical imperative under just doctoring, for all physicians.

In addition to helping decide what the adequate level of health care is, physicians should participate in a debate on the appropriate institutions for health care. While just doctoring does not necessarily support one set of institutions as opposed to another, it does require that physicians address these issues with the altruism and commitment they apply to individual patients. In particular, physicians should assess the ways in which the market in medical care must be regulated, and consider whether government control of the financing of health care may better service the goal of universal adequate access.

The Role of the Medical Profession

The above list of ethical requirements represents no small task for the medical profession. Indeed, I take a very broad view of the ethics of the profession. Although I recognize that many will disagree, it seems to me that each of these imperatives arises out of the nature of medical ethics in the liberal state. Perhaps the most salient feature of what I have described as just doctoring is its demand for comprehensive and collaborative action by the medical profession. An organized profession will, in fact, be far more capable of undertaking the set of tasks outlined above than would a disjointed or loosely organized profession. Is there a model for such an organized profession?

Some would say that the American Medical Association provides just this model. However, the AMA has rarely supported the sorts of ethical imperatives that arise out of just doctoring.[1] The AMA has addressed, for instance, the ethics of broadening access to health care. However, it is opposed to thoroughgoing governmental intervention in medicine, whereas just doctoring is attracted to government control of health care financing and would, perhaps, embrace it if it would bring equitable access to health care up to an adequate level. The AMA has also tirelessly opposed quality control programs that impose outside peer review of individual physicians, another issue that just doctoring supports. Thus, it is hard to imagine the organized medical profession in the United States undertaking the goals of just doctoring.

This insight raises an important point. A variety of commentators have argued that physicians are most interested in maintaining their own prerogatives, their own broad base of positive freedom. For instance, Robert Clark (see chapter 8) has argued that the market should be emphasized in health care so as to limit professional efforts to exact profits from the hospital (a physicians' cooperative). Some economists have supported this notion. Many in government believe that health care reforms must be premised on limits on the power of physicians. These positions evince a general skepticism about physician commitment to the welfare of patients as a group. Indeed, some may argue that the American Medical Association, and likely physicians in general, will attempt to block any progressive reforms in health care, suggesting that the profession is not trusted by some members of society.

There are reasons for the lack of trust. One of the best ways to understand it—the pun is unavoidable—is through a review of antitrust proceedings in medical care. This book is not the place to make a comprehensive analysis of antitrust law. Rather, our interest in antitrust law is to illustrate some of the bases for the distrust of the medical profession.

P. Areeda and D. F. Turner provide us with an excellent summary of the central aspects of antitrust laws.[2] They quote the Supreme Court on the object of the antitrust laws: "Congress was dealing with competition, which it ought to protect, and monopoly, which it sought to prevent."[3] The economic objectives of the antitrust laws are, however, somewhat more complex than this simple statement communicates. In particular, Areeda and Turner note that the objective of a procompetitive policy is

to maximize consumer economic welfare through efficiency in the use and allocation of scarce resources and via progressiveness in the development of new productive techniques and new products that put those resources to better use. At the same time, competitive policy also promotes "populist" goals that are commonly thought important. It disburses wealth; limits business size; broadens entrepreneurial opportunities; and substitutes the impersonal forces of the marketplace for the economic power of private individuals or groups to exploit or coerce those with whom they deal.[4]

They also argue, however, that courts usually give priority to competition over justifications for restrictive agreements that rest on concerns about economic distress. In addition, courts usually favor efficiency over those goals that might be considered more populist. Finally, when the choice is between competition and efficiency, the courts usually choose efficiency. Thus antitrust law is meant to promote competition but primarily when competition supports an efficient marketplace.[5]

The role that these laws play in the health care industry are instructive, for they demonstrate again the way in which courts have viewed the medical profession. In particular, antitrust litigation in health care shows the suspicion courts harbor toward the anticompetitive power of the medical profession. Therefore, populist tendencies of antitrust litigation tend to be emphasized in rulings on health care.

Antitrust litigation in the health care area is not new. As we have discussed, the Federal Trade Commission instituted antitrust suits against the American Medical Association several times in the 1930s and 1940s, largely as a result of interference from the organized profession in the development of prepaid group practices. However, through much of the century, the practice of learned professions was not thought to be commerce and thus was exempt from antitrust laws. In 1975, the Supreme Court decided that the practice of law could be subject to antitrust scrutiny in the case of *Goldfarb* v. *Virginia State Bar*.[6] Since then, the federal government has consistently subjected medical practice to antitrust scrutiny. Moreover, as procompetitive initiatives grow in medical care, antitrust plays a larger and larger role. An analysis of two key areas of antitrust litigation will demonstrate that the law as integrity and the American liberal state continue to distrust the medical profession and seek to curb the positive freedom of the profession.

Consider first the role of antitrust litigation in peer review. As discussed in chapter 6, peer review should be an important part of the medical profession's commitment to good quality care. Individual physicians should scrutinize the practice of other physicians, and those who have provided poor care should be educated or sanctioned. However, peer review can be a two-way street. If not done in a careful and ethical fashion, peer review can be used to discriminate against potential competitors. For instance, a powerful group of surgeons may decide they are facing too much competition from another surgeon. One way to remove this competition would be to subject the competing surgeon to unnecessary peer review.

We can see these sorts of tactics in the case of Dr. Timothy Patrick, a surgeon who worked in the Astoria Clinic in Astoria, Oregon. Dr. Patrick had joined a group practice.[7] He had eleven colleagues, including one other surgeon. He was paid a certain amount but billed a much larger amount. To increase his income, he requested that he receive as compensation a larger percentage of the total amount he was billing. The other practitioners refused. As a result, Dr. Patrick moved out of the Astoria Clinic and into practice by himself.

Thereafter occurred a series of events that eventually gave rise to a great deal of litigation. Practitioners at the Astoria Clinic and at Columbia Memorial Hospital alleged that Dr. Patrick was incompetent and frequently endangered patients in his medical practice. Dr. Patrick in turn alleged that the care he gave was consistently good, and that the concerns of the other physicians were with his status as a competitor, rather than with the quality of his practice. After a long series of charges and countercharges, Dr. Patrick sued for relief under the federal antitrust laws. He was awarded two million dollars following a jury trial, but the defendants appealed to the United States Circuit Court of Appeals, which overturned the jury verdict.[8]

Patrick's lawyers appealed to the Supreme Court, and in 1988 the Supreme Court ruled that Patrick had been a victim of antitrust violations by the other physicians in the clinic and his jury verdict and award were reinstated.[9] The Supreme Court was very clear that peer review had to be carried out in good faith and that the court would not tolerate hidden efforts to decrease competition.

Congress has now passed legislation that it hopes will promote peer review in spite of the *Patrick* decision.[10] Nonetheless, participants in peer review programs must be careful that their focus is strictly on the quality of care and not on more personal concerns.[11] The *Patrick* decision indicates that while society believes that peer review is important and that it leads to better quality care, they are also suspicious of physicians' efforts to control the practice of medicine through elimination of competitors.

This fear of the medical profession's monopolistic tendencies is also seen in cases regarding staff privileges. A good example is the case of *Weiss* v. *York Hospital*.[12] In this case, Weiss, the plaintiff, was an osteopath who was denied staff privileges at a hospital in Pennsylvania. Dr. Weiss alleged that his training was equivalent to the training received by medical doctors and that the refusal of the hospital to grant him privileges was motivated by competitive interests rather than by a real concern about his credentials or capacity to practice medicine. While the litigation focused to a large extent on the history of discrimination against osteopathic doctors and the overall market dominance of the defendant hospital, of critical importance to the plaintiff's case was the high-handed treatment that Dr. Weiss and his colleagues received from the medical staff executive committee at the defendant hospital.

While we have not discussed the issue of credentialing in great detail in this book, that process is one of the means by which a medical staff controls the quality of the care rendered at its hospital. Credentialing committees of hospitals review the applications of individuals who wish to practice at those hospitals and exclude those who might render poor care. In addition, these committees recredential physicians over time, again examining the quality of the practitioner. While this is a legitimate function, it can be used to monopolize access to hospitals and decrease competition. In more theoretical terms, it can be used as a way to increase the positive freedom of the physicians who are already practicing at a hospital and decrease the negative freedom of individual patients as consumers who might want to have their care provided by doctors who have not yet been credentialed.

It should be clear that courts will prohibit antitrust activities that occur under the guise of credentialing. In *Weiss* v. *York Hospital*, the court found that there was no legitimate basis for excluding osteopathic physicians from the staff and that the only rationale for such exclusion would be that staff physicians did not want any further competition. Again we see the law as integrity, the law of the liberal state, questioning the motives of physicians and ultimately finding it necessary to restrict the positive freedom of the profession. Some commentators, especially those who have long been suspicious of the medical profession's power, have continued to urge greater and broader applications of antitrust scrutiny in medical care.[13] They argue that it is necessary to limit the power of the medical profession if we are to bring about a better quality health care system in this country. It is clear, then, that antitrust litigation in health care demonstrates a certain distrust of the monopolistic power of the medical profession.

These commentators have a valid point of view, and there is little doubt it conflicts with the ethical imperatives created by just doctoring. Medical ethics as just doctoring creates a broad mandate for individual physicians and the profession as a whole to become more involved in political, legal, and economic issues in medicine. In contrast, those who argue that the medical profession's power must be controlled would no doubt require limits on the ability of physicians to address such issues. This conflict is not easily resolved. While from the point of view of just doctoring, I might urge that it is an ethical violation for physicians to engage in any activities that might increase monopoly power or decrease competition, clearly I am in favor of concerted action by the medical profession to bring about a better set of health care institutions. Others may reasonably fear that physicians will, in the name of ethics and commitment to better care, use this campaign to forward their own interests. Thus, while I urge a broader ethical agenda for physicians and base it on altruistic notions of the relationships between doctors and patients, others will argue that physicians will choose to modify purportedly ethical activity to their own advantage.

In essence, antitrust litigation against physicians, like many of the legal issues in medicine we have reviewed, reveals a need to decrease physicians' power and a need to increase the negative freedom of individual patients. Nevertheless, I have advocated generally greater efforts by physicians to involve themselves in political and legal issues in medicine. I maintain that rather than assuming the posture of mere technicians, physicians have an ethical duty to address issues of the organization of medical care and to take an active part in determining its structure. Even though I argue that this ethical duty is very much different from the ethical duties physicians may have assumed in the past, and I have tried to make medical ethics consistent with the liberal state, many might say that just doctoring simply creates greater opportunities for physicians' abuse of monopolistic power.

I recognize that these are serious objections to the theory of medical ethics as just doctoring. How do I answer them? On the one hand, I might argue that patients should trust the altruistic commitment of physicians and physicians' renewed understanding of what it means to be ethical in the practice of medicine. On the other hand, this may not be enough. Therefore, this question remains: How can patients be assured that physicians will assume a truly ethical stance consistent with just doctoring and not merely, as it appears they have in the past, turn these ethical propositions to their own advantage?

One answer obviously is education. Applications to medical schools have decreased greatly over the past decade. Perhaps students have begun to realize that physicians do not have the power they once had within the health care system, or perhaps they feel that medicine is less gratifying than it once was. I am optimistic, and I believe that those individuals who were interested in medicine only because they were interested in the economic gain have now decided upon other careers. This suggests that those who are now going to medical school are much more open to understanding the ethical nature of medical practice and thus could be trained to become just doctors. I hope this is the case.

In addition to educating students, medical societies and professional organizations must begin to debate the variety of issues discussed herein. Central, I have argued, must be the tenet that physicians move away from positions defined by their economic self-interest, and toward those more in alignment with the good of patients. Physicians must give up control, especially in economic decision making, and become patient advocates. This may be asking too much—I am unsure that it can occur.

What I am sure about is that medical practice and health institutions in this country are changing. Ethical physicians must address these changes and realize that traditional medical ethics is as outdated as the notion of an individual practitioner working in a fee-for-service arrangement in which there is no concern about health care cost. Medical care is changing and I believe that medical ethics must also change. I offer the notion of just doctoring as one point of view for a new medical ethics.

Notes

Chapter 1: The Liberal State

1. For a summary of this case, see A. M. Goldman, K. M. Stratton, and M. D. Brown, "What Actually Happened: An Informed Review of the Linares Incident," *Law, Medicine and Health Care* 17 (1989): 298–307.

2. Thomas Nagel, "Moral Conflict and Political Legitimacy," *Philosophy and Public Affairs* 16 (1987): 215–240.

3. *Webster's New Collegiate Dictionary* (Springfield, Mass.: Merriam & Co., 1974).

4. Isaiah Berlin, *Four Essays on Liberty* (London: Oxford University Press, 1969).

5. Ibid., 24.

6. John Stuart Mill, *On Liberty* (Northbrook, Ill.: AHM Publishing, 1947), 21.

7. Ibid., 35.

8. Charles Fried, *Right and Wrong* (Cambridge: Harvard University Press, 1978).

9. Berlin, *Four Essays on Liberty*, 38.

10. Robert Nozick, *Anarchy, State and Utopia* (New York: Basic Books, 1974), 164.

11. Bertrand de Jouvenal, *The Ethics of Redistribution* (Indianapolis: Liberty Press, 1990).

12. Of course, some theorists whom I would call conservatives might see themselves as true liberals, and might refer to my modern liberalism as socialism. For instance, H. Tristram Engelhardt, in developing a theory of bioethics, refers to the linchpin of public authority as a matter of peaceable, mutual negotiation. This is a liberal view, but I would understand Engelhardt

as a classic liberal or perhaps a conservative. See H. Tristram Engelhardt, *The Foundations of Bioethics* (New York: Oxford University Press, 1986), 44.

13. See, for example, C. B. McPherson, "Maximization of Democracy," in *Philosophy, Politics, and Society*, ed. P. Laslett and W. G. Runciman (New York: Barnes and Noble, 1967).

14. A. Hellegers and A. Jonsen, "Conceptual Foundations for an Ethic of Medical Care," in *Ethics and Health Policy*, ed. R. Branson and R. Veatch (Cambridge, Mass.: Ballinger Publishers Company, 1976), 38.

15. John Rawls, "Justice as Fairness: Political, Not Metaphysical," *Philosophy and Public Affairs* 14 (1985): 223–251.

16. See John Rawls, "The Idea of an Overlapping Consensus," *Oxford Journal of Legal Studies*, 7, no. 1 (1986): 1. Rawls reiterates that the overlapping consensus is not a mere *modus vivendi*, but substantive and constitutive of morality. See also John Rawls, "The Domain of the Political and the Overlapping Consensus," *New York University Law Review* 64 (May 1989): 233–255.

17. John Locke, *Second Treatise of Government* (New York: Dover, 1959), chaps. 9–12. See also Mill, *On Liberty*.

18. Herein I follow closely the arguments made by Ronald Dworkin, in "Liberalism," in *Public and Private Morality*, ed. S. Hampshire (Cambridge: Cambridge University Press, 1978).

19. Ibid., 72.

20. John Rawls, *A Theory of Justice* (Cambridge: Harvard University Press, 1971), 54.

21. T. M. Scanlon, "Contractualism and Utilitarianism," in *Utilitarianism and Beyond*, ed. A. Sen and B. Williams (New York: Cambridge University Press, 1982), 110. Joel Feinberg has noted that Rawls relies quite heavily on a theory of natural duty and contract theory in order to develop the concept of obedience. Rawls's natural duty theory states, in so many words, that one has a duty to partake in a just institution. One cannot avoid the rules of an institution if that institution is a just one. As J. Feinberg puts it: "That principle [of natural duty] which Rawls argues would be acknowledged in the original position and is in that sense 'derived from reason' requires individuals to 'support and comply with' already existing institutions and help bring about just arrangements. It is this principle which binds people to their political institutions." J. Feinberg, "Rawls and Institutionism," in *Reading Rawls*, ed. Norman Daniels (Oxford: Blackwell, 1975), 120. Citizens generate the institutions of society from an original set of just principles. In this manner, the justice of these institutions is put beyond question; if this were not so, then the citizens would have to debate the matter until the institutions were finally aligned with the two principles at the heart of justice as fairness. Since the original institutions must be just, the citizens have a duty to participate in just institutions and so they must obey the rules of the institutions.

Rawls's society, then, has strong restrictions on civil disobedience. He agrees with contract theoreticians who garner obedience through consent. Consent, used here as an agreement to fulfill the obligations of citizenship, is implicit in Rawls's society; if one did not consent at the outset, then debate would continue until consent was possible, given the constructive model of reasoning in the original position. As a result, Rawls faces difficulties in defining a viable theory of civil disobedience. He faces much the same problems as those faced by Locke, the ultimate contract theoretician. Neither can show how a person can selectively disobey laws: participation implies consent. See J. A. Simmons, "Tacit Consent and Political Obligation," *Philosophy and Public Affairs* 5 (1976): 274–291.

22. Rawls, *A Theory of Justice*, 54.

23. Ibid., 83.

24. Rawls does not, however, simply present these principles. He argues that they would be lexically ordered: the principle concerned with the right to equal liberty would take precedence over the one concerned with the restriction of inequality. Liberty can be limited only for the sake of liberty, not for the sake of equality. Rawls believes then that his citizens would opt for liberty over equality in the original position. From these lexically ordered principles, the citizens in the original position would go on to construct their society and the institutions that order it. In the constructive process, constant references would be made back to the lexically ordered principles that would stand as a basis for a final decision in any debate. As such, the principles would be embedded in the institutions, and the justice that issues from them would prevail. A profoundly liberal state emphasizing the virtues of individualism and liberty, and the importance of impartiality regarding the choice of individual moral principles would be constructed. Yet, there would also be concern for inequality.

25. R. Dworkin, *Law's Empire* (Cambridge, Mass.: Belknap Press, 1986).

26. Ibid., 1.

27. H. L. A. Hart, *Law, Liberty, and Morality* (Stanford: Stanford University Press, 1963), 20.

28. Patrick Devlin, *The Enforcement of Morals* (London: Oxford University Press, 1965).

29. Dworkin develops the notion of law as integrity to contrast with positivism in *Law's Empire*. See Dworkin, *Law's Empire*, especially chaps. 1–3.

30. Ibid., 126.

31. R. Wollheim, "Crime, Sin and Mr. Justice Devlin," *Encounter* 13 (1959): 13–24.

Chapter 2: The Medical Enterprise and Medical Ethics

1. D. Barnlund, "The Mystification of Meaning: Doctor-Patient Encounters," *Journal of Medical Education* 51 (1976): 716–725.

2. T. Szasz and J. Hollender, "The Basic Model of the Doctor-Patient Relationship," *Archives of Internal Medicine* 97 (1956): 85–90.

3. Robert Burt, *Taking Care of Strangers* (New York: Free Press, 1979), 103. This excellent monograph analyzes doctor-patient relationships in psy-

choanalytic terms, and extends Parsons's discussion of transference. As a result, some of Burt's conclusions may be quite different from those that issue from a political-philosophical analysis. These issues are, however, the subject of another essay.

4. See for example Jay Katz, *The Silent World of Doctors and Patients* (New York: Free Press, 1984). Szasz and Hollender assert that the participants in the relationship should have "equal power" and should be "mutually independent." These goals are very difficult to accomplish. The physician possesses a great deal of knowledge and information that the patient can barely begin to share without special efforts by the physician. A realistically ethical physician-patient relationship that respects the patient as a person means that the physician proposes something and the patient accepts. The key issue is the extent of the physician's proposal. Given her powerful advantage in knowledge, the proposal might be quite specific. Thus the mere assertion that the doctor and patient should be equal does little to demonstrate how or why the mutual participation model is to be reached.

5. H. S. Becker, "The Nature of a Profession," in *Sociological Work*, ed. H. S. Becker (Chicago: Aldine Publishing Co., 1970), 87.

6. E. Hughes, "Professions," *Daedalus* 92 (1963): 657–677.

7. Ibid., 658.

8. A. Buchanan, "Medical Paternalism," *Philosophy and Public Affairs* 7 (1976): 370–381.

9. C. J. Friedrich, "Authority, Reason, and Discretion," in *Nomos I: Authority*, ed. C. J. Friedrich (Cambridge: Harvard University Press, 1958).

10. Hannah Arendt has extended the concept of authority by describing its etymological roots. Hannah Arendt, *Between Past and Future; Six Exercises in Political Thought* (New York: Viking Press, 1961). The Greek and Latin roots indicate that "authority" originally approximated the meaning of the word "augmented." The person in authority is augmented by a set of ideas extraneous to his own personality or knowledge. These ideas or beliefs allow others to accept his authority.

Arendt's description derives at least partially from Max Weber's insights. Weber conceived of three types of authority: (1) de jure authority, which derives from rules and ordered activity; (2) de facto authority, which derives from one's own specific skills and abilities; and (3) charismatic authority, which results from one's personality and which is outside institutional constraints. Some have pointed out that Weber's authority types represent a spectrum of different sources of authority. Weber's primary point is that a conceptual relationship between a person's activity and a set of ideas or beliefs provides authority. Miriam Siegler and Humphrey Osmond have argued this in the medical context in "Aesculopian Authority," *Hastings Center Studies* (1973): 41–43, in which a physician has moral, sapiential, and charismatic authority. The latter type of authority has certain priestly or magical qualities.

11. Talcott Parsons's major works on this subject are *The Social System* (Glencoe, Ill.: Free Press, 1951) and "Social Change and Medical Organization in the United States: A Sociological Perspective," *Annals of the American Academy of Political and Social Science* 356 (1963): 21–42.

12. Talcott Parsons, *The Social Structure* (Glencoe, Ill.: Free Press, 1964), 43.

13. My characterization here is quite dependent on analysis by Jeffrey Berlant in *Profession and Monopoly: A Study of Medicine in the United States and Great Britain* (Berkeley, Los Angeles, London: University of California Press, 1975).

14. Ibid., 9.

15. Parsons, *The Social Structure*, 43.

16. Ibid., 44–46.

17. Parsons, "Social Change and Medical Organization," 23.

18. Ibid., 26.

19. Eliot Friedson, *Doctoring Together* (New York: Elsevier, 1975), 45.

20. Parsons, "Social Change and Medical Organization," 27.

21. A. Jonsen, "The Rights of Physicians: A Philosophical Essay" (unpublished essay filed with the Kennedy Institute Library, Georgetown University, dated June 1978), 14.

22. H. Tristram Engelhardt, *The Foundations of Bioethics* (New York: Oxford University Press, 1986), 23.

23. Berlant, *Profession and Monopoly*, chap. 3.

24. R. Kudlien, "Medical Ethics and Popular Ethics in Greece and Rome," *ClinoMedica* 5 (1970): 93.

25. Robert M. Veatch, *A Theory of Medical Ethics* (New York: Basic Books, 1981), 23.

26. Ibid., 149.

27. Ibid., 154.

28. Tom L. Beauchamp and James F. Childress, *Principles of Biomedical Ethics* (Oxford: Oxford University Press, 1983).

29. Berlant, *Profession and Monopoly*, 69.

30. Ibid., 70–75. Berlant believes that anticompetition and monopolization are the major reasons for the existence of ethical codes.

31. See Berlant, *Profession and Monopoly*, 100.

32. Ibid., 100.

33. Ibid., 107.

34. Ibid., 107.

35. Ibid., 108.

36. Veatch, *A Theory of Medical Ethics*, 5.

37. Beauchamp and Childress, *Principles of Biomedical Ethics*, 213.

38. There are, of course, many different ethical theories or principles that underlie the "patient comes first" value. Beauchamp and Childress, for example, outline a number of completely different principles based on certain ethical theories that justify physician behavior. These principles include, among others, justice, nonmalfeasance, beneficence, and autonomy. For now we will avoid this particular characterization of medical ethics.

39. Beauchamp and Childress, *Principles of Biomedical Ethics*, 177.

40. Paul Ramsey, *The Patient As Person* (New Haven: Yale University Press, 1970), 2.

41. Ibid., 5.

42. Ibid., 6.

43. Ibid., 6. Others have not shared this view, arguing that doctors' charity-in-relation is more akin to Aristotle's theory of virtue. See Beauchamp and Childress, *Principles of Biomedical Ethics*, 262.

44. B. Williams, "The Idea of Equality," in *Justice and Equality*, ed. Hugo Bedau (Englewood Cliffs, New Jersey: Prentice Hall, 1971), 127.

45. Immanuel Kant, *Groundwork of the Metaphysics of Morals*, ed., H. J. Paton (New York: Harper and Row, 1964), 61.

46. Ibid., 96.

47. Despite the apparent applicability of Kantian theory to the doctor-patient relation, medical ethics cannot claim a Kantian basis for one important reason. Kantian moral philosophy is based on universalizability. It applies to all citizens. The categorical imperative requires that each person be treated as an end in himself. Medical ethics is not meant to be universalizable. Rather it refers specifically to the relation between doctors and patients. The altruistic aspects of medical ethics do not reach beyond the doctor-patient encounter.

In this regard, medical ethics can be understood as a matter of role morality. Throughout this discussion I am quite dependent on David Luban's insightful discussion in *Lawyers and Justice* (Princeton: Princeton University Press, 1988). Role morality concerns those duties that arise out of one's role or "station." A role is a concept of functional anthropology and, as Erving Goffman has put it, "Consists of the activity the incumbent would engage in were he to act solely in terms of the normative demands upon someone in his position." See Erving Goffman, "Role Distance," in *Encounters: Two Studies in the Sociology of Interaction* (Indianapolis: Bobbs-Merrill, 1961), 85. For example, the lawyer's role morality might require that he act in an especially antagonistic manner when litigating a case on behalf of a client. Similarly, the physician may have to act in an especially benevolent fashion toward her sick and vulnerable patient.

Kantian ethics is more fundamental in that its imperatives apply to all people as people, not as actors within a certain role. Kantian moral agency is fundamental. One can move in and out of roles. The lawyer does not treat everyone as if he or she were his client, nor does he treat everyone as if each were the prosecutor or an adverse witness. Role morality assumes a secondary position when compared with the public morality envisioned by Kant. Thus public morality itself, especially Kantian morality, must be universalizable, whereas role morality is not.

More important for the purposes of my argument is the relationship of role morality to public morality in the liberal state. I would argue that public morality limits role morality in certain ways and yet tolerates role moralities insofar as they express imperatives that are more altruistic than the public morality can require.

The public morality of liberalism is based on equal concern and respect for each individual. This means that each individual must be allowed to pursue her own enterprises and to define her own conception of a good life. However, the liberal state must also ensure that this pursuit is not detrimental to the interests of other members of society. Specifically, the state must guard against inequality. Any role morality must respect these aspects of the public morality, for roles in the state are secondary to membership in the state.

Nonetheless, certain roles can require altruistic or virtuous behavior beyond that expected by the state. For instance, certain religious orders might require that their members earn money in the market and then give all of it away to charity. This is not a requirement for every citizen in the liberal state, but the state accepts these role duties. However, the state will not accept the demands the same religious order might make upon its members to oppose what they regard as murder by attacking abortion clinics. Thus role morality is limited by the public morality, but certain duties arising out of the role are acceptable, and even welcomed by the state. These role duties are not universalizable, however, in the same manner that the public morality is.

In short, medical ethics, which emphasizes the physician's duty to the patient, is not applicable to society at large. In this it differs fundamentally from Kantian moral philosophy. Medical ethics defines a role morality. When physicians care for patients they are held to a set of moral imperatives that are not part of the general set of moral relations between individuals in the liberal state. It is nevertheless important to note that the role morality of medical ethics does apply to all doctor-patient relationships. The patient's role as patient, not as an individual, and the doctor's role as doctor, not as a concerned citizen, define the ethical relationship. In this regard, the class of doctors bears some common responsibilities to the class of patients.

This means that if a physician finds certain aspects of the care of a patient morally repugnant, she must find equally repugnant the fact that these aspects exist for other doctors and patients. For example, a physician working in a small clinic in the inner city may find that many of her patients who carry the human immunodeficiency virus cannot afford to purchase AZT, a drug that can postpone the onset of AIDS. She finds that these financial constraints make it impossible for her to discharge her duties in an appropriate fashion. A physician at a well-heeled clinic might not face the same problem because her patients all have insurance. Nonetheless, the second physician can sympathize with the first and understand the problems with financing. More important, the second physician should find the situation of the inner-city patients as morally repugnant as their own doctor does. The fact that some patients are not being treated with complete respect offends medical ethics, even when the patients are not one's own. The doctor's role responsibilities are thus universalizable to the class of all patients, but they are focused on the particular patient. These are issues we will return to in subsequent chapters.

This raises another point. Kantian moral philosophy is only similar to, rather than being the basis of, medical ethics. Recognition of this fact frees my argument from a potentially serious conflict. I have argued that medical ethics is in many ways illiberal. Kant was in many ways quite liberal. Indeed his moral philosophy and its distinction between noumenon and phenomenon has been used as a critical element in the distinction between classic liberals and modern liberals. See Michael Sandel, *Liberalism and the Limits of Justice* (Cambridge: Cambridge University Press, 1982), chap. 1. Kant's insistence that all individuals be treated with equal respect and concern is quite compatible with the theory of liberalism developed in the previous chapter. Thus it would be difficult to argue medical ethics is illiberal and yet admit it is based in Kantian moral philosophy.

48. Hans Jonas, "Philosophical Reflections on Experimenting with Human Subjects," in *Contemporary Issues in Bioethics*, ed. Tom L. Beauchamp and Leroy Walters (Belmont, Calif.: Wadsworth Publishing Co., 1978), 417.

49. S. Twiss, "The Problem of Moral Responsibility in Medicine," *Journal of Medicine and Philosophy* 2 (1977): 338–352.

50. Ibid., 339.

51. See Edmund D. Pellegrino and David C. Thomasma, *For the Patient's Good* (New York: Oxford University Press, 1988).

52. Ibid., 27.

53. Ibid., 117.

54. Berlant, *Profession and Monopoly*, 204.

55. Ibid., 88.

56. Ibid., 225.

57. N. Davis, *History of the American Medical Association from Its Organization Up to 1855* (Philadelphia: Lippincott, Grambo and Co., 1855).

58. Berlant, *Profession and Monopoly*, 231.

59. R. Shyrock, *Medical Licensing in America: 1650–1965* (Baltimore: Johns Hopkins Press, 1987).

60. Paul Starr, *The Social Transformation of American Medicine* (New York: Basic Books, 1982), 184–185.

61. J. Duffy, *A History of Public Health in New York City, 1946–1966* (New York: Russel Sage Foundation, 1974).

62. Ibid., 230–245.

63. Starr, *Social Transformation of American Medicine*, 201.

64. G. Rosen, "Contract as Lodge Practice and Its Influence on Medical Attitudes to Health Insurance," *American Public Health Annals* 67 (1977): 374–378.

65. I. S. Falk, "Proposals for National Health Insurance in the U.S.A.: Origins and Evolution and Some Perceptions for the Future," *Milbank Memorial Fund Quarterly* 55 (1977): 161–191.

66. Shyrock, *Medical Licensing in America*, 63.

67. Starr, *Social Transformation of American Medicine*, 230–232.

68. One last chance for eliminating such control, or at least for changing its emphases, occurred with the rise of Progressivism. In the years 1910 to 1915, the Progressive Party attempted to resist laissez-faire policies. Some party members drew on developments then occurring in Great Britain and began to campaign for some sort of social insurance, including health insurance. For the first time, physicians began to question the assumption that the government should not be involved in the delivery of health care to the individual.

These developments set the stage for a very critical period in the history of the AMA and the American medical profession. In 1915 and 1916, the AMA was, surprisingly, quite open to the Progressive initiatives on health care.

Articles in the *Journal of the American Medical Association* and the AMA's directions to its committee on social insurance indicated that the association was certain that compulsory health insurance was in the offing. Thus the AMA seemed prepared to abandon its opposition to government involvement in medical care and accept that health care could best be served by social insurance. This would, of course, demand some changes in the existing fee-for-service system. It might also challenge the institutional arrangements that supported the doctor-patient relationship.

Enthusiasm for these proposals was, however, ephemeral. The profession had begun to divide into two groups. One, of which both Lambert and Rubinow were members, was composed of physicians who had received postgraduate education and had specialized professionally. They were at the leading edge of new developments in medical education and science. The other, larger, group was made up of general practitioners and led by Eden V. Delphy, who had no postgraduate training. Delphy's leadership was based on a fear that some government control of medicine would reduce physician prerogatives and control of therapy, and would change existing economic relationships. Drawing on a wellspring of support, Delphy's group took control of the House of Delegates.

69. "Minutes of the House of Delegates," *Journal of the American Medical Association* 74 (January-March 1920): 1319.

70. Falk, "Proposals for National Health Insurance," 161–191.

71. Editorial, *Journal of the American Medical Association* 99 (October-December 1932): 1950.

72. Starr, *Social Transformation of American Medicine*, 271.

73. Ibid., 272.

74. Ibid., 276.

75. T. Arnold, "Department of Justice: Statement About Group Health Insurance Cost," *Current History* (1938): 49.

76. Starr, *Social Transformation of American Medicine*, 305.

77. Congress definitely was aware of the AMA's success in defeating a California State health plan in 1945–1946. Starr, *Social Transformation of American Medicine*, 283.

78. Starr, *Social Transformation of American Medicine*, 297.

79. Ibid., 298.

80. Editorial, *Journal of the American Medical Association* 102 (April-June 1934): 2200–2201.

81. Starr, *Social Transformation of American Medicine*, 300.

82. The AMA campaign against the Group Health Associates was discussed in D. Hyde, et al., "The American Medical Association: Power, Purpose and Politics in Organized Medicine," *Yale Law Journal* 63 (1955): 938–978.

83. Starr, *Social Transformation of American Medicine*, 309.

84. Herman M. Somers and Anne R. Somers, *Doctors, Patients and Health Insurance: The Organization and Financing of Medical Care* (Washington: Brookings Institute, 1961), 300–320.

85. Starr, *Social Transformation of American Medicine*, 368.

86. *Handbook of Public Assistance*, Supplement D, 680 #D01540 (Washington: Government Printing Office, 1965).

87. E. Sparer, "The Legal Right to Health Care," *Hastings Center Report*, 6 (October 1976): 39–47, 43.

88. Starr, *Social Transformation of American Medicine*, 375.

89. Judith Feder, *Medicare: The Politics of Federal Hospital Insurance* (Lexington, Mass: Lexington Books, 1977).

90. Friedson, *Doctoring Together*, 45.

91. Ibid., 51.

92. Competition, or lack of it, is the subject of a great many recent essays and articles. See, for example, L. D. Brown, "Competition and Health Cost Containment: Cautions and Conjectures," *Milbank Memorial Foundation Quarterly* 59 (1981): 145–189; T. Marmor, et al., "Medical Care and Pro-competitive Reform," *Vanderbilt Law Review* 34 (1981): 1010–1040.

93. R. Gibson, "National Health Expenditures, 1979," *Health Care Financing Review* 2 (Summer 1980): 29–37.

94. Clark Havighurst, "Antitrust Enforcement in the Medical Services Industry: What Does It All Mean?" *Milbank Memorial Foundation Quarterly* 58 (Winter 1980): 89–124, 102.

95. Kenneth Arrow, "Uncertainty and the Welfare Economics of Medical Care," *American Economics Review* 53 (1963): 941–949.

96. R. Auger and D. Goldberg, "Prepaid Health Plans and Moral Hazard," *Public Policy* 22 (1974): 353–371.

Chapter 3: Medicine in the Liberal State

1. See Friedson, *Doctoring Together*, 125.

2. In subsequent chapters, we will return to more realistic encounters.

3. Alasdair MacIntyre, *After Virtue: A Study in Moral Theory* (Notre Dame, Ind.: University of Notre Dame Press, 1981).

4. G. Dworkin, "Paternalism," in *Morality and the Law*, ed. R. A. Wasserstrom (Belmont, Calif.: Wadsworth, 1971), 108.

5. D. W. Brock, "Paternalism and Autonomy," *Ethics* 98 (1988): 550–566.

6. James Childress, *Who Should Decide? Paternalism in Health Care* (New York: Oxford University Press, 1982).

7. Starr, *Social Transformation of American Medicine*, 381.

8. Public Health Service, *Health: United States 1981* (Washington: Government Printing Office, 1982).

9. Berlant, *Profession and Monopoly*, 70–75.

10. Ibid., 71.

11. Ibid., 72.

12. Congressional Budget Service, *Overview of Fiscal Year 1982 for Human Resources Programs* (Washington: Government Printing Office, 1982), 26.

13. *New York Times*, 29 September 1982, A-1. See also A. R. Somers,

"Sounding Board Moderating the Rise in Health Care Costs: A Pragmatic Beginning," *New England Journal of Medicine* 307 (1982): 944–946.

14. A. C. Enthoven, "Consumer Choice Health Plan," *New England Journal of Medicine* 298 (1978): 651–658.

15. Ibid., 652.

16. B. Roe, "The UCR Boondoggle: A Death Knell for Private Practice?" *New England Journal of Medicine* 305 (1981): 41–45.

17. See chapter 2.

18. Roe, "UCR Boondoggle," 41.

19. American Hospital Association, *Hospital Regulation: Report of the Special Committee on the Regulatory Process* (Chicago: American Hospital Association, 1977).

20. United States Senate, Committee on Finance, Report 92–1230 (United States Senate, Washington, D.C., 26 September 1972), cited in Friedson, *Doctoring Together*, 247.

21. M. Goran, "The PSRO Hospital Review System," *Medical Care* 13 (1975): 1–33.

22. Starr, *Social Transformation of American Medicine*, 402.

23. Jimmy Carter, State of the Union Address (Washington: 25 January 1978).

24. B. Mitchell and J. Schwartz, "Strategies for Financing National Health Insurance: Who Wins and Who Loses," *New England Journal of Medicine* 295 (1976): 866–871.

25. Ibid., 869.

26. Ibid., 870.

27. W. Blackstone, "On Health Care as a Legal Right," *Georgia Law Review* 10 (1976): 391–423.

28. Ralph Nader, "Responsibilities of Physicians to Society," *Federation Proceedings* 31 (1972): 44–54.

29. Starr, *Social Transformation of American Medicine*, 414.

30. See Enthoven, "Consumer Choice Health Plan," 651.

31. Ibid., 652.

32. One can expect encouragement of HMOs to be an integral part of any procompetition legislation (see below notes 39–49). For a comprehensive discussion of HMOs see H. Luft, *Health Maintenance Organizations: Dimensions of Performance* (New York: Wiley Press, 1981); A. C. Enthoven, *Health Plan: The Only Practical Solution to the Soaring Cost of Medical Care* (Reading, Mass.: Addison-Wesley Publishing Co., 1981).

33. E. Saward and A. Sorenson, "Competition, Profit, and the HMO," *New England Journal of Medicine* 306 (1982): 929–931.

34. John K. Iglehart, "Health Care and American Business," *New England Journal of Medicine* 306 (1982): 120–124.

35. John K. Iglehart, "Drawing the Lines for the Debate on Competition," *New England Journal of Medicine* 305 (1981): 291–296.

36. Ibid., 295.

37. R. Geist, "Incentive Bonuses in Prepayment Plans," *New England Journal of Medicine* 291 (1974): 1306–1308. See also, L. D. Brown, "Competition and Health Cost Containment: Cautions and Conjectures," *Milbank Memorial*

Fund Quarterly 59 (1981): 145–166; T. Marmor, et al., "Medical Care and Procompetitive Reform," *Vanderbilt Law Review* 4 (1981): 1010–1040.

38. John K. Iglehart, "The New Era of Prospective Payment for Hospitals," *New England Journal of Medicine* 307 (1982): 1288–1292.

39. Robert Fetter, et al., "Case Mix Definition by Diagnosis Related Groups," *Medical Care Supplement* 18 (1980): 1–24. See also, John Thompson, Robert Fetter, et al., "Case Mix and Resource Use," *Inquiry* 12 (1975): 300–312.

40. Donald W. Simborg, "DRG Creep: A New Hospital Acquired Illness," *New England Journal of Medicine* 304 (1981): 1602–1604.

41. Thompson and Fetter, "Case Mix and Resource Use," 303.

42. See Simburg, "DRG Creep," 1603.

43. Iglehart, "Prospective Payment for Hospitals," 1288.

44. The Department of Health and Human Services pursued the DRG initiative with vigor, proposing a standard payment schedule and several guidelines for instituting DRGs. The guidelines included: adjustment of rates to fit local variations; prohibition of direct billing for costs not allowed by the plan; and an annual update of payment rates. Iglehart, "Prospective Payment for Hospitals," 1290.

45. Ibid., 1290.

46. John K. Iglehart, "Medicare Begins Prospective Payment of Hospitals," *New England Journal of Medicine* 308 (1983): 1428–1432.

47. I do not oppose such cost control techniques. I only wish to make clear what I see as their repercussions for doctors and patients.

48. Somers, "Moderating the Rise in Health Care Costs," 945.

49. David Kinzer, "Massachusetts and California—Two Kinds of Hospital Cost Control," *New England Journal of Medicine* 308 (1983): 838–841. D. Blumenthal and B. Caper, "What Price Cost Control? Massachusetts' New Hospital Payment Law," *New England Journal of Medicine* 308 (1983): 542–544.

50. Kinzer, "Two Kinds of Hospital Cost Control," 838.

51. E. P. Melia, L. M. Aucoin, L. J. Duhl, et al., "Competition in the Health Care Marketplace—A Beginning in California," *New England Journal of Medicine* 308 (1983): 788–792.

52. Kinzer, "Two Kinds of Hospital Cost Control," 839.

53. See N. Lurie, D. Ward, M. Shapiro, and R. H. Brook, "Termination from Medi-Cal—Does It Affect Health?" *New England Journal of Medicine* 311 (1984): 480–484.

54. U.S. Department of Health and Human Services: Report of the Graduate Medical Education National Advisory Committee to the Secretary, Vol. 1, September 1980: DHHS Pub. No. 81-651 (Washington: General Printing Office, 1981).

55. D. N. Mendelsohn, W. B. Schwartz, and F. A. Sloan, "Why There Will be Little or No Physician Surplus Between Now and the Year 2000," *New England Journal of Medicine* 318 (1988): 892–897. Compare with E. Ginzburg, "Physician Supply in the Year 2000," *Health Affairs* (Summer 1989): 84–90.

56. See Mendelsohn, et al., "No Physician Surplus," 893.

57. A. Gittlesohn and J. E. Wennberg, "Variations in Medical Care Among Small Areas," *Scientific American* 246 (1982): 120–126.

58. The following is drawn from Alvin Tarlov, "The Shattuck Lecture—the Increasing Supply of Physicians, the Changing Structure of the Health-Services System, and the Future of the Practice of Medicine," *New England Journal of Medicine* 308 (1983): 1235–1244.

59. Ibid., 1240.

60. Ibid., 1241.

61. Ibid., 1241.

62. Ibid., 1241.

63. B. Steinwald, "The Role of the Proprietary Hospital," *Law and Contemporary Problems* 35 (1970): 817–839. See also, American Hospital Association, *Hospital Statistics* (Chicago: American Hospital Association, 1980).

64. See B. Ferber, "An Analysis of Chain Operated For-Profit Hospitals," *Health Services Research* 6 (1971): 49–60.

65. See Arnold Relman, "Investor-Owned Hospitals and Health Care Costs," *New England Journal of Medicine* 309 (1983): 370–372.

66. See A. I. Levenson, "The Growth of Investor Owned Psychiatric Hospitals," *American Journal of Psychiatry* 139 (1982): 902–907.

67. Nearly one-half of the nongovernmental psychiatric beds in this country are privately owned. We will not spend a great deal of time discussing this special case.

68. See R. M. Cunningham, "Changing Philosophies in Medical Care and the Rise of the Investor Owned Hospital," *New England Journal of Medicine* 307 (1982): 817–819.

69. See Edmund D. Pellegrino, "Medical Care Quality and the Public Trust," cited in Cunningham, "Changing Philosophies," 818.

70. R. Baird, "On Profits and Hospitals," *Journal of Economic Issues* 5 (1971): 57.

71. R. Kinkhead, "Humana's Hard Sell Hospitals," *Fortune* (17 November 1981): 68–81.

72. See Ferber, "Chain Operated For-Profit Hospitals," 49.

73. See E. Ginzberg, "The Destabilization of Health Care," *New England Journal of Medicine* 315 (1986): 757–760.

74. See Levenson, "Growth of Investor Owned Psychiatry Hospitals," 905.

75. See Arnold Relman, "The New Medical Industrial Complex," *New England Journal of Medicine* 303 (1980): 963–970.

76. Ibid., 967.

77. See L. Jones, "Side Effect Seen in Ban on Self-Referrals," *American Medical News* 17 (March 1989).

78. American Medical Association, *Current Opinions of the Judicial Council of the American Medical Association—1982* (Chicago: American Medical Association, 1982), ix.

79. Ibid., sec. 6.10.

80. Ibid., sec. 8.07.

81. M. Siegler, "A Right to Health Care: Ambiguity, Professional Responsibility, and Patient Liberty," *Journal of Philosophy and Medicine* 4 (1979): 148–157.

82. The reaction of many physicians has been to embrace the liberal state wholeheartedly and to assert a libertarian ethic for patient care. First and foremost physicians assert the importance of their rights. Some observers, such as W. Ruddick, assert these rights in an effort to help return to the isolated doctor-patient relationship of the past. He argues that the advocacy of such rights can reestablish the mutual trust between patients and physicians. W. Ruddick, "Doctors' Rights and Work," *Journal of Medicine and Philosophy* 4 (June 1979): 192–203. His choice of the concept of rights is odd in light of the fact that he advocates a duty-based relationship, but this merely demonstrates the manner in which rights language can cause confusion.

83. R. Sade, "Medical Care as a Right: A Refutation," *New England Journal of Medicine* 285 (1976): 1288–1292.

84. R. Sade, "Is Health Care a Right?," *Image* 7 (1977): 11.

85. Ibid., 13.

86. Ibid., 15.

87. Sade, "Medical Care as a Right," 1289.

88. Ibid., 1290.

89. G. Annas, "The Patient Rights Advocate: Why and What and Who: A Joint Discussion Paper," presented at the Boston College Law School, April 1973, 10.

90. G. Outka, "Social Justice and Equal Access to Health Care," *Perspectives in Biology and Medicine* 18 (1975): 185–202, 194.

91. Ibid., 194.

92. Ibid., 194.

93. R. Masters, "Is Contract an Adequate Basis for Medical Ethics?" *Hastings Center Report* 5 (1975): 24–28.

Chapter 4: Just Doctoring: Medical Ethics for the 1990s

1. Dr. Thomas Duffy has used certain psychoanalytic insights to characterize this change in attitude. Duffy is a hematologist-oncologist and cares for many patients with life-threatening diseases. See Thomas Duffy, "Agamemnon's Fate and the Medical Profession," *Western New England Law Review* 9 (1987): 21–31.

2. Michael D. Bayles, *Professional Ethics* (Belmont, Calif.: Wadsworth Publishing Co., 1981), 11–12.

3. Robert M. Veatch, *A Theory of Medical Ethics* (New York: Basic Books, 1987), chapter 4.

4. See Bayles, "Professional Ethics," 7–13.

5. See Eliot Friedson, *Professional Powers: A Study of the Institutionalization of Formal Knowledge* (Chicago: University of Chicago Press, 1988), 110.

6. In this regard I am in agreement with Veatch. See Veatch, *A Theory of Medical Ethics*, chapter 4.

7. See T. A. Brennan, "Ensuring Access to Health Care for All: The Problem of AIDS as an Occupational Disease," *Duke Law Journal* (1988): 247–283.

8. M. Abrams and P. Volberding, "Clinical Care and Research in AIDS," *Hastings Center Report* 15 (1985): 16–18.

9. See John Rawls, "The Domain of the Political and Overlapping Consensus," *New York University Law Review* 64 (May 1989): 233–255.

10. M. Sandel, *Liberalism and the Limits of Justice* (New York: Cambridge University Press, 1982), 1.

11. Ibid., 6.

12. Ibid., 11.

13. Ibid., 17.

14. Ibid., 61.

15. Ibid., 145.

16. A. Gutman, "Communitarian Critics of Liberalism," *Philosophy and Public Affairs* 14 (1985): 308–322.

17. Ibid., 310.

18. Ibid., 312.

19. Michael Walzer, *Spheres of Justice* (New York: Basic Books, 1983).

20. Ibid., 89.

21. Veatch, *A Theory of Medical Ethics*, 149.

22. Ibid., 87.

23. Edmund D. Pellegrino and David C. Thomasma, *For the Patient's Good* (New York: Oxford University Press, 1988).

24. Ibid., 27.

25. Ibid., chapter 5.

26. Jay Katz, *The Silent World of Doctors and Patients* (New York: Free Press, 1984).

27. Tom L. Beauchamp and Ruth Faden, *A History and Theory of Informed Consent* (New York: Oxford University Press, 1986).

28. Katz, *The Silent World of Doctors and Patients*, 119.

29. Ibid., 175.

30. Ibid., 198.

31. Pellegrino and Thomasma, *For the Patient's Good*, 101.

32. Pellegrino and Thomasma distinguish between the covenant models of Ramsey, May, and Veatch. Their discussion here is quite insightful. Pellegrino and Thomasma, *For the Patient's Good*, 104.

33. Ibid., 114.

34. Ibid., 64.

35. Veatch, *A Theory of Medical Ethics*, 285.

Chapter 5: Informed Consent

1. Some have argued that informed consent suits push the Szasz-Hollender model of informed consent toward mutual participation. In this essay, we will regard mutual participation as the relationship of buyer to seller, both bearing rights that define their liberties. We will not refer to mutual participation as Ramsey-like teamwork between two ends in themselves.

2. See chapters 1 and 2. This focus helps us to avoid those criticisms of analyses of informed consent that center on the lack of empirical data showing that patients want more information.

3. See Alan Donagan, "Informed Consent in Theory and Experimentation," *Journal of Philosophy and Medicine* 2 (1977): 307–327.

4. Many cases define the limits of informed consent when emergency treatment is necessary. In this situation and in others, the liberal notion of individual liberty is more complicated and efforts to maintain autonomy more difficult to characterize. As we have seen, Mill was willing to allow such infringements on liberty in order to prevent harm. These kinds of cases can be separated in a nonarbitrary fashion from the normal doctor-patient relationship, and so need not confuse the following analysis.

5. It is true that the plaintiff's attorney normally decides what theory of law to bring to a suit. Most attorneys in the past, however, would bring both battery and negligence claims. As we shall see, the ascendance of the latter is due to increasingly favorable judicial decisions on its behalf.

6. See *Slater* v. *Boken*, 95 Eng. Rep. 860 (K.B. 1707). In this case the court held that trespass would occur if an unauthorized surgical procedure took place.

7. William L. Prosser, *Handbook of the Law of Torts*, 4th ed. (St. Paul, Minn.: West Publication Co., 1971), 102–106.

8. Fowler V. Harper and Fleming James, *The Law of Tort*, 4th ed. (Boston: Little, Brown, 1956), 213.

9. Jay Katz, "Informed Consent—A Fairy Tale?" *University of Pittsburgh Law Review* 39 (1977): 137–145. See also, Marcus Plante, "An Analysis of Informed Consent," *Fordham Law Review* 36 (1968): 639–658.

10. Prosser, *Handbook of the Law of Torts*, 165.

11. Arnold J. Rosoff, *Informed Consent: A Guide for Health Care Providers* (Rockville, Md.: Aspen Systems, 1981).

12. Marcus Plante, "The Decline of Informed Consent," *Washington & Lee Law Review* 35 (1978): 92–133. Compare, A. Meisel, "Exceptions to Informed Consent Doctrine: Striking a Balance Between Competing Issues in Medical Decision-Making," *Wisconsin Law Review* (1979): 413. (Meisel sees informed consent as reconciliation with individualism in medicine.)

13. *Pratt* v. *Davis*, 118 Ill. App. 161, 79 N.E. 562 (1905).

14. The details here are quite grisly. It appears that after a minor operation, the patient returned to Pratt's sanatorium. The court notes that "counsel for appellee assert in their brief that she was chloroformed in her bed without

her knowledge," and then operated on. Pratt was using the wondering "hyster" theory of epilepsy when he operated—a theory that had long since lost legitimacy, *Pratt v. Davis*, 118 Ill. App. 165, 79 N.E. 562 (1905).

15. *Pratt v. Davis*, 118 Ill. App. 162, 79 N.E. 562 (1905).

16. Ibid., 162.

17. *Mohr v. Williams*, 95 Minn. 261, 104 N.W. 12 (1905).

18. Ibid., 262.

19. Ibid., 263.

20. *Schloendorff v. New York Hospital*, 211 N.Y. 125, 105 N.E. 92 (1914).

21. Ibid., 126.

22. See chapter 3.

23. *Bennan v. Parsonnet*, 83 N.J.L. 20, 83 A. 948 (1912).

24. Ibid., 22.

25. Ibid., 24.

26. The court in *Bennan v. Parsonnet* thus accepts that trust and duty-bound behavior, the tenets of medical ethics, legitimate the doctor's authority in the doctor-patient relationship. (See chapter 3.)

27. *Hunt v. Bradshaw*, 242 N.C. 517 88 S.E. 2d 762 (1955).

28. Ibid., 766.

29. This is not to say that the plaintiff lost every consent suit that sounded in negligence. In *Borg v. Charles T. Miller Hospital*, 251 Minn. 427, 88 N.W. 2d 186 (1958), the court ruled that the plaintiff deserved a new trial on the grounds that the physicians acted negligently in failing to advise Borg that his spermatic cords would be cut in a prostatectomy. Nonetheless, *Hunt v. Bradshaw* appears to be representative of pre-Salgo informed consent suits.

30. *Salgo v. Leland Stanford University Board of Trustees*, 154 Cal. App. 2d 56, 317 P. 2d 170 (1957).

31. Ibid., 180–181.

32. Ibid., 180–181.

33. Ibid., 180–181. In this passage, Judge Bray closely followed the amicus curiae brief submitted by the American College of Surgeons. The amalgamation of positions he incorporates into his informed consent proposition is apparent in his cited cases: *Hunt v. Bradshaw*, (deference to physicians) and *Schloendorff v. Society of New York Hospital*, (strict battery standard).

34. Katz, "Informed Consent: A Fairy Tale," 152.

35. *Natanson v. Kline*, 186 Kan. 393, 350 P. 2d 1093 (1960).

36. 350 P. 2d, 1097. Schroeder cites, with approval, the case of *Borg v. Charles T. Miller Hospital*.

37. Ibid., 1103.

38. Ibid., 1104.

39. Ibid., 1105.

40. Ibid., 1105.

41. Katz, "Informed Consent: A Fairy Tale," 150.

42. *Shetter v. Rochelle*, 490 P. 2d 74, 78 (1966).

43. Ibid., 78.

44. *Mason v. Ellsworth*, 3 Wash. App. 298, 474 P. 2d 909 (1970).

45. Katz, "Informed Consent: A Fairy Tale," 154. Another barrier to pa-

tient's recovery in an informed consent action is the issue of causation. The negligence standard not only emphasizes the importance of expert testimony, but it also demands that a patient demonstrate that the failure to inform was the proximate cause of the injury. In other words, the plaintiff must be able to demonstrate that she would not have consented had she been informed fully about the procedure. This requirement led Justice Abe, in stinging dissent to the decision of *Nishi* v. *Hartwell*, to state that if "all cases under the doctrine of informed consent shall be tried under the negligence theory, it may amount to nullification of all such claims because it may be almost impossible, if not absolutely impossible in many cases, to prove damages under the generally recognized rule of proximate cause." *Nishi* v. *Hartwell*, 52 Hawaii 188, 473 P.2d 116 (1970). Justice Abe's dissent relies heavily on an article by Marcus L. Plante entitled, "An Analysis of informed Consent," *Fordham Law Review* 36 (1968): 639–658.

In any case, courts continued to employ the negligence standard backed by medical testimony on the extent of a physician's duty. Physicians' autonomy remained unchallenged by the judiciary. A classic example of post-*Natanson* reasoning is found in *Dow* v. *Kaiser Foundation*, 90 Cal. Rptr. 747 (1970). The court states that "in order for a patient to vitiate his voluntary consent to treatment on the basis that the doctor breached his duty of disclosure, it was proved the doctor *willfully* and *without good medical reason*, withheld *material* information." Another innovation is that the patient has a duty to ask for information. See *Russel* v. *Horwick*, 116 So. 2d 904 (1964). See also *Scott* v. *Bradford*, 606 P. 2d 554 (1979).

It is notable that the negligence standard, which requires the plaintiff to demonstrate that the defendant had a *duty* to inform, and that the damage was a consequence of the breach of *that* duty, is a much more complex standard than the battery standard. The latter requires only proof of unconsented touching.

46. *Canterbury* v. *Spence* 150 App. D.C. 263, 464 F. 2d 772 (D.C. Cir. 1972), *cert. denied, Spence* v. *Canterbury*, 409 U.S. 1064, 34 L. Ed. 2d 518 (1972).

47. Ibid., *Canterbury* v. *Spence*, 464 F. 2d 772, 778.

48. Ibid., 784.

49. Ibid., 786.

50. Ibid., 785.

51. Ibid., 786. Judge Robinson recognized that introducing medical expert testimony and therapeutic privilege defenses are procedurally equivalent. See Katz, "Informed Consent: A Fairy Tale," 156.

52. *Canterbury* v. *Spence* 464 F. 2d, 787. Judge Robinson argued that it is primarily up to the physician to determine whether a patient is reasonable or not. "Indeed with knowledge of, or ability to learn, his patient's background and current condition, he is in a position superior to that of most others—attorneys, for example—who are called upon to make judgment on pain of liability in damages for an unreasonable miscalculation." 464 F. 2d, 787.

53. There is some question whether the facts of *Canterbury* v. *Spence* will stand up to the radical explanation offered here. Was Canterbury victimized by

the medical profession? It seems that a case can be made that he was. Dr. Spence's cursory explanation of the operation to the plaintiff and his mother was probably in line with standard procedure, but certainly reflected the dehumanization of the patient in medical institutions as well as a disrespect for Canterbury's right to self-determination. Yet, Canterbury lost. Walter Murphy, the defendant's lawyer, cited two reasons for the jury verdict: (1) Canterbury submitted to another laminectomy four years later; and (2) jurors would not want their physicians to detail all the horrors of an operation.

54. *Haven* v. *Randolph*, 342 F. Supp. 538 (D.Ct. D.C. 1972).

55. Ibid., 539.

56. *Haven* v. *Randolph*, 161 App. D.C. 150, 494 F. 2d 1069 (D.C. Cir. 1974).

57. *Henderson* v. *Milowsky*, 193 App. D.C. 269, 595 F. 2d 654 (D.C. Cir. 1978).

58. *Cobbs* v. *Grant*, 8 Cal. 3d 229, 104 Cal. Rptr. 505, 502 P. 2d 1 (1972).

59. Ibid., 10.

60. Ibid., 9. Justice Mosk cites Note, "Physician and Surgery," *Harvard Law Review* 75 (1962): 1445–1465 (an early work that discussed many of the same subjects presented here). See also, Donald G. Hagman, "The Medical Patient's Right to Know," *University of California at Los Angeles Law Review* 17 (1971): 758.

61. *Cobbs* v. *Grant*, 502.

62. Ibid., 502.

63. See, for example, *Archen* v. *Galbraith*, 18 Wash. App. 369, 567 P. 2d 1155 (1977), in which the doctor failed to tell the patient of various alternatives to surgery in thyroid cancer treatment.

64. *Hernandez* v. *Smith*, 552 F. 2d 142 (5th Cir. 1977) (the hospital and staff failed to warn a pregnant woman that the hospital did not have facilities for Caesarian sections).

65. *Bly* v. *Rhoades*, 216 Va. 645, 222 S.E.2d 783 (1976); see also *Wooley* v. *Henderson*, 418 A.2d 1123 (1980), in which a reasonable medical practitioner is the best standard. See also, David E. Seidelson, "Medical Malpractice in Full Disclosure Jurisdictions," *Duquense Law Review*, 14 (1976): 309–362.

66. See A. D. Twerski and N. B. Cohen, "Informed Decision-Making and the Law of Torts: The Myth of Justiciable Causation," *University of Illinois Law Review* (1988): 607–655.

67. A. Meisel and A. Kabnick, "Informed Consent to Medical Treatment: An Analysis of Recent Legislation," *University of Pittsburgh Law Review* 41 (1980): 420–462.

68. *Harnish* v. *Children's Hospital*, 387 Mass. 152, 439 N.E.2d 240 (Mass. 1982).

69. See A. Meisel, "A Dignitary Tort as a Bridge between the Idea of Informed Consent and the Law of Informed Consent," *Law, Medicine & Health Care* 16 (1988): 210–218.

70. D. H. Novack, et al., "Physicians' Attitudes Toward Using Deception to Resolve Difficult Ethical Problems," *JAMA* 261 (1989): 2980–2985.

71. See S. E. Bedell, "Choices about Cardiopulmonary Resuscitation in the Hospital. When do Physicians Talk with Patients?" *New England Journal of Medicine* 310 (1984): 1089–1093.

72. *Trogan* v. *Fruchtman*, 58 Wisc.2d 596, 207 N.W.2d 297 (1973).

73. Ibid., 299.

74. Ibid., 299.

75. J. E. Wennberg, "Dealing with Medical Practice Variations: A Proposal for Action," *Health Affairs* 3 (1984): 6–32.

76. B. A. Barnes, J. E. Wennberg, and M. Zubkoff, "Professional Uncertainty and the Problem of Supplier-Induced Demand," *Social Science and Medicine* 16 (1982): 811–824.

77. D. Hanley, et al., "An Assessment of Prostatectomy for Benign Urinary Tract Obstruction," *JAMA* 259 (1988): 3027–3030.

78. Hanley, et al., "An Assessment of Prostatectomy," 3029.

79. See Wennberg, "Dealing with Medical Practice Variations," 32.

80. M. R. Chassin, et al., "The Use and Misuse of Upper Gastrointestinal Endoscopy," *Annals of Internal Medicine* 109 (1988): 664–670.

81. J. F. Morrissey, "The Problem of the Inappropriate Endoscopy," *Annals of Internal Medicine* 109 (1988): 605–606.

Chapter 6: Physicians and Quality of Medical Care

1. This is, of course, only one of several possible explanations for the increase of medical injury litigation. See P. Weiler and T. Brennan, "The Harvard Medical Practice Study" (forthcoming, 1991).

2. L. Wyszewianski, "Quality of Care: Past Achievements and Future Challenges," *Inquiry* 25 (1988): 13–22.

3. R. I. Lee and L. W. Jones, *The Fundamentals of Good Medical Care* (Chicago: University of Chicago Press, 1933).

4. A. Donabedian, "Twenty Years of Research on the Quality of Medical Care, 1965–1984," *Evaluation and the Health Professions* 8 (1985): 243–265.

5. See L. Wyszewianski, "Quality of Care," 15.

6. Charles E. Rosenberg, *The Care of Strangers* (New York: Basic Books, 1987).

7. J. F. Horty and D. M. Mulholland, "The Legal Status of the Hospital Medical Staff," *St. Louis University Law Journal* 22 (1978): 485–500.

8. Timothy J. Jost, "Private Regulation of Health Care," *Boston College Law Review* 24 (1983): 835–900.

9. Ibid., 851.

10. See *Modaber* v. *Culpepper Memorial Hospital*, 674 F.2d 1023 (1982).

11. 42 U.S.C. Sec. 1395 et seq. (1976).

12. Charles L. Bosk, *Forgive and Remember* (Chicago: University of Chicago Press, 1979).

13. California Medical Association, *Report of the Medical Insurance Feasibility Study* (San Francisco: Sutter Publishing, 1977).

14. See K. Steel, P. M. Gertman, C. Crecenzi, and J. Anderson, "Iatrogenic Illness on A General Medical Service at a University Hospital," *New England Journal of Medicine* 304 (1981): 638–642; N. P. Couch, N. L. Tilney, A. A. Rayner, F. D. Moore, "The High Cost of Low-Frequency Events: The Anatomy and Economics of Surgical Mishaps," *New England Journal of Medicine* 304 (1981): 634–637.

15. Oliver Wendell Holmes, *The Common Law* (Boston: Little, Brown and Co., 1881).

16. Guido Calabresi, *The Costs of Accidents: A Legal and Economic Analysis* (New Haven: Yale University Press, 1970). See also, Richard A. Posner, *Economic Analysis of Law*, 2d ed. (Boston: Little, Brown and Co., 1987).

17. George Priest, "Understanding the Liability Crisis," in *New Directions in Liability Law, Proceedings of the Academy of Political Science*, ed. W. Olsen (New York: Academy of Political Science, 1987), 196–211.

18. George Priest, "The Invention of Enterprise Liability: A Critical History of the Intellectual Foundations of Modern Tort Law," *Journal of Legal Studies* 14 (1985): 461–527. Priest's is not the only theory. Others have focused on American risk adversity and its sometimes absurd results. See Peter Huber, *Liability: The Legal Revolution and its Consequences* (New York: Basic Books, 1988).

19. See *Henningsen* v. *Bloomfield Motors Inc.*, 32 N.J. 358, 161 A.2d 69 (1960); *Greenman* v. *Yuba Power Products, Inc.*, 59 Cal. 2d 57, 377 P. 2d 897, 27 Cal. Rptr. 697 (1963).

20. See generally, Friedrich Kessler, "Contracts of Adhesion—Some Thoughts about Freedom of Contract," *Columbia Law Review* 43 (1943): 629–652; Friedrich Kessler, "Some Reflections on Types of Thinking about Law and Justice," *Tulane Law Review* 19 (1944): 32–62.

21. There is little doubt that malpractice litigation has increased over the past quarter century. Weiler has mustered much of the evidence regarding this increase. See Paul Weiler, *Legal Policy for Medical Injuries: The Evidence, the Issues and the Options* (Philadelphia: American Law Institute, 1988). He notes that the costs for medical liability insurance have risen from $60 million in 1960 to $7 billion in 1989, an increase that far outstrips the rise in medical care costs or the consumer price index. He also notes that the frequency and the severity (the amount of damages) of suits have risen. The usual measure of the frequency of malpractice litigation is the number of claims per physicians per year. This fraction was around one per 100 physicians annually in 1960, and had risen to eighteen per 100 physicians in 1985. Some subspecialties such as neurosurgery and obstetrics were as high as 50 per 100 physicians per year in selected geographic areas.

With regard to severity, the average jury verdict in malpractice litigation in San Francisco and Chicago increased from $50,000–100,000 in the mid-1960s, to $400,000–600,000 in the mid-1970s, to $1,200,000 in the early

1980s. Settlements of cases out of court increased in a similar manner. In New York and Florida in the mid-1980s, the average settlement was over $100,000.

These increases in severity and frequency of suits fueled the increase in premiums of malpractice insurance. This concern over rising premium costs led both doctors and insurers to assert there was a tort crisis. It is notable that there appear to have been two malpractice tort crises, one in the mid-1970s and the other in the mid- to late-1980s. Both abated when the number and severity of suits dropped off, and premiums came down as a result of cycles in the insurance underwriting business. Kenneth Abraham, *Distributing Risk* (New Haven: Yale University Press, 1986).

22. 25 Cal. 2d 486, 154 P. 2d 687 (1944).

23. Ibid., 488.

24. See Warren A. Seavy, "Res Ipsa Loquitur: Tabula in Naufragio," *Harvard Law Review* 63 (1950): 643–667.

25. 62 Cal. 2d 154, 41 Cal. Rptr. 577, 397 P. 2d 161 (1966).

26. Indeed, the decision of the majority prompted Justice Tobriner to assert that it was wrong to rely on notions of negligence if patients were to be compensated.

27. Throughout I have distinguished informed consent cases from malpractice cases.

28. 519 P. 2d 981 (Washington 1974).

29. It appears that many ophthalmologists do test for glaucoma in patients under forty years of age. See Jerry Wiley, "The Impact of Judicial Decisions on Professional Conduct: An Empirical Study," *Southern California Law Review* 55 (1981): 345–382.

30. 354 Mass. 102, 235 N.E. 2d 793 (1968).

31. See Allan H. McCoid, "The Care Required of Medical Practitioners," *Vanderbilt Law Review* 12 (1961): 549–567. See also *King* v. *Williams*, 270 S.E.2d 618 (1981).

32. *Darling* v. *Charleston Memorial Hospital*, 33 Ill. 2nd 326, 211 N.E. 2d 253 (1965), cert. denied, 383 U.S. 946 (1966).

33. See *Jackson* v. *Power*, 743 P. 2d 1376 (1987). Diane M. Janulis and Alan D. Hornstein, "Damned If You Do, Damned If You Don't: Hospital Liability for Physician's Malpractice," *Nebraska Law Review* 64 (1985): 689–720.

34. See Peter A. Bell, "Legislative Intrusion into the Common Law of Medical Malpractice: Thoughts About the Deterrent Effect of Tort Liability," *Syracuse Law Review* 35 (1984): 939–982.

35. See D. Dewees, P. Coyte, and M. Trebilcock, *Canadian Medical Malpractice Liability: An Empirical Analysis of Recent Trends* (Toronto: University of Toronto, 1989); C. Ham, R. Dingwall, P. Fenn, and D. Harris, *Medical Negligence: Compensation and Accountability* (Oxford: Center for Sociolegal Studies, 1988), 7–12.

36. This is not to say that all tort reform is intended to overcome frivolous litigation. Some of it is intended to limit what would be valid tort claims, usually because litigation has curbed socially desirable activities. For instance,

the Price-Anderson Act restricts nuclear energy plant liability so as to encourage this source of energy generation.

37. See, for example, R. H. Palmer and M. C. Reilly, "Individual and Institutional Variables Which May Serve as Indicators of Quality of Medical Care," *Medical Care* 17 (1979): 693–717; A. Donabedian, *Explorations in Quality Assessment and Monitoring, Vol. I: The Definition of Quality and Approaches to Its Assessment* (Ann Arbor: Health Administration Press, 1980).

38. K. B. Johnson, "Beyond Tort Reform," *JAMA* 257 (1987): 827–828.

39. American Medical Profession, *Professional Liability in the 1980s* (Chicago: American Medical Association, 1986).

40. Harvard Medical Practice Study, *Patients, Lawyers and Doctors* (Boston: Harvard Medical School, 1990), chap. 9.

41. See Otis R. Bowen, "Congressional Testimony on Senate Bill S-1804," *JAMA* 257 (1987): 813–819.

42. L. R. Tancredi and J. A. Barondess, "The Problem of Defensive Medicine," *Science* 200 (1978): 879–882.

43. R. Reynolds, J. A. Rizzo, and M. L. Gonzalez, "The Cost of Medical Professional Liability," *JAMA* 257 (1987): 2776–2781.

44. See Johnson, "Beyond Tort Reform," 828. Moreover, given the customary practice standard of liability, there are pressures for physicians to follow the most expensive processes in treatment, leading to huge "defensive medicine" costs.

45. Nathan Hershey, "The Defensive Practice of Medicine," *Milbank Memorial Fund Quarterly* 50 (1972): 69–98.

46. Staff of Duke Law Journal, "Defensive Medicine," *Duke Law Journal* 1971 (1971): 929–949.

47. Tancredi and Barondess, "The Problem of Defensive Medicine," 879–882.

48. S. Williams, et al., "Physicians' Perceptions about Unnecessary Diagnostic Testing," *Inquiry* 19 (1982): 363–370.

49. K. K. Shy, E. B. Larson, and D. A. Luthy, "Evaluating a New Technology: the Effectiveness of Electronic Fetal Heart Rate Monitoring," *Annual Review of Public Health* 8 (1987): 165–190.

50. Reynolds, Rizzo, and Gonzalez, "The Cost of Medical Professional Liability," 2779.

51. J. E. Harris, "Defensive Medicine: It Costs, But Does It Work?" (editorial) *JAMA* 257 (1987): 2801–2802.

52. See, for example, "Report of the Special Task Force on Professional Liability and Insurance and the Advisory Panel on Professional Liability," *JAMA* 257 (1987): 810–820.

53. Throughout this discussion I am heavily dependent on Randall Bovbjerg, "Legislation on Medical Malpractice: Further Developments and a Preliminary Report Card," *University of California Davis Law Review* 22 (1989): 499–556.

54. See Ind. Code Ann. Sec. 16-9. 5-5-1 (West, 1984).

55. See Patricia Danzon, "The Frequency and Severity of Medical Mal-

practice Claims: New Evidence," *Law and Contemporary Problems* 49 (1986): 57–79.

56. See John F. Fleming, "The Collateral Source Rule and Loss Allocation in Tort Law," *California Law Review* 54 (1966): 1459–1478.

57. See *Jones* v. *State Board of Medicine*, 555 P.2d 399 (Idaho, 1976).

58. Mich. Comp. Laws Ann. Sec 600. 2912 (a) (1985).

59. See, for example, Ralph Nader, "The Assault on Injured Victims' Rights," *Denver University Law Review* 64 (1988): 625–640.

60. David R. Smith, "Battling a Receding Tort Frontier: Constitutional Attacks on Medical Malpractice Laws," *Oklahoma Law Review* 38 (1985): 195–242.

61. See, for example, *Boyd* v. *Bulala*, 647 F. Supp. 781 (W.D. Va, 1986).

62. See Justice William J. Brennan, "The Bill of Rights and the States: The Revival of State Constitutions as Guardians of Individual Rights," *New York University Law Review* 61 (1986): 535–558.

63. Weiler, "Legal Policy," 65.

64. H. H. Hiatt, B. A. Barnes, T. A. Brennan, et al., "A Study of Medical Injury and Medical Malpractice: An Overview," *New England Journal of Medicine* 321 (1989): 480–484.

65. See W. J. Curran, "Medical Peer Review of Physician Competence and Performance: Legal Immunity and the Antitrust Laws," *New England Journal of Medicine* 316 (1987): 597–598.

66. See Note, "Discovery of Peer Review Records," *University of Missouri at Kansas City Law Review* 53 (1985): 663–689; C. F. Goldberg, "The Peer Review Privilege: A Law in Search of a Valid Policy," *American Journal of Law and Medicine* 10 (1984): 151–192. Defamation is considered to be a growth industry in tort law. See A. C. Blakley, "Employer-Employee Relations: Employment Torts Come of Age: Increasing Risks of Liability for Employers and Their Insurers," *Tort and Insurance Law Journal* 24 (2) (1989): 268–282.

67. Throughout this discussion I am very dependent on an unpublished paper written by Laura Keidan, Harvard Law School 1989, entitled "Physician Discipline: Cure for the Malpractice Crisis?" (on file with author).

68. See generally, R. J. Feinstein, "The Ethics of Professional Regulation," *New England Journal of Medicine* 312 (1985): 801–804.

69. 42 U.S.C.A. 11101–11152 (West Supp. 1988).

70. Keidan, "Physician Discipline."

71. Florida Stat. 458.307 (West Supp. 1988); California Business and Professional Code 2001 (West Supp. 1989); New York Public Health Law 230(1) (McKinney Supp. 1989); Texas Review Civ. Stat. Ann. art 4495b et seq.

72. K. N. Lohr, K. D. Lordy, and S. O. Thier, "Current Issues in the Quality of Care," *Health Affairs* 7 (1988): 5–18.

73. See Office of Technology Assessment, *The Quality of Medical Care* (Washington: United States Government Printing Office, June 1988).

74. J. H. Eichorn, J. B. Cooper, D. J. Cullen, et al., "Standards for Patient Monitoring During Anesthesia at Harvard Medical School," *JAMA* 256 (1986): 1017–1020.

75. Personal Communication with James Holzer, Vice President, Harvard University Risk Management Foundation, July 10, 1989.

76. See Troyen Brennan, "Practice Guidelines and Malpractice: Collision or Cohesion," *Journal of Health Politics, Policy and Law* (forthcoming, 1991).

77. See A. F. Southwick and D. A. Slee, "Quality Assurance in Health Care; Confidentiality of Information and Immunity for Participants," *Journal of Legal Medicine* 5 (1984): 343–397.

78. In our study of adverse events in New York, the Department of Health had to exercise a great deal of influence over hospitals selected for our sample in order to gain their participation. They were fearful that our research might encourage lawsuits.

79. See P. Weiler and T. A. Brennan, "Medical Malpractice," in *A Call for Action: Final Report of the Pepper Commission* (Washington: Government Printing Office, 1990).

80. D. A. Hastings, "Legal Issues Raised by Private Review Activities of Medical Peer Review Organizations," *Journal of Health Politics, Policy and Law* 8 (1983): 293–313.

81. All of this raises questions about the appropriate role for physicians in quality assurance. Some believe that physicians ought to be regulated by state and local authorities through external controls. Vladeck, for example, argues that external controls, enforced through close surveillance, offer the best hope for improving the quality of care. See B. C. Vladeck, "Quality Assurance Through External Controls," *Inquiry* 25 (1988): 100–107. Others find such regulation, at least those nascent programs, to be burdensome and inefficacious. See K. E. Raske and D. Eisenman, "Hospitals Under the Regulatory Knife: Directions in Medical Malpractice," *New York State Journal of Medicine* 86 (July 1986): 356–360. They argue that medicine, as a learned profession, has a long history of self-regulation and can learn to adapt to a new environment requiring more open accountability. See J. A. Sbarbaro and E. Casper, "A Case for Independent Judgment: The Medical Society in Perspective for the 1990s," *Denver University Law Review* 65 (1989): 259–266.

82. See D. M. Berwick, "Continuous Improvement as an Ideal in Health Care," *New England Journal of Medicine* 320 (1989): 53–56.

83. M. Tribus, *Deming's Way* (Cambridge, Mass.: Massachusetts Institute of Technology Center for Advanced Engineering Study, 1985).

84. See generally, Jules Coleman, "Moral Theories of Torts: Their Scope and Limits: Part II," *Law and Philosophy* 2 (1893): 5–36.

85. An administrative system may sound farfetched to the hard-bitten among us. It is interesting to note, however, that such a system of no-fault administrative compensation exists today in both Sweden and New Zealand. In these countries, compensation for medical injuries has been split from efforts to deter substandard practice. For a discussion of Sweden's efforts with regard to medical discipline and no-fault compensation, see Marilyn M. Rosenthal, *Dealing with Medical Malpractice: The British and Swedish Experience*, (Durham, N.C.: Duke University Press, 1986). For an overview of New Zealand, see Walter Gellhorn, "Medical Malpractice Litigation (U.S.)— Medical Mishap Compensation (N.Z.)," *Cornell Law Review* 73 (1988): 170–

212. Although there are significant differences between these two countries' approaches, I will discuss them in broad enough strokes so that I will not need to touch on those differences.

Chapter 7: The Challenge of AIDS

1. Allan H. McCoid, "The Care Required of Medical Practitioners," *Vanderbilt Law Review* 12 (1959): 549–567.

2. Arthur F. Southwick, *The Law of Hospital and Health Care Administration* (Ann Arbor: Health Administration Press, 1978), 97.

3. *Hammonds* v. *Aetna Casualty and Sur. Co.*, 237 F. Supp. 96, 98-9 (N.D. Ohio 1965).

4. *Payton* v. *Weaver*, 131 Cal. App.3d 38, 182 Cal. Rptr. 225, 229 (1982).

5. *McCulpin* v. *Bessmer*, 241 Iowa 727, 43 N.W.2d 121 (1950); *Ricks* v. *Budge*, 91 Utah 307, 64 P.2d 208 (1937).

6. Taunya L. Banks, "The Right to Medical Treatment," in *AIDS and the Law*, ed. Harlon Dalton and Scott Burris (New Haven: Yale University Press, 1986).

7. The state of Washington has attempted to address this issue by requiring continuing medical education on HIV disease for all practitioners. This approach has been supported by primary care internists. See D. W. Northfelt, R. A. Hayward, and M. F. Shapiro, "The Acquired Immunodeficiency Syndrome is a Primary Care Disease," *Annals of Internal Medicine* 109 (1988): 773–775.

8. George Annas, "Legal Risks and Responsibilities of Physicians in the AIDS Epidemic," *Hastings Center Report* 18 (1988): 26–32.

9. Clark Havighurst, "The Changing Locus of Decision-making in the Health Care Sector," *Journal of Health Policy, Politics and Law* 11 (1986): 697–735.

10. *Manlove* v. *Wilmington General Hospital* 174 A. 2d 135 (Del. 1961); Charles Dougherty, "The Right to Health Care: First Aid in the Emergency Room," *Public Law Forum* 4 (1984): 101–120; *Hiser* v. *Randolph*, 126 Ariz. 608, 617 P.2d 774 (Ct. App. 1980).

11. *Harper* v. *Baptist Medical Center*, 341 So. 2d 133 (Ala. 1976).

12. A. Schiff, H. Ansell, R. Schlossen, et al., "Transfers to Public Hospitals: A Prospective Study of 467 Patients," *New England Journal of Medicine* 314 (1986): 552–554; H. Treiger, "Preventing Patient Dumping: Sharpening the COBRA's Teeth," *New York University Law Review* 61 (1987): 1186–1206.

13. Martin Hirsch, "The Rocky Road to Effective Treatment of Human Immunodeficiency Virus (HIV) Infection," *Annals of Internal Medicine* 110 (1989): 1–3.

14. P. S. Arno, et al., "Economic and Policy Implications of Early Inter-

vention in HIV Disease," *Journal of the American Medical Association* 262 (1989): 1493–1498.

15. M. E. St. Louis, K. J. Ranch, L. R. Peterson, et al., "Seroprevalence Rates of Human Immunodeficiency Virus Infection at Sentinel Hospitals in the United States," *New England Journal of Medicine* 323 (1990): 213–218.

16. J. W. Curran, et al., "Epidemiology of HIV Infection and AIDS in the United States," *Science* 239 (1988): 610–616.

17. G. C. Kelen, et al., "Unrecognized Human Immunodeficiency Virus Infection in Emergency Department Patients," *New England Journal of Medicine* 318 (1988): 1645–1650.

18. J. W. Jason, et al., "HTLV-III/LAV Antibody and Immune Status of Household Contacts and Sexual Partners of Persons with Hemophilia," *Journal of the American Medical Association* 255 (1986): 212–215; G. H. Friedland, et al., "Lack of Transmission of HTLV-II/LAV Infection to Household Contacts of Patients with AIDS or AIDS-Related Complex with Oral Candidiasis," *New England Journal of Medicine* 314 (1986): 344–349.

19. Update, "Human Immunodeficiency Virus Infections in Health Care Workers Exposed to Blood of Infected Patients," *MMWR* 36 (1987): 285–289.

20. J. L. Baker, et al., "Unsuspected Human Immunodeficiency Virus in Critically Ill Patients," *JAMA* 257 (1987): 2609–2611.

21. T. Barker, "Physician Sues Johns Hopkins after Contracting AIDS," *American Medical News*, June 19, 1987, 20; T. Brennan, "The Acquired Immunodeficiency Syndrome as an Occupational Disease," *Annals of Internal Medicine* 107 (1987): 581–583.

22. *Prego v. City of New York*, 141 Misc. 2d 709 (NY Sup. 1988), aff'd. 147 A.D. 2d 165 (N.Y. A.D. 2d Dept. 1989).

23. Lynn Peterson, "AIDS: The Ethical Dilemma for Surgeons," *Law, Medicine and Health Care*, 17 (1989): 139–144.

24. P. Vaught, "AIDS Clinic Being Weighed by Chicago Dental Society," *New York Times* 21 July 1987, B-2.

25. K. Henry, S. Campbell, B. Jackson, et al., "Long Term Follow-Up of Health Care Workers with Work-Site Exposure to Human Immunodeficiency Virus," *JAMA* 263 (1990): 1765–1760.

26. J. R. Allen, "Health Care Workers and Risk of HIV Transmission," *Hastings Center Report* 18 (1988): 2–5. See generally, C. Becker, ed., *Occupational HIV Infection: Risks and Risk Reduction* (Philadelphia: Hanley & Belfus, 1989).

27. Carol M. Mangione, Steven R. Cummings, and Julie L. Gerberding, "Occupational Exposure to HIV Infection: Prevalence and Rates of Under-Reporting of Medical Housestaff," *American Journal of Medicine*. In press.

28. See Julie Gerberding, et al., "Risk of Transmitting the Human Immunodeficiency Virus, Cytomegalovirus and Hepatitis B Virus to Health Care Workers Exposed to Patients with AIDS and AIDS-Related Conditions," *Journal of Infectious Diseases* 156 (1987): 1–8.

29. B. Gerbert, et al., "Why Fear Persists: Health Care Professionals and AIDS," *JAMA* 260 (1988): 3481–3483.

30. E. Emanuel, "Do Physicians Have an Obligation to Treat Patients with AIDS?" *New England Journal of Medicine* 318 (1988): 1686–1688.

31. A. Zuger and S. H. Miles, "Physicians, AIDS and Occupational Risk: Historic Traditions and Ethical Obligations," *JAMA* 258 (1987): 1924–1928.

32. J. D. Arras, "The Fragile Web of Responsibility: AIDS and the Duty to Treat," *Hastings Center Report* 18 (1988): 11–16.

33. J. Reed and P. Evans, "The Deprofessionalization of Medicine: Causes, Effects and Responses," *JAMA* 258 (1987): 3279–3282.

34. See R. Sade, "Medical Care as a Right: A Refutation," *New England Journal of Medicine* 285 (1971): 1288–1292.

35. S. Staver, "Arizona Medical Doctors Can Refuse AIDS Patients," *American Medical News* (November 1987): 6.

36. Others have sought alternative bases than beneficence for a duty to treat. See Edmund Pellegrino, "Ethical Obligations and AIDS," *JAMA* 258 (1987): 1957–1959.

37. See H. W. Jaffe, et al., "The Acquired Immunodeficiency Syndrome in a Cohort of Homosexual Men. A Six Year Follow-up Study," *Annals of Internal Medicine* 103 (1985): 210–214.

38. See A. M. Hardy, et al., "The Economic Impact of the First 10,000 Cases of Acquired Immunodeficiency Syndrome in the United States," *JAMA* 255 (1986): 209–211.

39. See Guido Calabresi, *The Costs of Accidents* (New Haven: Yale University Press, 1970).

40. Troyen A. Brennan, "Ensuring Access to Care for the Sick: The Challenge of the Acquired Immunodeficiency Syndrome as an Occupational Disease," *Duke Law Journal* (1988): 29–70.

41. James Robert Chelius, *Workplace Safety and Health: The Role of Workers' Compensation* (Washington: American Enterprise Institute, 1977).

42. Peter S. Barth and H. Allan Hunt, *Workers' Compensation and Work-Related Illnesses and Diseases* (Cambridge, Mass.: MIT Press, 1980).

43. Kenneth Abraham, *Distributing Risk* (Princeton: Princeton University Press, 1986), 227.

44. See C. E. Becker, J. E. Cone, and J. Gerberding, "Occupational Infection with Human Immunodeficiency Virus (HIV): Risks and Risk-Reduction," *Annals of Internal Medicine* 110 (1989): 653–656.

45. See Carol M. Mangione, et al., "Occupational Exposure to HIV Infection."

46. See generally, Larry O. Gostin, "Hospitals, Health Care Professionals, and AIDS: The Right to Know the Health Status of Professionals and Patients," *Maryland Law Review* 48 (1989): 12–42.

47. See J. M. Steckelberg and F. R. Cockerill, "Serologic Testing for Human Immunodeficiency Virus Antibodies," *Mayo Clinic Proceedings* 63 (1988): 373–380. AIDS testing usually involves use of two separate tests. There is usually a window period of up to three months after infection before the antibodies to the virus can be detected, although recent evidence suggests that some long-term carriers of the virus may test negative.

48. See generally Milton C. Weinstein and Harvey Fineberg, *Clinical Decision Analysis* (Philadelphia: Saunders, 1980), 84–85.

49. K. B. Meyers and S. G. Pauker, "Screening for HIV: Can We Afford the False Positive Rate?" *New England Journal of Medicine* 317 (1987): 238–241.

50. G. D. Kelen, T. DiGiovanna, L. Bissou, et al., "Human Immunodeficiency Virus in Emergency Department Patients: Epidemiology, Clinical Presentations and Risk to Health." *JAMA* 262 (1989): 516–522.

51. M. E. St. Louis, K. J. Ranch, L. R. Peterson, et al., "Seroprevalence Rates of Human Immunodeficiencies Virus Infection at Sentinel Hospitals in the United States," *New England Journal of Medicine* 323 (1990): 213–218.

52. The emphasis here is on consent. One might support mandatory testing, but still require that the patient be fully informed of all the risks of the test.

53. D. Dyer, "Testing for HIV: The Medicolegal View," *British Medical Journal* 295 (1987): 871–872.

54. Henry K. Willenbring and K. Crossley, "Human Immunodeficiency Virus Antibody Testing. A Description of Practices and Policies at U.S. Infectious Disease-Teaching Hospitals," *JAMA* 259 (1988): 1819–1822.

55. Joel D. Howell, "What is the Difference Between an HIV and a CBC?" *Hastings Center Report* 18 (1988): 18–20.

56. L. O. Gostin, "Hospitals, Health Care Professionals, and AIDS: The Right to Know the Health Status of Professionals and Patients," *Maryland Law Review* 48 (1989): 12–54.

57. Martin Hirsch, "The Rocky Road to Effective Treatment of Human Immunodeficiency Virus (HIV) Infection," *Annals of Internal Medicine* 110 (1989): 1–3.

58. G. P. Schultz and M. Reuter, "AIDS Legislation in Missouri: An Analysis and a Proposal," *Missouri Law Review* 53 (1988): 599–621.

59. Renslow Sherer, "Physicians Use of HIV Antibody Test. The Need for Consent, Counseling, Confidentiality and Caution," *JAMA* 259 (1988): 264–265.

60. P. M. Marzuk, et al., "Increased Risk of Suicides in Persons with AIDS," *JAMA* 259 (1988): 1333–1337.

61. M. Sherzer, "Insurance" in *AIDS and the Law*, ed. H. L. Dalton and S. Burris (New Haven: Yale University Press, 1987).

62. A. S. Leonard, "AIDS in The Workplace," in *AIDS and the Law*, ed. Dalton and Burris.

63. Note, "Preserving the Public Health: A Proposal to Quarantine Recalcitrant AIDS Carriers," *Boston University Law Review* 68 (1988): 415–470; See also E. S. Janus, "AIDS in the Law: Setting and Evaluating Threshold Standards for a Course in Public Health Intervention," *William Mitchell Law Review* 14 (1988): 504–573.

64. This is not to say that in other nonliberal states, quarantine and other types of use of the police power might be acceptable. See R. Bayer and C. Helton, "Controlling AIDS in Cuba. The Logic of Quarantine," *New England*

Journal of Medicine 320 (1989): 1022–1024. The privacy rights that are based on interpretations of our Constitution are designed to maintain the individual's right to be free from governmental institution. See *Griswold* v. *Connecticut*, 381 U.S. 479 (1965).

65. Note, "The Constitutional Implications of Mandatory Testing for Acquired Immunodeficiency Syndrome-AIDS," *Emory Law Journal* 37 (1988): 217–248.

66. B. Mishu, W. Schaffner, J. M. Horan, et al., "A Surgeon with AIDS. Lack of Evidence of Transmission to Patients," *JAMA* 264 (1990): 467–470.

67. Richard Knox, "Dentist Transmits HIV to Patient," *Boston Globe*, 29 July 1990, 16.

68. Larry O. Gostin, "HIV Infected Physicians and the Practice of Seriously Invasive Procedures." *Hastings Center Report* 19 (1989): 32–39.

69. K. B. Rothenberg and J. J. Potterat, "Strategies for Management of Sex Partners," in *Sexually Transmitted Diseases*, ed. K. K. Holmes, et al. (New York: McGraw-Hill International Book Company, 1984): 965–972.

70. G. W. Rutherford and J. M. Woo, "Contact Tracing and the Control of Human Immunodeficiency Virus Infection," *JAMA* 259 (1988): 3609–3610.

71. Larry O. Gostin, "Traditional Public Health Strategies," *AIDS and the Law*, ed. Dalton and Burris, 56.

72. R. F. Wykoff, et al., "Contact Tracing to Identify Human Immunodeficiency Virus Infection in a Rural Community," *JAMA* 259 (1988): 3563–3566.

73. P. E. Munday, et al., "Contact Tracing in Hepatitis B Infection," *British Journal of Venereal Diseases* 59 (1983): 314–316.

74. T. A. Brennan, "Research Records, Litigation and Confidentiality: The Case of Research on Toxic Substances," *IRB* 4 (1983): 6–8.

75. R. Winslade, "Confidentiality of Medical Records," *Journal of Legal Medicine* 3 (1982): 497–533.

76. Missouri General Statutes Sections 287. 140(5) et seq.

77. *McIntosh* v. *Milano* 168 N.J. Super 466, 403 A.2d 500 (1979).

78. *Watts* v. *Cumberland County Hospital System, Inc.*, 330 S.E. 2d 242 (1985).

79. *Davis* v. *Rodman*, 227 S.W. 612 (1921).

80. 551 P.2d 334, 17 Cal. 3rd 425 (1976).

81. Note, "Between a Rock and a Hard Place: AIDS and the Conflicting Physician's Duties of Preventing Disease Transmission and Safeguarding Confidentiality," *Georgetown Law Journal* 76 (1988): 169–202, fn 63.

82. California Health and Safety Code Sec. 199.21(c) (West Supp., 1988).

83. Massachusetts Gen. Laws, Chapter 111, Section 70 F (1986).

84. Anonymous, "State Health Officials Group Urges Adoption of Guarantees," *AIDS Policy & Law* 2 (1987): 1.

85. See Henry T. Greely, "AIDS and the American Health Care Financing System," *University of Pittsburgh Law Review* 51 (1989): 73–163.

Chapter 8: Limits on Care

1. My view stands in contrast to V. L. Willman's, "Medical Perspectives in Allocating Resources," *Public Law Forum* 4 (1984): 51–55.

2. In 1950, national health expenditures were $12.7 billion, equivalent to $82 per capita. Health care expenditures were 4.4 percent of the Gross National Product (GNP). By 1970, the total expenditures rose to $74.7 billion, which amounted to $358 per capita, or 7.5 percent of the GNP. By 1982, after a full decade of inflation in the health care market, expenditures were up to $322 billion, amounting to $1,365 per capita, or 10.5 percent of the GNP. Hospital care has constituted a significant part of the increase in health care costs. Expense per inpatient day rose from $41 per day in 1965, to $96 per day in 1972. By 1982, the inpatient day costs were $348 and rose further to $432 in 1984. See J. Phillips and D. Wineberg, "Medicare Prospective Payment: A Quiet Revolution," *West Virginia Law Review* 87 (1984): 27–61.

3. Ibid., 27.

4. M. L. Barer, R. G. Evans, and R. Labelle, "Fee Controls as Cost Controls: Tales from the Frozen North," *The Milbank Memorial Quarterly* 66 (1988): 1–61.

5. See Richard Morriss Titmuss, *Commitment to Welfare* (London: Allen and Unwin, 1968).

6. See M. Pauly and T. Redisch, "The Not for Profit Hospital as Physicians Cooperative," *American Economic Review* 63 (1973): 87–97. See also Robert Clark, "Does the Nonprofit Form Fit the Hospital Industry?" *Harvard Law Review* 93 (1982): 1416–1490.

7. See Willard Manning, et al., "Health Insurance and the Demand for Medical Care: Evidence from a Randomized Experiment," *American Economic Review* 77 (1987): 251–262.

8. Lawrence Brown, "Common Sense Meets Implementation: Certificate of Need Regulation in the States," *Journal of Health Politics, Policy and Law* 8 (1983): 480–494.

9. John M. Eisenberg, et al., "Substituting Diagnostic Services: New Tests Only Partially Replace Older Ones," *JAMA* 262 (1989): 1196–1200.

10. T. W. Maloney and D. E. Rogers, "Medical Technology—A Different View of the Contentious Debate over Costs," *New England Journal of Medicine* 301 (1979): 1413–1419.

11. See J. K. Iglehart, "Health Policy Report. Another Chance for Technology Assessment," *New England Journal of Medicine* 309 (1983): 509–512.

12. Even in these cases, as a doctor who works in emergency rooms, I find it hard to differentiate between when I am being defensive, and when I am just being cautious, or doing the best for the patient.

13. See, for example, Robert G. Evans, "Illusions of Necessity: Evading Responsibility for Choice in Health Care," *Journal of Health Politics, Policy and Law* 10 (1985): 439–467.

14. Since Medicaid was expanding so quickly, in 1972 Congress developed a capital expenditure review program for states receiving Medicare/Medicaid and other federal funds. See Brown, "Common Sense," 480. As part of this initiative, states were to set up Certificate of Need (CON) programs, designed to review the appropriateness of new capital expenditures by hospitals. See generally, D. Salkever and T. Bice, *Hospital Certificate of Need Controls; Impact on Investment Cost and Use* (Washington: American Enterprise Institute for Public Policy Research, 1979). In a more direct effort to constrain costs, states set hospital reimbursement rates prospectively, usually constraining the amount a hospital budget could rise on an annual basis. See C. Eby and D. Cohodes, "What Do We Know About Rate-Setting?" *Journal of Health Politics, Policy and Law* 10 (1985): 299–327.

15. See Eli Ginzberg, "The Destabilization of Health Care," *New England Journal of Medicine* 315 (1986): 757–761.

16. See Paul Starr, *Social Transformation*, 431–438.

17. See Randall Bovbjerg, "Competition versus Regulation," *Vanderbilt Law Review* 34 (1981): 908–943.

18. The administration was influenced by Enthoven's classic article on consumer's choice of health plans. See A. C. Enthoven, "Consumer-Choice Health Plan," *New England Journal of Medicine* 298 (1978): 709–720. Health maintenance organizations were thought to provide a great deal of procompetitive effects in any health care market. See H. Luft, S. Maerkis, and J. Trauner, "The Competitive Effects of Health-Maintenance Organizations: Another Look at the Evidence from Hawaii, Rochester and Minneapolis/St. Paul," *Journal of Health Politics, Policy and Law*, 10 (1986): 625–658. Since the concept of managed care promised lower costs for consumers, other more traditional insurance policies had to adapt. They did so by offering different packages of benefits and also by developing preferred provider organizations (PPOs), through which they could control the resource use of individual providers. In addition, commercial insurers made greater use of utilization review (UR), attempting to police directly health care resources.

19. The Supreme Court aided this effort by rethinking the role of the McCarran-Ferguson Act vis-à-vis the innovative provision of health services, and by reinterpreting the role of the Employee Retirement Income Security Act (ERISA) in determining the shape of health care packages offered by employers. See generally, S. Law, "Negotiating Physician Fees," *New York University Law Review* 61 (1988): 1–59. In particular, Law's analysis of the decision of *Union Labor Life Insurance Company* v. *Pireno*, 458 U.S. 119 (1981) is that the Supreme Court has decided that state regulation of insurance must be constrained owing to the value of anti-trust claims in developing a market in medical care.

20. See David Kinzer, "The Decline and Fall of Deregulation," *New England Journal of Medicine* 318 (1988): 112–116. We will return to this issue in chapter 9.

21. *Social Security Amendments of 1983*, Public Law No. 98-21, 97 Stat. 65. The prospective payment system was based on a classification of diagnosis known as the Diagnosis Related Groups, DRGs. This concept, which had

been tested in New Jersey, provided specific reimbursement for a given DRG. Prospective payment meant that the hospital could expect only a certain amount of money for any given DRG.

22. See J. Phillips and D. Wineberg, "Medicare Prospective Payment: A Quiet Revolution," *West Virginia Law Review* 87 (1984): 27–61.

23. J. Feder, J. Hadley, and S. Zuckerman, "How Did Medicare's Prospective Payment System Affect Hospitals?" *New England Journal of Medicine* 317 (1987): 867–873.

24. D. A. Dolenc and C. J. Dougherty, "DRG's: The Counterrevolution in Financing Health Care," *Hastings Center Report*, 15 (1985): 19–29; T. Halper, "DRG's and the Idea of the Just Price," *Journal of Medicine and Philosophy* 12 (1987): 155–164.

25. A. Sager, E. Leventhal, and D. Easterling, "The Impact on Medicare's Prospective Payment System on Wisconsin Nursing Homes," *JAMA* 257 (1987): 1762–1766.

26. L. M. Fleck, "DRG's: Justice and the Invisible Rationing of Health Care Resources," *Journal of Medicine and Philosophy* 12 (1987): 165–196.

27. S. D. Horn and J. E. Backofen, "Ethical Issues in the Use of a Prospective Payment System: The Issue of a Severity of Illness Adjustment," *Journal of Medicine and Philosophy* 12 (1987): 145–153.

28. A. R. Dyer, "Patients, Not Costs, Come First." *Hastings Center Report* 16 (1986): 5–7.

29. C. E. Begley, "Prospective Payment and Medical Ethics," *Journal of Philosophy and Medicine* 12 (1987): 107–122.

30. 70 N.J. 10 (1976).

31. E. Emanuel, "A Review of the Ethical and Legal Aspects of Terminating Medical Care," *American Journal of Medicine* 84 (1988): 291–301.

32. *In re Dinnerstein*, 38 N.E. 2nd 134 (1978); *In re Spring*, 399 N.E. 2nd 493 (1979).

33. *In re Conroy*, 98 N.J. 321 (1985); *In re Jobes*, 108 N.J. 394 (1987).

34. On refusal of therapy, see *Brophy* v. *New England Sinai Hospital*, 398 Mass. 417 (1986); *In re Peter*, 108 N.J. 365 (1987).

35. *In re Saikewicz*, 370 N.E.2d 417 (1977); see also W. Curran, "Law-Medicine Notes: The Saikewicz Decision," *New England Journal of Medicine* 298 (1978): 499–500; G. Annas, "Reconciling Quinlan and Saikewicz: Decision-making for the Terminally Ill Incompetent," *Journal of Law and Medicine* 4 (1979): 301–334.

36. Charles H. Baron, "Medical Paternalism and the Rule of Law: A reply to Dr. Relman," *American Journal of Law and Medicine* 4 (1979): 337–365; Larry O. Gostin, "A Right to Choose Death: The Judicial Trilogy of Brophy, Bouvia and Conroy," *Law, Medicine and Health Care* 14 (1986): 198–202.

37. See, for example, L. J. Schneiderman and R. G. Spragg, "Ethical Decisions in Discontinuing Mechanical Ventilation," *New England Journal of Medicine* 318 (1988): 984–988.

38. T. Tomlinson and H. Brody, "Ethics and Communication in Do-Not-Resuscitate Orders," *New England Journal of Medicine* 318 (1988): 43–46. No Code status means that a person will not undergo cardiopulmonary resusci-

tation in the event of cardiac arrest. An effort to resuscitate a patient is known as a "code."

39. L. J. Blackhall, "Must We Always Use CPR?" *New England Journal of Medicine* 317 (1987): 1281–1285.

40. Bernard Lo, et al., "Do Not Resuscitate Decisions: A Prospective Study at Three Teaching Hospitals," *Archives of Internal Medicine* 145 (1985): 1115–1117.

41. Troyen A. Brennan, "Ethics Committees and Decisions to Limit Care: The Experience at the Massachusetts General Hospital," *JAMA* 268 (1989): 803–807; Troyen A. Brennan, "Incompetent Patients with Limited Care in the Absence of Family Consent: Socioeconomic and Clinical Parameters," *Annals of Internal Medicine* 109 (1989): 819–820.

42. S. Braithwaite and D. C. Thomasma, "New Guidelines on Foregoing Life-sustaining Treatment in Incompetent Patients: An Anti-cruelty Policy," *Annals of Internal Medicine* 104 (1986): 711–715.

43. A. S. Brett and L. B. McCullough, "When Patients Request Specific Interventions: Defining the Limits of the Physician's Obligation," *New England Journal of Medicine* 315 (1986): 1347–1351.

44. B. Lo and A. R. Jonsen, "Clinical Decisions to Limit Treatment," *Annals of Internal Medicine* 93 (1980): 764–768.

45. *In re Westchester County Medical Center on behalf of O'Connor*, 72 N.Y. 2d 517, 531 N.E. 2d 607 (1988).

46. *Cruzan* v. *Director, Missouri Department of Health*, 58 L.W. 4916 (1990). I do not wish to advocate Missouri's approach to the Cruzan case. Indeed, I think that patient autonomy and the biological facts of the persistent vegetative state should argue for a low evidentiary threshold for patient's previous statements about heroic care. Nonetheless, I continue to fear how the substituted judgment principle may be misinterpreted by the medical profession. See Troyen A. Brennan, "Silent Decisions: Limits of Consent and Care of the Terminally Ill," *Law, Medicine and Health Care* 1988 (16): 204–210.

47. L. L. Emanuel and E. J. Emanuel, "The Medical Directive: A New Comprehensive Advance Care Document," *JAMA* 261 (1988): 3288–3293.

48. In effect, I am drawing a distinction between an individual physician's decision to ration, and broader policy decisions to allocate resources that lead to limits on care.

49. Eli Ginzberg, "The High Cost of Dying," *Inquiry* 17 (1980): 295–308; J. Lubitz and R. Prihoda, "Use and Cost of Medicare Services in the Last Two Years of Life," *Health Care Financing Review* 5 (1984): 117–131.

50. A. S. Detsky, et al., "Prognosis, Survival and the Expenditure of Hospital Resources for Patients in Intensive Care Units," *New England Journal of Medicine* 305 (1981): 667–672.

51. J. Henderson, M. J. Goldacre, and M. Griffith, "Hospital Care for the Elderly in the Last Year of Life," *BMJ* 301 (1990): 17–19.

52. S. H. Miles, R. Cranford, and A. Schultz, "The Do Not Resuscitate Order in a Teaching Hospital," *Annals of Internal Medicine* 96 (1982): 660–664.

53. Katz, *The Silent World of Doctors and Patients*.

54. Stuart Younger, "Do-Not-Resuscitate Orders: No Longer Secret, but Still a Problem," *Hastings Center Report* 17 (1987): 24–33.

55. Daniel Callahan, *Setting Limits: Medical Goals in an Aging Society* (New York: Simon and Schuster, 1987).

56. Anne A. Scitovsky, "Medical Care in the Last Twelve Months of Life: The Relationship Between Age, Functional Status and Medical Care Expenditures," *Milbank Memorial Quarterly* 66 (1988): 640–659.

57. Larry Churchill, *Rationing Health Care in America: Perceptions and Principles of Justice* (Notre Dame, Ind.: University of Notre Dame Press, 1987).

58. J. F. Kilner, "Age as a Basis for Allocating Lifesaving Medical Resources: An Ethical Analysis," *Journal of Health Politics, Policy and Law* 13 (1988): 405–432.

59. For example, the Uniform Anatomical Gift Act that has been adopted by many states was meant to streamline and standardize the provision of organs from those who have died. See James F. Blumstein, "Government's Role in Organ Transplantation Policy," *Journal of Health Politics, Policy and Law* 14 (1989): 5–40.

60. Public Law #92-603, section 299i (1972).

61. Peter H. Schuck, "Government Funding for Organ Transplant," *Journal of Health Politics, Policy and Law* 14 (1989): 169–190.

62. Public Law #98-507 (1984).

63. There is also funding of organ transplantation through private insurers, and especially through Blue Cross programs. Eligibility for Blue Cross funding is quite complex and will not be discussed in this book. See Richard A. Knox, "Heart Transplant, To Pay or Not To Pay," *Science* 209 (1980): 570–575.

64. R. C. Fox and J. P. Swazey, *The Courage to Fail: The Social View of Organ Transplant and Dialysis* (Chicago: University of Chicago Press, 1974).

65. See Robert W. Evans, "The Heart Transplant Dilemma," *Issues in Science and Technology* 2 (1986): 91–101.

66. 51 Fed. Reg. 37, 164 (1986).

67. Clark Havighurst and Nancy King, "Liver Transplantation in Massachusetts: Public Policy Making as Morality Play," *Indiana Law Review* 19 (1986): 955–980; R. A. Rettig, "The Politics of Organ Transplantation: A Parable of our Times," *Journal of Health Politics, Policy and Law* 14 (1989): 191–208.

68. Henry J. Aaron and William B. Schwartz, *The Painful Prescription: Rationing Hospital Care* (Washington: The Brookings Institute, 1984), 35.

69. As in the United States, the physician's control over such decisions may be diminshing in Great Britain. See Richard G. Lee and Frances H. Miller, "The Doctor's Changing Role in Allocating U.S. and British Medical Services." *Law, Medicine and Health Care* 1990 (18): 69–76.

70. Churchill, *Rationing Health Care*, 122.

71. These issues are discussed in some detail in James F. Childress, "Ethical

Criteria for Procuring and Distributing Organs for Transplantation," *Journal of Health Politics, Policy and Law* 1989 (14): 87–113.

72. See generally Eugene Braunwald, et al., *Harrison's Principles of Internal Medicine* (New York: McGraw Hill, 1987).

73. Ralph M. Crawshaw, et al., "Oregon Health Decisions: An Experiment with Informed Community Consent," *JAMA* 254 (1985): 3213–3216.

74. A. L. Otten, "Local Groups Attempt to Shape Policy on Ethics and Economics of Health Issues," *Wall Street Journal* 25 May 1988, 1. This model has been exported to other states.

75. See generally chapter 5.

76. See L. P. Welch, et al., "Cost Effectiveness of Bone Marrow Transplantation in Acute Nonlymphocytic Leukemia," *New England Journal of Medicine*, 321 (1989): 807–811.

77. Several other roadblocks remain for the Oregon plan. First, they must obtain a Medicaid waiver from the Federal Health Care Financing Administration. See D. S. Lund, "HCFA Chief Unsure About Oregon's Medicaid Waiver," *American Medical News*, 15 June 1990, 11. Second, provisions of the Employment Retirement Income Security Act of 1974 may hamper implementation. See D. S. Lund, "Oregon Faces New Hurdle in Access Plan," *American Medical News*, 27 July 1990, 14.

78. Blue Cross reimburses hospitals for costs incurred by Blue Cross subscribers. Blue Shield provides reimbursement directly to providers. Most commercial insurers provide cash directly to the insured who in turn pay the health care institutions and providers.

79. Charles Phelps, *Taxing Health Insurance: How Much is Enough?* (Santa Monica: The Rand Corporation, 1983); Mark Pauly, "Taxation, Health Insurance and Market Failure," *Journal of Economic Literature*, 24 (1986): 629–636.

80. 42 U.S.C. Section 1395c, 1395o (1982) Supp. III 1985.

81. 42 U.S.C. Section 1395, 1395i, 1395o.

82. Eleanor D. Kinney, "National Coverage Under the Medicare Program: Problems and Proposals for Change," *St. Louis University Law Journal* 32 (1988): 872–898.

83. Maxwell Mehlman, "Health Care Cost Containment and Medical Technology: A Critique of Waste Theory," *Case Western Reserve Law Review* 36 (1986): 778–886.

84. Judith Feder, *Medicare: The Politics of Federal Hospital Insurance* (Lexington, Mass.: Lexington Books, 1977).

85. Social Security Act, Title XIX, 42 U.C.S. Section 1396 et seq. (1982 and Supp. 1985).

86. T. Joe, J. Meltzer, and P. Yu, "Arbitrary Access to Care: The Case for Reforming Medicaid," *Health Affairs*, 10 (1988): 61–79.

87. Ibid., 62.

88. See generally, "Health Care Financing Administration," *The Medicare and Medicaid Data Book* (Washington: HCFA, 1983).

89. Ibid., 7–10.

90. Robert Blendon and Thomas Moloney, ed., *New Approaches to the Medicaid Crisis* (New York: Free Press, 1982).

91. See A. Torres and A. M. Kenney, "Expanding Medicaid Coverage for Pregnant Women: Estimates of the Impact and Cost," *Family Planning Perspectives* 21 (1989): 19–23.

92. Department of Health and Human Services, *Better Health for Our Children: A National Strategy, Vol. III* (Washington: Government Printing Office, 1983).

93. National Study Group on State Medicaid Strategies, *Restructuring Medicaid, An Agenda For Change* (Washington: The Center for the Study of Social Policy, 1984).

94. John Holahan and Joel W. Cohen, *Medicaid: The Tradeoff Between Cost Containment and Access to Care* (Washington: Urban Institute Press, 1986).

95. Congress has paid significant attention to the problems of the uninsured. See in particular, *Essential Health Care*, Hearing Before the Committee on Labor and Human Resources, United States Senate, S.HRG.100-267 (May 1987); Congressional Research Service (CRS), *Insuring the Uninsured: Options and Analysis*, Special Committee on Aging of the United States Senate, Serial No. 100-0 (October 1988); Special Committee on Aging of the United States Senate, *Health Insurance and the Uninsured: Background Data and Analysis*, Serial No. 100-i (May 1988).

96. CRS, 11.

97. There are several reasons given for the increase in the population of uninsured from 1979 to 1986. The main reason is that the work force changed with the percent of nonunion employees in the work force increasing, especially in agricultural and service industries. These sectors of the economy are typically near the top in percentage of individuals uninsured. There have also been a number of demographic changes in the population. The percent of the population under eighteen is declining. These individuals were traditionally covered as dependents under their parents' plans. Economic incentives have also changed. Noncash compensation increased throughout the 1970s as high inflation and high tax rates made inflation resistant nontaxable compensation more attractive. With low inflation in the mid 1980s, and a changing tax structure reducing incentives for employees to favor noncash compensation, there is less incentive to provide insurance as a benefit at work.

There is an extensive literature on the uninsured population. See, for example, Gail Wilensky, "Filling the Gaps in Health Insurance: Impact on Competition," *Health Affairs* 7 (Summer 1988): 133–152; Randall Bovbjerg and Peter Kopit, "Coverage and Care for the Medically Indigent; Public and Private Options," *Indiana Law Review*, 19 (1986): 857–910; A. Davis and J. Rowland, "Uninsured and Undeserved: Inequalities in Health Care in the United States," *Milbank Memorial Fund Quarterly* (1983): 183–205.

98. M. E. Moyer, "Revised Look at the Number of Uninsured Americans," *Health Affairs* 8 (Summer 1989): 102.

99. This is considerably less than the 37 million that were reported in earlier reports. The individuals who conduct federal surveys believe that the

reasons for the change were that the health insurance questions were reordered on the most recent survey, that the questions were asked of more adults, and that additional questions were added to the survey on the coverage of children by Medicaid or by private health insurance.

100. See generally, I. S. Falk, "Proposals for National Health Insurance in the USA: Origins and Evolution, and Some Perceptions for the Future," *Milbank Memorial Fund Quarterly* 55 (1977): 161–191.

101. See R. J. Maxwell, "Financing Health Care: Lessons from Abroad," *British Medical Journal* 296 (1988): 1423–1426.

102. Massachusetts has recently embarked on an experiment in this regard. See Alan Sager, "Prices of Equitable Access: The New Massachusetts Health Insurance Law," *Hastings Center Report* 18 (1988): 21–28.

103. See generally, David U. Himmelstein, et al., "A National Health Program for the United States: A Physician's Proposal," *New England Journal of Medicine* 320 (1989): 102–108.

104. For an illuminating discussion of the differences between businesspeople and academics who propose organizational changes in health care delivery, see J. B. Johnston and U. E. Reinhardt, "Addressing the Health of a Nation: Two Views," *Health Affairs* 8 (1989): 6–22.

105. See James F. Blumstein, "Thinking About Government's Role in Medical Care," *St. Louis University Law Journal* 32 (1988): 853–873.

106. See Charles Phelps, "Cross-Subsidies and Charge Shifting in American Hospitals," in *Uncompensated Health Care: Rights and Responsibilities*, ed. Frank Sloan, James Blumstein, and James F. Perrin (Baltimore: Johns Hopkins University Press, 1986).

107. See generally Bradford H. Gray, ed., *For Profit Enterprise in Health Care* (Washington: National Academy Press, 1986).

108. See Theodore R. Marmor and Rudolph Klein, "America's Health Care Dilemma Wrongly Considered," *Health Matrix* 4 (1986): 19–24.

109. See Robert G. Evans, "Tension, Compression and Shear: Directions, Stresses and Outcomes of Health Care Cost Control," *Journal of Health Politics, Policy and Law* 15 (1990): 101–128.

Chapter 9: The Economic and Political Structure of Medical Practice

1. See Charles E. Rosenberg, *The Care of Strangers* (New York: Basic Books, 1988).

2. *Internal Revenue Service Code* sec. 501 C3 (1985).

3. Robert Clark, "Does the Non-Profit Form Fit the Hospital Industry?" *Harvard Law Review* 93 (1981): 1416–1480.

4. However, profit-seeking institutions can issue stocks to raise capital. See Joseph Newhouse, "Toward a Theory of Non Profit Institutions: An Economic Model of a Hospital," *American Economic Review* 68 (1970): 64–84.

5. See Henry Hansmann, "The Role of Non-Profit Enterprise," *Yale Law Journal* 89 (1980): 835–884.

6. Rosenberg, *The Care of Strangers.*

7. See M. V. Pauly and J. Radisch, "The Not-for-Profit Hospital as a Physician's Cooperative," *American Economic Review* 63 (1973): 47–57.

8. See Pauly and Radisch, "Not-for-Profit Hospital."

9. See Clark, "The Non Profit Form."

10. See Mark S. Freeland, et al., "Health Spending in the 1980's; Integration of Clinical Practice Management," *Health Care Financing and Review* 6 (Spring 1984): 1–12; *HHS News* (12/20/90) 1–4.

11. See M. Roemer and N. Shain, *Hospitalization under Insurance* (Chicago: American Hospital Association, 1959).

12. See *Health Planning and Resources Development Act* (Public Law 93-641): 1974.

13. Lawrence D. Brown, "Common Sense Meets Implementation: Certificate of Needs Regulation in the States," *Journal of Health Politics, Policy and Law* 8 (1983): 480–513.

14. C. Eby and D. Cohodes, "What Do We Know about Rate Setting?" *Journal of Health Politics, Policy, and Law* 10 (1985): 299–313.

15. E. P. Melia, et al., "Competition in the Health Care Marketplace: A Beginning in California," *New England Journal of Medicine* 308 (1983): 778–782.

16. Clark Havighurst, "The Changing Locus of Decision Making in the Health Care Sector," *Journal of Health Politics, Policy, and Law* 11 (1986): 697–728.

17. See Eli Ginzberg, "The Destabilization of Health Care," *New England Journal of Medicine* 315 (1986): 749–750.

18. Arnold Relman, "Dealing with Conflicts of Interest," *New England Journal of Medicine* 313 (1985): 749–750; Arnold Relman, "Practicing Medicine in the New Business Climate," *New England Journal of Medicine* 316 (1987): 1150.

19. Mark V. Pauly, "Is Medical Care Different? Old Questions, New Answers," *Journal of Health Politics, Policy, and Law* 13 (1988): 227–237.

20. Alain C. Enthoven, "Effective Management of Competition in the FEHDP," *Health Affairs* 8 (1989): 33–50.

21. See R. Mayer and G. G. Mayer, "HMO's: Origin and Development," *New England Journal of Medicine* 312 (1985): 590–594.

22. During the Depression, much larger scale models developed. In Oklahoma and in Los Angeles, physicians and employers developed prepaid group practices for the benefit of employees or members of unions. The first urban HMO was the Group Health Association of Washington, D.C., which was organized out of the Homeowners Loan Corporation.

23. In 1942, Kaiser had approached Garfield to develop a health care program for workers at Kaiser's shipbuilding plant in the San Francisco area. This plan was to take form as the Kaiser-Permanente Health Care Program, which now has over five million members.

24. See H. S. Luft, S. C. Maerki, and J. B. Trauner, "The Competitive

Effects of Health Maintenance Organizations: Another Look at the Evidence from Hawaii, Rochester, and Minneapolis/St. Paul," *Journal of Health Politics, Policy, and Law* 10 (1986): 625–645.

25. See Willard G. Manning, et al., "A Controlled Trial of a Prepaid Group Practice on Use of Services," *New England Journal of Medicine* 310 (1984): 1505–1510; as well as Luft, Maerki, and Trauner, "Competitive Effects of Health Maintenance Organizations."

26. See G. P. Wilensky and L. F. Rossiter, "Patient's Self-selection in HMO's," *Health Affairs* 6 (1986): 66–80.

27. See S. B. Jones, "Can Multiple Choice Be Managed to Constrain Health Care Cost," *Health Affairs* 8 (1989): 51–60.

28. See R. Feldman, J. Kralewsky, and B. Dod, "Health Maintenance Organizations: Beginning or the End?" *Health Services Research* 24 (1989): 191–211.

29. See H. Scovern, "Hired Help: A Physician's Experience in a For-Profit Staff Model HMO," *New England Journal of Medicine* 319 (1988): 787–790; see also, Arnold S. Relman, "Salaried Physicians and Economic Incentives," *New England Journal of Medicine* 319 (1988): 784.

30. See A. L. Hillman, M. V. Pauly, and J. J. Kerstein, "How Do Financial Incentives Affect Physicians' Clinical Decisions and the Financial Performance of Health Maintenance Organizations?" *New England Journal of Medicine* 321 (1989): 86–92.

31. Relman, "Dealing with Conflicts of Interest."

32. See J. K. Iglehart, "Second Thoughts about HMO's for Medicare Patients," *New England Journal of Medicine* 316 (1987): 1487–1492. Recent data suggest that HMOs for Medicaid and Medicare beneficiaries have functioned rather well. See K. M. Longwell and J. P. Hadley, "Evaluation of Medicare Competition Demonstrations," *Health Care Financing Review* 1989 (11): 65–80; D. A. Freund, et al., "Evaluation of Medicaid Competition Demonstrations," *Health Care Financing Review* 1989 (11): 81–97.

33. See *California Business and Professional Code*, sec. 650 (West Supplement 1988).

34. This terminology is somewhat unfortunate as the "referrals" often entail nothing more than a laboratory test, or further examination.

35. 41 *United States Code*, sec. 1395 NN (B) (1982).

36. 42 *United States Code*, sec. 132A-7A (B) (West Supplement 1988).

37. See Mark H. Hall, "Institutional Control of Physician Behavior: Legal Barriers to Health Care Cost Containment," *University of Pennsylvania Law Review* 137 (1988): 431–506.

38. See T. N. McDowell, "Physicians' Self-Referral Arrangements: Legitimate Business or Unethical Entrepreneurs," *American Journal of Law and Medicine* 15 (1988): 63–89.

39. See Office of the Inspector General, Department of Health and Human Services, *Financial Arrangements between Physicians and Health Care Businesses* (May 1989), cited in McDowell, "Physician Self-Referral Arrangements," 69.

40. See *United States v. Greber*, 760 F.2d 68 (3rd Circuit, 1985).

41. See P. J. Feldstein, T. M. Wickizer, and J. R. C. Wheeler, "Cost Containment: The Effects of the Utilization Review Program on Health Care Use and Expenditures," *New England Journal of Medicine* 318 (1988): 1310–1314.

42. *Wickline v. State*, 228 Cal. 661 (Cal. App. 2 Dist. 1986).

43. See Troyen A. Brennan, "Ensuring Adequate Health Care for the Sick: The Challenge of the Acquired Immunodeficiency Syndrome as an Occupational Disease," *Duke Law Journal* 1 (1988): 29–70.

44. See A. J. McClurg, "Your Money or Your Life: Interpreting the Federal Act against Patient Dumping," *Wake Forest Law Review* 24 (1989): 173–210.

45. See *Essential Health Care; Hearing before the Committee on Labor and Human Resources*, United States Senate, S. HRG. 100-267 (May 1987); *Health Insurance and the Uninsured: Background Data and Analysis*, Special Committee on Aging in the United States Senate, Serial Number 100-I (May 1988).

46. Norman Daniels, "Rights to Health Care and Distributive Justice," *Journal of Philosophy of Medicine* 4 (1979): 180.

47. Gene Outka, "Social Justice and Equal Access to Health Care," *Perspectives in Biology and Medicine* 18 (1975): 187–197.

48. Daniels, "Rights to Health Care," 181.

49. P. Greene, "Health Care and Justice in Contract Theory Perspective," in *Ethics and Health Policy*, ed., Robert Veatch and Roy Branson (Cambridge, Mass.: Ballinger Co., 1976).

50. Daniels, "Rights to Health Care," 185.

51. Greene, "Health Care and Justice," 48.

52. Kenneth Arrow, "Some Ordinalist-Utilitarian Notes on Rawls' Theory of Justice," *Journal of Philosophy* 70 (1973): 245–263.

53. Outka, "Social Justice and Equal Access," 187.

54. Greene, "Health Care and Justice," 48.

55. The existence of right to health care does not mean that right must be constitutionally protected. Indeed, there is little evidence that the federal constitution supports a right to health care. An analysis of cases decided within the past decade (which deal with rights to welfare benefits) demonstrates this point. See *Dandridge v. Williams*, 397 U.S. 471 (1970); *San Antonio Independent School District v. Rodriguez*, 411 U.S. 1 (1973); and *Board of Education of the Hendrick Hudson Center School District Board of Education, Westchester County v. Rowley*, 102 S.Ct. 3045 (1983).

56. See James S. Blumstein, "Thinking about Government's Role in Medical Care," *St. Louis University Law Journal* 32 (1988): 853–867.

57. See Ronald Bayer, "Ethics, Politics and Access to Health Care: A Critical Analysis of the President's Commission for the Study of Ethical Problems in Medicine and Biomedical and Behavioral Research," *Cardozo Law Review* 6 (1984): 303–320.

58. Indeed, while the constitutional law of our liberal state does not provide any basis for a right to health care, common law, the law as integrity, has slowly evolved a limited set of legal obligations for providing health care to the indigent. For instance, while the doctor-patient relationship has long been

based on contract law, physicians have been prohibited by the common law from "abandoning" critically ill patients. Allan H. McCoid, "The Care Required of Medical Practitioners," *Vanderbilt Law Review* 12 (1959): 549–571; see also, *Hurley* v. *Eddingfield*, 156 Indiana 416, 59 N.E. 1058 (1901). Moreover, hospitals that offer emergency services cannot refuse to admit and treat individuals who are suffering from emergencies. Troyen A. Brennan, "Ensuring Adequate Health Care for the Sick: The Challenge of the Acquired Immunodeficiency Syndrome as an Occupational Disease," *Duke Law Journal* 1 (1988): 29–70.

Over the years, this common-law duty to treat emergency patients in emergency rooms has evolved and grown. In particular, courts will no longer require that there be any previous relationship between the treating physician and the patient who seeks the emergent care. See *Hiser* v. *Randolph*, 126 Arizona 608, 617 P. 2d 774 (1980). Thus the liberal state does find legal obligations for practitioners to treat persons who are emergently ill, irrespective of their ability to pay.

59. 701 F.2d 717 (W.D. Mo. 1988).

60. British Medical Association, *Special Report on the Government's White Paper, Working for Patients* (London: British Medical Association, 1989).

61. G. Bevan, W. Holland, and N. Mays, "Working for Which Patient and at Which Cost," *Lancet* 1 (1989): 947–949; Editorial, T. Smith, "BMA Rejects NHS Review But . . . Doctors Must Develop a Coherent Alternative," *British Medical Journal* 298 (1989): 1405–1406.

62. See, for example, David U. Himmelstein and S. Woolhandler, "A National Health Program for the United States: A Physician's Proposal," *New England Journal of Medicine* (320) 1989: 102–107; American College of Physicians, "Access to Health Care: Executive Summary and Position Paper," *Annals of Internal Medicine* 112 (1990): 641–662.

63. In the following discussion, I rely heavily on the insightful writing of Robert Evans. Sources include, but are not limited to, the following: Robert G. Evans, *Strained Mercy: The Economics of Canadian Health Care* (Toronto: Butterworths, 1984); Robert G. Evans, "Tension, Compression and Shear: Directions, Stresses and Outcomes of Health Care Cost Control," *Journal of Health Care Politics, Policy and Law* 15 (1990): 101–128; M. L. Barer, Robert G. Evans, and R. J. Labelle, "Fee Controls as Cost Control: Tales from the Frozen North," *Milbank Quarterly* 60 (1988): 1–61; R. G. Evans, "Finding the Levers, Find the Courage: Lessons from Cost Containment in North America," *Journal of Health Politics, Policy and Law* 11 (1988): 585–615.

64. Office of National Cost Estimates, "National Health Expenditures, 1988," *Health Care Financing Review* 11 (1990): 1–7.

65. Although the exact size of this savings is debatable. Compare J. P. Newhouse, G. Anderson, and L. L. Roos, "Hospital Spending in the United States and Canada: A Comparison," *Health Affair* 7 (1988): 1–11; Robert G. Evans, "Perspectives: Canada," *Health Affairs* 7 (1988): 12–16.

66. See Newhouse, et al., "Hospital Spending." The emphasis is on discernible, as these kinds of outcomes are very difficult to measure.

67. See R. L. Kravitz, L. S. Linn, and M. F. Shapiro, "Physician Satis-

faction Under the Ontario Health Insurance Plan," *Medical Care* 28 (1990): 502–512.

68. A. Enthoven and R. Kronick, "A Consumer Choice Health Plan for the 1990s: Universal Health Insurance and Assistance Designed to Promote Quality and Economy (2)," *New England Journal of Medicine* 320 (1989): 100.

69. A. Enthoven and R. Kronick, "A Consumer Choice Health Plan for the 1990s: Universal Health Insurance and Assistance Designed to Promote Quality and Economy (1)," *New England Journal of Medicine* 320 (1989): 29–37.

70. There have been some proposals along these lines in Canada. See Evans, *Strained Mercy*, 344.

71. Various states have tried to increase access by requiring employers to provide health care insurance. Massachusetts has recently followed Hawaii's lead and has enacted legislation that requires employers to provide health care insurance for workers. Those who are unemployed will have their health care funded by the state, thus creating universal access to health care within the state. See Alan Sager, "Prices of Equitable Access: The New Massachusetts Health Insurance Law," *Hastings Center Report* 18 (1988): 21–25. New York has recently followed suit with the Department of Health advocating a universal New York health care system under its administration. See New York State Department of Health, *Universal New York Health Care: A Proposal* (Albany: Department of Health, 1989).

Broad plans for coverage of the costs of health care are not restricted to state initiatives. In the past three years, Congress has developed several plans to increase access to health care. See E. Richard Brown, "Principles for a National Health Program: Framework for Analysis and Development," *Milbank Memorial Fund Quarterly* 66 (1988): 573–617. Senator John Chaffee has introduced a bill that would expand Medicaid to cover all citizens who are below the poverty line. Those whose incomes fall between 100 and 250 percent of the poverty line would be able to purchase Medicaid on a sliding scale basis. Senator Edward Kennedy and Representative Henry Waxman have introduced proposals similar to those passed in Massachusetts and considered in New York, requiring all employers to purchase health insurance for employees so that each employee would have at least a comprehensive benefit package. Even more comprehensive is Representative Ronald Dellum's legislation, which envisions a national health service that would be government owned and operated and would be financed by a variety of taxes. All health professionals would be salaried under this system.

An employment-based program was also embraced by the Pepper Commission. See United States Bipartisan Commission on Comprehensive Health Care, *A Call for Action: Final Report* (Washington: Government Printing Office, 1990).

Chapter 10: Concluding Thoughts: Trust and Antitrust

1. As discussed by Paul Starr, and more recently by Frank D. Campion in the *American Medical Association and US Health Policy Since 1940* (Chicago: Chicago Review Press, 1984).

2. P. Areeda and D. F. Turner, *Anti-trust Law: An Analysis of Anti-trust Principles and Their Application* (Boston: Little, Brown and Company, 1978).

3. *Standard Oil Co.* v. *FTC*, 340 U.S. 231, 249 (1951).

4. Areeda and Turner, *Anti-trust Law*, 7.

5. See J. G. Van Cise, W. T. Lifland, and L. T. Sorkin, *Understanding the Anti-trust Laws*, 9th ed. (New York: New York City Practicing Law Institute, 1986).

6. 421 U.S. 773 (1975).

7. See M. Holoweiko, "What Competition Can Do to Peer Review," *Medical Economics* 41 (19 August 1985): 122–128.

8. See *Patrick* v. *Burget*, 800 F.2d 1498 (9th Cir., 1986).

9. *Patrick* v. *Burget*, 108 S.Ct. 1658 (1988).

10. See J. R. Bierig and R. M. Portman, "The Health Care Quality Improvement Act of 1986," *St. Louis University Law Journal* 32 (1988): 977–1014.

11. James F. Blumstein and Frank Sloan, "Antitrust in Hospital Peer Review," *Law and Contemporary Problems* 51 (1988): 7–93.

12. 745 F.2d 786 (3rd Cir., 1984).

13. See Clark Havighurst, "Doctors and Hospitals: Antitrust Perspective on Traditional Relationships," *Duke Law Journal* 1 (1984): 1071–1120.

Index

Designer: U.C. Press Staff
Compositor: Auto-Graphics, Inc.
Text: 10/13 Galliard
Display: Galliard
Printer: Bookcrafters, Inc.
Binder: Bookcrafters, Inc.